Lecture Notes in Artificial Intelligence 7911

Subseries of Lecture Notes in Computer Science

T0202496

LNAI Series Editors

Randy Goebel
University of Alberta, Edmonton, Canada
Yuzuru Tanaka
Hokkaido University, Sapporo, Japan
Wolfgang Wahlster
DFKI and Saarland University, Saarbrücken, Germany

LNAI Founding Series Editor

Joerg Siekmann
DFKI and Saarland University, Saarbrücken, Germany

Thomas Drugman Thierry Dutoit (Eds.)

Advances in Nonlinear Speech Processing

6th International Conference, NOLISP 2013
Mons, Belgium, June 19-21, 2013
Proceedings

Springer

Volume Editors

Thomas Drugman
Thierry Dutoit
University of Mons, TCTS Lab
31, Bouldevard Dolez, 7000 Mons, Belgium
E-mail: {thomas.drugman, thierry.dutoit}@umons.ac.be

ISSN 0302-9743 e-ISSN 1611-3349
ISBN 978-3-642-38846-0 e-ISBN 978-3-642-38847-7
DOI 10.1007/978-3-642-38847-7
Springer Heidelberg Dordrecht London New York

Library of Congress Control Number: 2013939661

CR Subject Classification (1998): I.2.7, I.5, H.5, I.6, G.1

LNCS Sublibrary: SL 7 – Artificial Intelligence

Typesetting: Camera-ready by author, data conversion by Scientific Publishing Services, Chennai, India

Printed on acid-free paper

Springer is part of Springer Science+Business Media (www.springer.com)

Preface

NOLISP, an ISCA tutorial and workshop on non-linear speech processing, is a biannual event whose aim is to present and discuss new ideas, techniques, and results related to alternative approaches in speech processing that may depart from the mainstream. In order to work at the front-end of the subject area, the following domains of interest have been defined for the NOLISP workshops:

1. Non-linear approximation and estimation
2. Non-linear oscillators and predictors
3. Higher-order statistics
4. Independent component analysis
5. Nearest neighbors
6. Neural networks
7. Decision trees
8. Non-parametric models
9. Dynamics for non-linear systems
10. Fractal methods
11. Chaos modeling
12. Non-linear differential equations

The initiative of organization of NOLISP 2013 at the University of Mons (UMONS) came from the speech processing research group at TCTS Lab. The fact that this was the sixth edition of NOLISP gives evidence that the workshop has already become an established international event.

The Organizing Committee would like to sincerely thank our sponsors Acapela Group and Nuance, as well as FNRS, University of Mons, and ISCA for their financial support.

April 2013

Thomas Drugman
Thierry Dutoit

Sponsors

acapela group

NUANCE

fnrs
LA LIBERTÉ DE CHERCHER

UMONS
Université de Mons

International Speech Communication Association

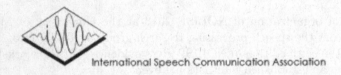

Table of Contents

Speech and Audio Analysis

Speech Synthesis

Speech-Based Biomedical Applications

Automatic Speech Recognition

Speech Enhancement

Evaluation of Automatic Glottal Source Analysis

John Kane and Christer Gobl

Phonetics and Speech Laboratory,
School of Linguistic, Speech and Communication Sciences,
Trinity College Dublin, Ireland

Abstract. This paper documents a comprehensive evaluation carried out on automatic glottal inverse filtering and glottal source parameterisation methods. The experiments consist of analysis of a wide variety of synthetic vowels and assessment of the ability of derived parameters to differentiate breathy to tense voice. One striking finding is that glottal model-based parameters compared favourably to parameters measured directly from the glottal source signal, in terms of separation of breathy to tense voice. Also, certain combinations of inverse filtering and parameterisation methods were more robust than others.

1 Introduction

The production of voiced speech can be considered as: the sound source created by the vibration of the vocal folds (glottal source) inputted through the resonance structure of the vocal tract and radiated at the lips. Most acoustic descriptions typically used in speech processing involve characterisation of mainly the vocal tract contribution to the speech signal. However, there is increasing evidence that development of independent feature sets for both the vocal tract and the glottal source components can yield a more comprehensive description of the speech signal. Recent developments in speech synthesis [1], voice quality modification [2], voice pathology detection [3] and analysis of emotion in speech [4] have served to highlight the potential of features related to the glottal source.

However, approaches for analysing the estimated glottal source are at times believed to lack robustness in certain cases. For instance, higher pitch voices are known to be problematic for inverse filtering [5] and particularly when combined with a low first formant frequency. There can be strong source-filter interaction effects [6] which seriously affect the linear model of speech exploited in inverse filtering. Furthermore, precise glottal source analysis is often said to require the use of high-quality equipment to record in anechoic or studio settings [5]. Despite these claims, some studies have found that glottal source parameters derived from speech recorded in less than ideal recording conditions contribute positively to certain analyses [7].

It follows that the purpose of this paper is to investigate the performance of both inverse filtering and parameterisation steps typically used in glottal source analysis. The evaluation of glottal source analysis methods is known to be problematic as it is not possible to obtain 'true' reference values. To deal with this,

T. Drugman and T. Dutoit (Eds.): NOLISP 2013, LNAI 7911, pp. 1–8, 2013.

the current study presents two different evaluation procedures in order to provide a more thorough impression of the performance of the various methods. Some similar work was recently carried out in [8] and the current study builds on this by incorporating model-fitting based parameterisation methods.

2 State-of-the-Art

A description of the state-of-the-art in terms of automatic glottal inverse filtering and glottal source parameterisation methods was previously given in [9] and [5]. For the evaluation in the present study the following glottal inverse filtering methods are evaluated: a closed-phase inverse filtering method (CPIF, [10]), iterative and adaptive inverse filtering (IAIF, [11]) and mixed-phase decomposition based on the complex-cepstrum (CCEPS, [12]). Note that for these methods glottal closure instants (GCIs) are detected using the SE-VQ algorithm [13]. For the CPIF method, the glottal closed phase is determined by detecting glottal opening instants (GOIs) using the algorithm described in [14].

The glottal source parameterisation methods are divided into two groups: direct measures and model fitting. The direct measures used in the current study are: the normalised amplitude quotient (NAQ, [15]), the quasi-open quotient (QOQ, [16]) and the difference between the first two harmonics of the narrowband glottal source spectrum (H1-H2, [21]). These three parameters are chosen as they were shown to be particularly effective at discriminating breathy to tense voice in a previous study [17]. Two algorithms are included which involve fitting the Liljencrants-Fant (LF) glottal source model [22] to the glottal source signal. A standard time domain method is used (Strik-LF, [18]) and an algorithm based on dynamic programming (DyProg-LF) described in [26]. One further algorithm is used in the evaluation which provides an estimate of the *Rd* parameter of the LF model by minimising a phase-based error criterion (Degott-LF, [20]).

3 Experimental Setup

As any single evaluation of glottal source analysis has its shortcomings, the approach here is to evaluate both on synthetic and natural speech data.

3.1 Synthetic Testing

A frequently used evaluation procedure (see e.g., [18,8]) is to do analysis of synthetic vowel segments where there are known reference values. This has the advantage of allowing straightforward quantitative evaluation where systematic modifications to both vocal tract and glottal source model settings can be investigated. The disadvantage, however, is that the stimuli will be a simplified version of real speech and will not contain some of the known difficulties for glottal source analysis (e.g., the presence of aspiration noise, source-filter interaction effects, etc.). In this paper, analysis is carried out on a large range of synthetic vowel segments with wide variation of glottal source and vocal tract filter model settings. This is done in a similar fashion to that in [8]. The LF glottal source model is used to generate the synthetic source signal and is varied using f_0 and three parameters which can be used to characterise its shape: Ra, Rk and Rg. With each setting 10 LF pulses are concatenated to create the source signal. An all-pole vocal tract model is used to modulate the source signal. Eight vowel settings are used based on the analysis of spoken vowels (i.e. one vocal tract model used to characterise each of the eight vowels). Note that the first formant frequency (F1) is derived from the vocal tract model, and we consider error rates as a function of F1. In total 198,720 synthetic signals (each containing 10 concatenated synthetic glottal pulses) are generated for analysis. A small proportion of these variations result in improper LF model configurations (i.e. when $Rk > 2Rg - 1$ or when $Ra > 1 - \frac{1+Rk}{2Rg}$), and these signals are not analysed.

In order to evaluate the performance of automatic inverse filtering the following three parameters are considered: NAQ, QOQ and H1-H2. These parameters are calculated from the synthetic source signal, as reference values. Then for each synthetic vowel the three inverse filtering methods: CPIF, IAIF and CCEPS, are used to estimate the source signal, which is subsequently parameterised. Relative error scores are then computed for each parameter and then are analysed as a function of f_0 values and first formant frequency (F1, derived from the all-pole settings).

3.2 Voice Quality Differentiation

One useful application of glottal source analysis is to automatically differentiate voice quality. Furthermore, as NAQ, QOQ, and H1-H2 have been shown to be suitable for separating breathy to tense voice (see for example: [17,15,16,21]) it is reasonable to assume that quality of inverse filtering can be somewhat evaluated on the basis of how well the extracted glottal source parameter differentiates the voice quality. Such an approach has been used in previous studies [23,8] and can allow quantitative evaluation on natural speech.

The speech data consist of all-voiced spoken sentences from two separate databases. The use of all-voiced sentences allowed evaluation independent of the effects of using automatic voicing decision algorithms. Furthermore, as voicing transitions often display characteristics associated with laxer phonation this would affect the results. The speech data from 6 speakers (3 male and 3 female) were selected from the speech database first described in [13]. Participants were asked to read a set of phonetically balanced TIMIT sentences in six different phonation types (though only the 5 all-voiced breathy, modal and tense samples are used here, i.e. 6-speakers × 5-sentences × 3-phonation types). Following a final perceptual evaluation 10 of the intended tense utterances were not perceived as such, and hence were discarded from the analysis. A further 10 all-voiced sentences produced by 3 male speakers in breathy, modal and tense voice, were recorded and added to the sentence dataset (giving a total of 60 breathy, 60 modal and 50 tense utterances). The three male speakers are all experienced in voice-related research and individual utterances were re-recorded in several iterations until the sentences were deemed to properly represent the stated voice quality mode for the entire utterance. All audio was captured in a semi-anechoic studio using high quality recording equipment: a B & K 4191 free-field microphone and a B & K 7749 pre-amplifier. The signals were digitised at 44.1 kHz and were subsequently downsampled to 16 kHz.

For each included speech segment inverse filtering is carried out using CPIF, IAIF and CCEPS, and parameterised using NAQ, QOQ and H1-H2. Furthermore, *Rd* and OQ parameters are derived from the model fitting by the **Strik-LF** and **DyProg-LF** methods, following IAIF inverse filtering. *Rd* is also derived using **Degott-LF**, which does not require prior inverse filtering. In order to have a balanced dataset it is desirable to have a fixed number of datapoints per sentence. To address this, parameter contours are derived using each of the methods. These contours are then resampled to 10 samples which can capture variations in the parameter contour but still maintaining a constant number of datapoints. An explained variance metric is then derived as the squared Pearson's R coefficient by treating median parameter values as the dependent variable and voice quality label as the independent variable. A similar evaluation procedure was carried out in [17].

4 Results

4.1 Synthetic Testing

The results from the synthetic testing are shown in Figure 1, with mean relative error plotted as a function of f_0 setting and F1 (derived from the vocal tract models). The NAQ parameter is shown to be rather insensitive to variations in f_0 (Figure 1a). Below around 240 Hz the IAIF method produces the lowest relative error; however from after this point the three inverse filtering methods yield similar results. Although these results corroborate previous findings in [8] for the performance of NAQ on synthetic data other studies on natural speech have found that NAQ becomes less effective with wide f_0 variation [19].

For F1, NAQ is shown to be insensitive to its variation. Again IAIF provides the lowest relative error scores, although there is a sudden increase for the vowel setting with an F1 of 344 Hz. This can be explained by the fact that this is a /u/ vowel setting with a very low second formant. IAIF may at times treat this as a single formant resulting in incomplete formant cancellation thus affecting NAQ. For QOQ, the closed-phase inverse filtering method (CPIF) provided the lowest relative error scores. This is particularly true for higher f_0 values, with both IAIF and CCEPS showing significant increases in relative error from around 200 Hz. There is a clear effect of certain vowel settings on IAIF and CCEPS, but they are clearly not as a result of F1. CPIF is not affected by the different vowel settings. In the case of H1-H2, however, CPIF gave clearly the highest relative error values. It is apparent from the analysis that even though the extracted time domain waveform, using CPIF, is suitable for deriving time domain parameters, it is considerably less so for the frequency domain one. The CPIF method is unable to reliably extract the relative amplitude of the first few harmonics.

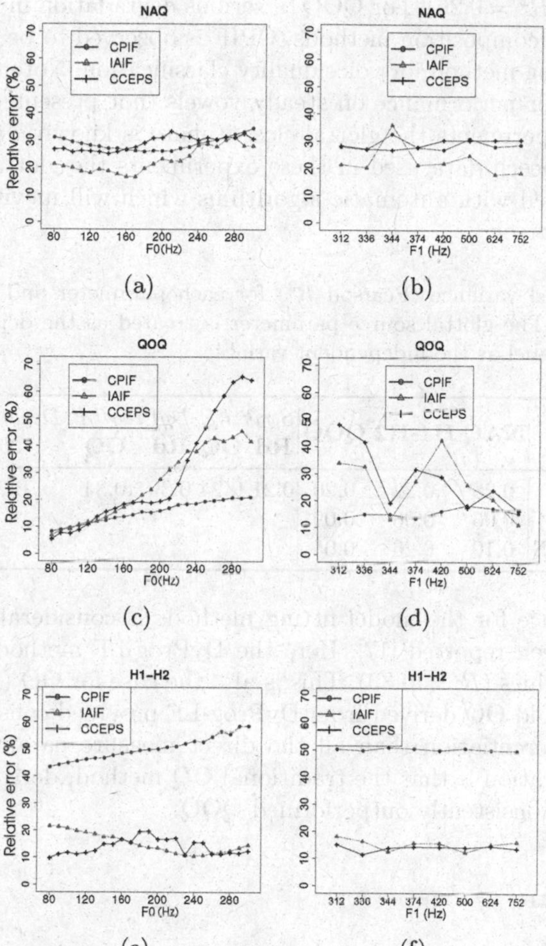

Fig. 1. Mean relative error score for NAQ (top row), QOQ (middle row) and H1-H2 (bottom row) as a function of f_0 (left column) and F1 (right column), for the three inverse filtering methods: CPIF (blue), IAIF (red) and CCEPS (black)

4.2 Voice Quality Differentiation

The results from the voice quality differentiation experiments are summarised Table 1. As expected, overall differentiation of voice quality is reduced when analysing the continuous speech considered here compared to vowel data analysed in [17] (note that our analysis of the same vowel data, not presented here, closely corroborates the trends seen in [17]). This is likely due to the difficulty in inverse filtering some parts of continuous speech (e.g., certain voiced consonants). However, similar trends to those in [17] are maintained with NAQ derived following IAIF giving the best performance for the direct measure parameters

($R^2 = 0.28$). Once more CCEPS is the most suitable decomposition method for applying H1-H2 ($R^2 = 0.26$). For QOQ, a serious degradation in performance is observed for all decomposition methods. CPIF is observed to be the least effective inverse filtering method for voice quality classification. Note that it displays considerably better performance on steady vowels (not presented here). In the synthetic data experiments the glottal closed phase is known *a priori*, whereas for the natural speech data used in these experiments the glottal closed phase has to be estimated with automatic algorithms which will inevitably display a certain degree of error.

Table 1. Explained variance (Pearson R^2) for each parameter and inverse filtering type combination. The glottal source parameter is treated as the dependent variable and voice quality label as the independent variable.

	NAQ	**H1-H2**	**QOQ**	*Strik-LF*		*DyProg-LF*		*Degott-LF*
				Rd	**OQ**	**Rd**	**OQ**	**Rd**
IAIF	0.28	0.22	0.20	0.21	0.24	0.39	0.34	0.28
CPIF	0.06	0.06	0.09					
CCEPS	0.10	0.26	0.05					

The performance for the model fitting methods is considerably better than has previously been reported [17]. Here the DyProg-LF method gave the best performing *Rd* values ($R^2 = 0.39$). This is also the case for OQ ($R^2 = 0.34$) and in fact both *Rd* and OQ derived from DyProg-LF provided considerably better voice quality differentiation than all the direct measure parameters. Another interesting observation is that the traditional OQ method, derived using model fitting methods, consistently outperformed QOQ.

5 Discussion

Perhaps the most striking finding in this study is the strong performance of LF model based parameters at differentiating breathy to tense voice. Whereas the standard time domain LF model fitting algorithm (Strik-LF, [18]) gave comparable performance to that in [17], more recent algorithms for deriving LF model parameters (DyProg-LF, [26] and Degott-LF, [20]) compared favourably with direct measure parameters. This is particularly the case for continuous speech, where direct measure parameters suffered a serious degradation in performance. Specifically for DyProg-LF, both the *Rd* and OQ parameters still provided strong differentiation of the voice quality in continuous speech. The reason for the apparent robustness of the DyProg-LF method to continuous speech can be explained by the suitability of dynamic programming for maintaining sensible parameter contours even in "*difficult*" speech regions.

Although differentiation of voice quality does not directly measure the accuracy of derived parameter values, strong performance does suggest that the particular method is characterising salient glottal features.

Evidence from the testing on synthetic speech signals indicates that certain glottal inverse filtering methods are more suited to certain parameters. For instance, closed-phase inverse filtering (CPIF) is shown to be particularly suitable for deriving NAQ and QOQ, both time domain parameters. These parameters derived following CPIF are also rather insensitive to changes in f_0 and vocal tract filter setting. However, for the frequency domain parameter, H1-H2, the CPIF output is clearly less suitable. This finding may corroborate those in [8] where CPIF is shown to produce higher levels of spectral distortion than the other inverse filtering methods. However, the findings for IAIF conflict with those in [8], as in the present results IAIF had a similar performance to the other methods in terms of relative error on NAQ and QOQ, whereas in [8] it was considerably worse. In fact IAIF displayed relatively stable performance across the experiments and is shown to be particularly useful in combination with NAQ for breathy-tense discrimination and accuracy on synthetic speech signals.

6 Conclusion

This study presents a general assessment of automatic glottal inverse filtering and glottal source parameterisation methods. To overcome the known difficulty of quantitative evaluation of glottal source analysis methods two different experiments are conducted which, in combination, provide a more comprehensive impression of the performance of the methods. Testing on synthetic signals revealed that different glottal inverse filtering methods are more suited to certain parameter estimation methods. The experiments on voice quality differentiation show that more recent LF model fitting methods are more suited to the continuous speech data than direct measures.

Acknowledgments. This research is supported by the Science Foundation Ireland Grant 09/IN.1/I2631 (FASTNET) and the Irish Department of Arts, Heritage and the Gaeltacht (ABAIR project).

References

1. Degottex, G., Lanchantin, P., Roebel, A., Rodet, X.: Mixed source model and its adapted vocal-tract filter estimate for voice transformation and synthesis. Speech Communication 55(2), 278–294 (2013)
2. Degottex, G., Roebel, A., Rodet, X.: Pitch transposition and breathiness modification using a glottal source model and its adapted vocal-tract filter. In: Proceedings of ICASSP, pp. 5128–5131 (2011)
3. Drugman, T., Dubuisson, T., Dutoit, T.: On the mutual information between source and filter contributions for voice pathology detection. In: Proceedings of Interspeech, pp. 1463–1466 (2009)
4. Lugger, M., Yang, B.: The relevance of voice quality features in speaker independent emotion recognition. In: Proceedings of ICASSP, pp. 17–20 (2007)
5. Walker, J., Murphy, P.: A review of glottal waveform analysis. In: Stylianou, Y., Faundez-Zanuy, M., Esposito, A. (eds.) COST 277. LNCS, vol. 4391, pp. 1–21. Springer, Heidelberg (2007)

6. Lin, Q.: Speech production theory and articulatory speech synthesis, Ph. D. Thesis (1990)
7. Székely, É., Kane, J., Scherer, S., Gobl, C., Carson-Berndsen, J.: Detecting a targeted voice style in an audiobook using voice quality features. In: Proceedings of ICASSP, pp. 4593–4596 (2012)
8. Drugman, T., Bozkurt, B., Dutoit, T.: A comparative study of glottal source estimation techniques. Computer Speech and Language 26, 20–34 (2011)
9. Alku, P.: Glottal inverse filtering analysis of human voice production - A review of estimation and parameterization methods of the glottal excitation and their applications. Sadhana 36(5), 623–650 (2011)
10. Yegnanarayana, B., Veldhius, R.: Extraction of vocal-tract system characteristics from speech signals. IEEE Transactions on Audio Speech and Language Processing 6(4), 313–327 (1998)
11. Alku, P., Bäckström, T., Vilkman, E.: Glottal wave analysis with pitch synchronous iterative adaptive inverse filtering. Speech Communication 11(2-3), 109–118 (1992)
12. Drugman, T., Bozkurt, B., Dutoit, T.: Complex cepstrum-based decomposition of speech for glottal source estimation. In: Proceedings of Interspeech, pp. 116–119 (2009)
13. Kane, J., Gobl, C.: Evaluation of glottal closure instant detection in a range of voice qualities. Speech Communication 55(2), 295–314 (2013)
14. Drugman, T., Thomas, M., Gudnason, J., Naylor, P., Dutoit, T.: Detection of Glottal Closure Instants From Speech Signals: A Quantitative Review. IEEE Transactions on Audio Speech and Language processing 20(3), 994–1006 (2012)
15. Alku, P., Bäckström, T., Vilkman, E.: Normalized amplitude quotient for parameterization of the glottal flow. Journal of the Acoustical Society of America 112(2), 701–710 (2002)
16. Hacki, T.: Klassifizierung von Glottisdysfunktionen mit Hilfe der Elektroglottographie. Folia Phoniatrica 41, 43–48 (1989)
17. Airas, M., Alku, P.: Comparison of multiple voice source parameters in different phonation types. In: Proceedings of Interspeech, pp. 1410–1413 (2007)
18. Strik, H.: Automatic parameterization of differentiated glottal flow: Comparing methods by means of synthetic flow pulses. Journal of the Acoustical Society of America, 2659–2669 (1998)
19. Gobl, C., Ní Chasaide, A.: Amplitude-based source parameters for measuring voice quality. In: Proceedings of the ISCA Tutorial and Research Workshop VOQUAL 2003 on Voice Quality: Functions, Analysis and Synthesis, Geneva, pp. 151–156 (2003)
20. Degottex, G., Roebel, A., Rodet, X.: Phase minimization for glottal model estimation. IEEE Transactions on Audio Speech and Language processing 19(5), 1080–1090 (2011)
21. Hanson, H.M.: Glottal Characteristics of female speakers: Acoustic Correlates. Journal of the Acoustical Society of America 10(1), 466–481 (1997)
22. Fant, G., Liljencrants, J., Lin, Q.: A four-parameter model of glottal flow. In: STL-QPSR, Speech, Music, and Hearing, KTH, Stockholm, vol. 26(4), pp. 1–13 (1985)
23. Kane, J., Kane, M., Gobl, C.: A spectral LF model based approach to voice source parameterisation. In: Proceedings of Interspeech, pp. 2606–2609 (2010)
24. Laver, J.: The Phonetic Description of Voice Quality. Cambridge University Press (1980)
25. Gobl, C.: Modelling aspiration noise during phonation using the LF voice source model. In: Proceedings of Interspeech, pp. 965–968 (2006)
26. Kane, J., Gobl, C.: Automating manual user strategies for precise voice source analysis. Speech Communication 55(3), 397–414 (2013)

NMF-Based Spectral Analysis for Acoustic Event Classification Tasks

Jimmy Ludeña-Choez[1,2] and Ascensión Gallardo-Antolín[1]

[1] Dept. of Signal Theory and Communications, Universidad Carlos III de Madrid, Avda. de la Universidad 30, 28911 - Leganés (Madrid), Spain

[2] Facultad de Ingenierías, Universidad Católica San Pablo, Arequipa, Perú

{jimmy,gallardo}@tsc.uc3m.es

Abstract. In this paper, we propose a new front-end for Acoustic Event Classification tasks (AEC). First, we study the spectral contents of different acoustic events by applying Non-Negative Matrix Factorization (NMF) on their spectral magnitude and compare them with the structure of speech spectra. Second, from the findings of this study, we propose a new parameterization for AEC, which is an extension of the conventional Mel Frequency Cepstrum Coefficients (MFCC) and is based on the high pass filtering of acoustic event spectra. Also, the influence of different frequency scales on the classification rate of the whole system is studied. The evaluation of the proposed features for AEC shows that relative error reductions about 12% at segment level and about 11% at target event level with respect to the conventional MFCC are achieved.

Keywords: Acoustic Event Classification, Non-Negative Matrix Factorization, Auditory Filterbank.

1 Introduction

In recent years, the problem of automatically detecting and classifying acoustic non-speech events has attracted the attention of numerous researchers. Although speech is the most informative acoustic event, other kind of sounds (such as laughs, coughs, keyboard typing, etc.) can give relevant cues about the human presence and activity in a certain scenario (for example, in an office room). This information could be used in different applications, mainly in those with perceptually aware interfaces such as smart-rooms [1]. Additionally, acoustic event detection and classification systems, can be used as a pre-processing stage for automatic speech recognition (ASR) in such way that this kind of sounds can be removed prior to the recognition process increasing its robustness. In this paper, we focus on acoustic event classification (AEC).

A design of a suitable feature extraction process for AEC is an important issue. Several front-ends have been proposed in the literature, some of them based on short-term features, such as Mel-Frequency Cepstral Coefficients (MFCC) [1], [2], [3], [4], log filterbank energies [3], Perceptual Linear Prediction (PLP) [5], log-energy, spectral flux, fundamental entropy and zero-crossing rate [1].

T. Drugman and T. Dutoit (Eds.): NOLISP 2013, LNAI 7911, pp. 9–16, 2013.

Other approaches are based on the application of different temporal integration techniques over these short-term features [6], [7].

However, as pointed in [3] these features are not necessarily the more appropriate for AEC tasks because they have been design according to the spectral characteristics of speech which are quite different from the spectral structure of acoustic events. To deal with this issue, in [3], it is proposed a boosted feature selection method to construct a more suitable parameterization for AEC.

In this work, we follow a different approach. First, we study the spectral characteristics of different acoustic events by applying Non-Negative Matrix Factorization (NMF) on their spectral magnitude and compare them with the structure of speech spectra. As NMF provides a way to decompose a signal into a convex combination of non-negative building blocks (called Spectral Basis Vectors, SBV) by minimizing a cost function, the resulting SBVs carry the information about the most relevant spectral components of each acoustic event. Second, from the findings of this study, we propose a new parameterization for AEC, which is an extension of the conventional MFCC and is based on the high pass filtering of acoustic event spectra. Also, the influence of different frequency scales (Mel, ERB, Bark and linear) on the classification rate of the whole system is studied.

This paper is organized as follows: Section 2 introduces the mathematical background of NMF. In Section 3 we present the spectral analysis of acoustic events using NMF. Section 4 is devoted to the explanation to our proposed parameterization and Section 5 describes the experiments and results to end with some conclusions and ideas for future work in Section 6.

2 Non-negative Matrix Factorization (NMF)

Given a matrix $V \in \mathbb{R}_+^{F \times T}$, where each column is a data vector, NMF approximates it as a product of two matrices of nonnegative low rank W and H, such that

$$V \approx WH \tag{1}$$

where $W \in \mathbb{R}_+^{F \times K}$ and $H \in \mathbb{R}_+^{K \times T}$ and normally $K \leq min\,(F, T)$. This way, each column of V can be written as a linear combination of the K basis vectors (columns of W), weighted with the coefficients of activation or gain located in the corresponding column of H. NMF can be seen as a dimensionality reduction of data vectors from an $F-$dimensional space to the $K-$dimensional space. This is possible if the columns of W uncover the latent structure in the data [8]. The factorization is achieved by an iterative minimization of a given cost function as, for example, the Euclidean distance or the generalized Kullbak Leibler (KL) divergence,

$$D_{\mathrm{KL}}\,(V \| WH) = \sum_{ij} \left(V_{ij} log \frac{V_{ij}}{(WH)_{ij}} - (V - WH)_{ij} \right) \tag{2}$$

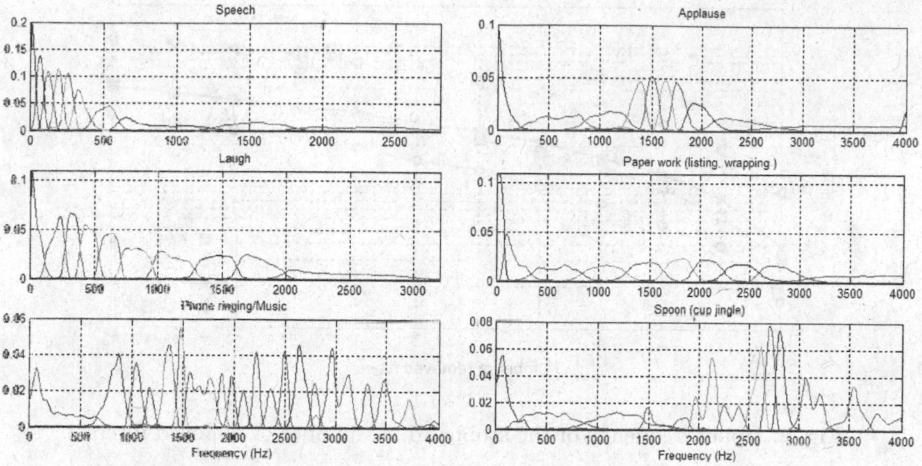

Fig. 1. Spectral Basis Vectors (SBVs) for speech and different acoustic events

In this work, we consider the KL divergence because it has been recently used with good results in speech processing tasks, such as speech enhancement and denoising for ASR tasks [9] [10] or feature extraction [11]. In order to find a local optimum value for the KL divergence between V and (WH), an iterative scheme with multiplicative update rules can be used as proposed in [8] and stated in (3),

$$W \leftarrow W \otimes \frac{\frac{V}{WH} H^T}{1 H^T} \qquad H \leftarrow H \otimes \frac{W^T \frac{V}{WH}}{W^T 1} \tag{3}$$

where 1 is a matrix of size V, whose elements are all ones and the multiplications $\otimes$ and divisions are component wise operations. NMF algorithm produces a sparse representation of the data, reducing the redundancy.

3 NMF-Based Spectral Analysis of Acoustic Events

In order to gain insight into the spectral content of the different Acoustic Events (AEs) considered, a NMF-based spectral analysis of each of these acoustic classes have been carried out.

For doing this, for a given AE, NMF is applied to the short-term spectrum magnitude of a subset of the audio files belonging to this particular class. The spectral basis vectors of this AE, W_e, are obtained minimizing the KL divergence between the magnitude spectra $|V_e|$ and their corresponding factored matrices $W_e H_e$ using the learning rules in (3). Note that the matrix W_e contains the SBVs that can be seen as the building blocks which represent each AE, as it is verified that $|V_e| \approx W_e H_e$.

The SBVs of five different non-speech sounds (applause, laugh, paper work, phone ringing and spoon cup jingle) are represented in Figure 1. The SBVs of

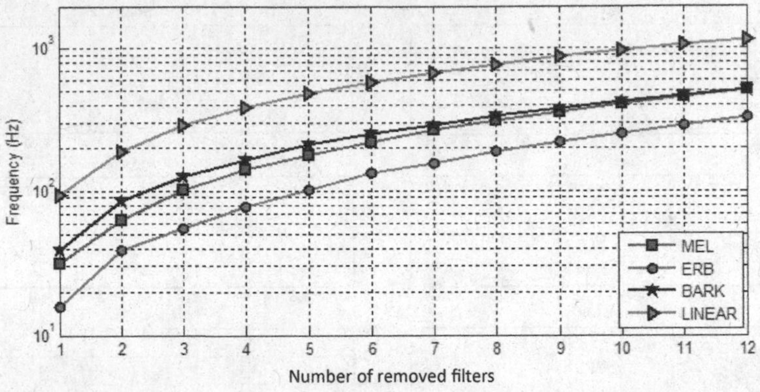

Fig. 2. Upper frequency of the stopband vs. number of removed filters

speech are also represented for comparison purposes. In all cases, 10 SBVs were obtained by applying NMF to the short-term spectrum magnitude computed over 20 ms windows with a frameshift of 10 ms. From this figure, the following observations can be extracted:

- The spectral content of the AEs are very different each other and with respect to speech. In fact, while the spectral components of speech are concentrated in low frequencies, the non-speech sounds present, in general, a relevant spectral content in medium-high frequencies,
- In all cases, low frequency components are presented to a greater or lesser extent, so this part of the spectrum seems not to very discriminative when comparing different types of AEs (including speech).
- Comparing the SBVs of the non-speech sounds, it can be observed that large differences can be found in the medium-high part of the spectrum, suggesting that these frequency bands are more suitable (or at least, they can not be negligible) than the lower part of the spectrum for discriminating between different acoustic events.

4 Parameterization Derived from the High-Pass Filtering of the Acoustic Event Spectrum

The analysis of the SBVs of the different acoustic events shown in Section 3 motivated us to derive a modified version of the conventional MFCC in which the special relevance of the medium-high frequencies of the spectrum is taking into account. This can be accomplished by filtering the short-term spectrum of the signal (using the appropriate high-pass filter) prior to the application of the auditory filterbank (in the case of MFCC, a mel-scaled triangular filterbank). However, in this work, we adopt a straightforward method which consists of modifying the auditory filterbank by means of the explicit removal of a certain number of the filters placed on the low frequency bands of the spectrum.

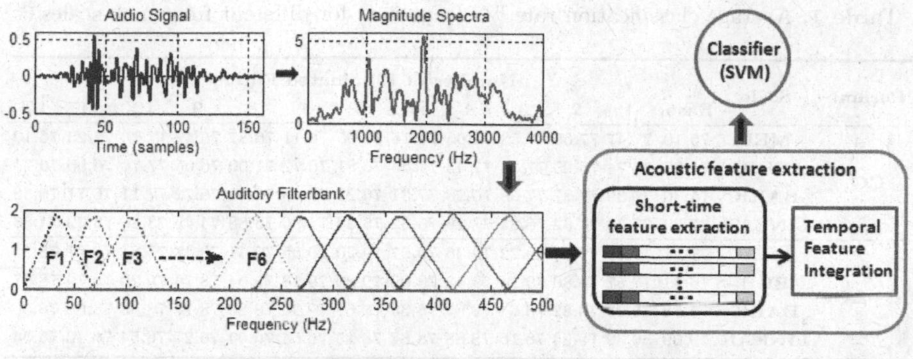

Fig. 3. Block diagram of the proposed method

In addition, in order to analyse the influence of the filter positions for AEC, several well-known frequency scales are considered: Mel, ERB, Bark and linear.

In Figure 2 it can be observed the upper frequency of the complete stopband as a function of the number of removed filters in the auditory filterbank for the four scales considered.

Once the speech spectrum is filtered following the procedure previously described and the remaining log filterbank energies are computed, a Discrete Cosine Transform is applied over them as in the case of the conventional MFCC yielding to a set of cepstral coefficients. Finally, it is applied a temporal feature integration technique which consists of dividing the sequence of cepstral coefficients into segments and computing the statistics of these parameters (in this case, mean, standard deviation and skewness) over each segment. These segment-based parameters are the input to the acoustic event classifier, which is based on Support Vector Machines (SVM). This process is summarized in Figure 3.

5 Experiments

5.1 Database and Experimental Protocol

The database used for the experiments consists of a total of 2,114 instances of target events belonging to 12 different acoustic classes: applause, coughing, chair moving, door knock, door slam, keyboard typing, laughter, paper wrapping, phone ringing, steps, spoon/cup jingle and key jingle. The composition of the whole database was intended to be similar to the one used in [3]. Audio files were obtained from different sources: websites, the FBK-Irst database [12] and the UPC-TALP database [13]. The speech sounds used for the computation of the speech SBVs shown in Figure 1 were extracted from the ShATR database [14].

Since this database is too small to achieve reliable classification results, we have used a 6-fold cross validation to artificially extend it, averaging the results afterwards. Specifically, we have split the database into six disjoint balanced

Table 1. Average classification rate [%] (segment) for different frequency scales

Param.	Scale	Number of Eliminated Filters												
		Base.	1	2	3	4	5	6	7	8	9	10	11	12
CC	MEL	75.10	77.47	77.66	77.58	77.63	78.16	76.95	78.11	76.87	76.12	77.23	77.23	76.10
	ERB	74.02	74.74	75.95	77.38	77.43	77.53	76.81	76.77	77.09	76.66	77.76	76.90	76.71
	BARK	74.30	77.39	77.27	77.68	76.96	77.31	76.27	77.43	76.91	76.72	77.11	76.77	76.59
	LINEAR	77.29	77.30	77.62	76.84	77.26	75.52	75.33	74.96	73.88	74.43	73.36	73.22	71.83
CC+ΔCC	MEL	77.57	79.43	79.45	79.22	79.36	79.07	79.20	79.55	79.41	78.47	77.81	78.77	78.55
	ERB	76.51	77.57	78.80	79.14	79.42	78.69	79.22	79.13	79.04	78.74	79.20	78.79	78.97
	BARK	77.58	78.98	79.32	78.64	78.65	78.33	78.62	79.25	78.86	78.77	78.03	78.08	78.56
	LINEAR	79.09	80.39	79.94	78.16	78.88	78.82	78.15	76.64	76.54	76.27	76.54	76.42	75.54

groups. One different group is kept for testing in each fold, while the remainder are used for training.

The AEC system is based on a one-against-one SVM with RBF kernel and a majority voting scheme for the final decision [7]. For each one of these experiments, a 5-fold cross validation was used for computing the optimal values of RBF kernel parameters.

5.2 Results

For the baseline experiments, 12 cepstral coefficients were extracted every 10 ms using a Hamming analysis window of 20 ms long and an auditory filterbank composed of 40 spectral bands. Four different frequency scales were considered: Mel (yielding to the conventional MFCC), ERB, Bark and linear. Also, the log-energy of each frame and the first derivatives (where indicated) were computed and added to the cepstral coefficients. The final feature vectors consisted of the statistics of these short-term parameters (mean, standard deviation and skewness) computed over segments of 2 s length with overlap of 1 s.

Table 1 and Table 2 show, respectively, the results achieved in terms of the average classification rate at segment level (percentage of segments correctly classified) an at target event level (percentage of target events correctly classified) by varying the number of eliminated low frequency bands in the auditory filterbank. Results for the baseline systems (when no frequency bands are eliminated) are also included. Both tables contain the classification rates for the four frequency scales considered (Mel, ERB, Bark and linear) and for two different set of acoustic parameters (CC: cepstral coefficients + log-energy and CC+ΔCC: cepstral coefficients + log-energy + its derivatives).

As can be observed for the CC parameterization, the performance of the Mel, ERB and Bark scales are quite similar, being the Mel scale slightly better. The behaviour with respect to the elimination of low frequency bands follows the same trends for the three scales. In all cases, the high pass filtering of the acoustic event spectrum outperforms the baseline: for the Mel scale, the best performance is achieved when the number of eliminated filters varies from 3 to 7, for the ERB

Table 2. Average classification rate [%] (target event) for different frequency scales

Param.	Scale	Number of Eliminated Filters												
		Base.	1	2	3	4	5	6	7	8	9	10	11	12
CC	MEL	81.07	82.28	82.04	82.42	82.42	81.89	81.31	83.20	81.27	80.78	80.69	81.75	79.72
	ERB	79.43	80.73	81.46	82.09	82.57	82.52	82.71	82.42	82.28	81.46	83.29	81.51	80.73
	BARK	80.83	81.94	82.47	82.33	80.83	81.07	80.98	81.84	80.73	81.07	80.98	81.55	80.98
	LINEAR	82.04	80.98	81.12	80.49	80.44	79.19	78.51	77.89	76.29	77.16	77.02	76.24	74.70
CC+ ΔCC	MEL	81.41	82.62	83.39	83.58	83.49	83.15	82.38	82.71	82.81	80.06	81.12	81.55	81.22
	ERB	80.73	80.98	82.18	82.67	83.24	82.62	82.76	81.89	82.04	81.80	82.71	81.75	82.57
	BARK	81.84	82.76	82.71	81.41	82.62	81.84	82.04	82.09	81.55	81.80	81.22	81.41	81.22
	LINEAR	82.81	82.38	82.42	81.60	81.36	80.78	80.35	79.33	79.24	79.04	79.38	78.71	77.16

scale, from 3 to 10 and for the Bark sale, from 2 to 7. From Figure 2, it can be seen that these ranges of eliminated filters roughly correspond to a stopband from 0 Hz to 100-275 Hz. The linear scale outperforms the classification rates achieved with the other scales in the baseline experiment (when no frequency bands are removed). However, no further improvements are obtained when low frequency filters are eliminated from the auditory filterbank. This can be explained for the higher bandwidth of the low frequency filters in the linear scale with respect to the other scales.

In summary, when using CC parameters, the best performance is obtained with the Mel scale when the seven first low frequency filters are not considered in the cepstral coefficients computation. In this case, the difference in performance with respect to the baseline is statistically significant at 95% confidence level and the relative error reduction with respect to the respective baseline is around 12% at segment level and around 11% at target event level.

Similar observations can be drawn for the CC+ΔCC parameterization: best results are obtained when low frequencies (below 100-275 Hz) are not considered in the feature extraction process. When comparing to CC, it can be observed that CC+ΔCC achieves improvements about 1% absolute over CC, However, these differences are not statistically significant.

6 Conclusion

In this paper, we have presented a new parameterization method for acoustic event classification tasks, motivated by the study of the spectral characteristics of non-speech sounds. First, we have analysed the spectral contents of different acoustic events by applying NMF on their spectral magnitude and compared them with the structure of speech spectra, concluding that medium and high frequencies are specially important for the discrimination between non-speech sounds. Second, from the findings of this study, we have proposed a new front-end for AEC, which is an extension of the MFCC parameterization and is based on the high pass filtering of acoustic event spectra. We have compared the proposed features to the conventional MFCC for an AEC task, obtaining relative error reductions about 12% at segment level and about 11% at target event level.

For future work, we plan to use feature selection techniques for automatically determining the most discriminative frequency bands for AEC. Other future lines include the unsupervised learning of auditory filter banks by means of NMF.

Acknowledgments. This work has been partially supported by the Spanish Government grants TSI-020110-2009-103, IPT-120000-2010-24 and TEC2011-26807. Financial support from the Fundación Carolina and Universidad Católica San Pablo, Arequipa (Jimmy Ludeña-Choez) is thankfully acknowledged.

References

1. Temko, A., Nadeu, C.: Classification of acoustic events using SVM-based clustering schemes. Pattern Recognition 39, 684–694 (2006)
2. Zieger, C.: An HMM based system for acoustic event detection. In: Stiefelhagen, R., Bowers, R., Fiscus, J.G. (eds.) RT 2007 and CLEAR 2007. LNCS, vol. 4625, pp. 338–344. Springer, Heidelberg (2008)
3. Zhuang, X., Zhou, X., Hasegawa-Johnson, M.A., Huang, T.S.: Real-world acoustic event detection. Pattern Recognition Letters 31, 1543–1551 (2010)
4. Kwangyoun, K., Hanseok, K.: Hierarchical approach for abnormal acoustic event classification in an elevator. In: IEEE Int. Conf. AVSS, pp. 89–94 (2011)
5. Portelo, J., Bugalho, M., Trancoso, I., Neto, J., Abad, A., Serralheiro, A.: Non speech audio event detection. In: IEEE Int. Conf. on Acoustics, Speech, and Signal Processing (ICASSP), pp. 1973–1976 (2009)
6. Meng, A., Ahrendt, P., Larsen, J.: Temporal feature integration for music genre classification. IEEE Trans. on Audio, Speech, and Language Processing 15, 1654–1664 (2007)
7. Mejía-Navarrete, D., Gallardo-Antolín, A., Peláez, C., Valverde, F.: Feature extraction assesment for an acoustic-event classification task using the entropy triangle. In: Interspeech, pp. 309–312 (2011)
8. Lee, D., Seung, H.: Algorithms for non-negative matrix factorization. Nature 401, 788–791 (1999)
9. Wilson, K., Raj, B., Smaragdis, P., Divakaran, A.: Speech denoising using nonnegative matrix factorization with priors. In: IEEE Int. Conf. on Acoustics, Speech, and Signal Processing (ICASSP), pp. 4029–4032 (2008)
10. Ludeña-Choez, J., Gallardo-Antolín, A.: Speech denoising using non-negative matrix factorization with kullback-leibler divergence and sparseness constraints. In: Torre Toledano, D., Ortega Giménez, A., Teixeira, A., González Rodríguez, J., Hernández Gómez, L., San Segundo Hernández, R., Ramos Castro, D. (eds.) IberSPEECH 2012. CCIS, vol. 328, pp. 207–216. Springer, Heidelberg (2012)
11. Schuller, B., Weninger, F., Wollmer, M.: Non-negative matrix factorization as noise-robust feature extractor for speech recognition. In: IEEE Int. Conf. on Acoustics, Speech, and Signal Processing (ICASSP), pp. 4562–4565 (2010)
12. FBK-Irst database of isolated meeting-room acoustic events, ELRA Catalog no. S0296
13. UPC-TALP database of isolated meeting-room acoustic events, ELRA Catalog no. S0268
14. The ShATR multiple simultaneous speaker corpus, `http://www.dcs.shef.ac.uk/spandh/projects/shatrweb/index.html`

Efficient GCI Detection for Efficient Sparse Linear Prediction

Vahid Khanagha and Khalid Daoudi

INRIA Bordeaux Sud-Ouest (GEOSTAT Team)
200 Avenue de la vielle tour, 33405 Talence, France
{vahid.khanagha,khalid.daoudi}@inria.fr
http://geostat.bordeaux.inria.fr/

Abstract. We propose a unified non-linear approach that offers an efficient closed-form solution for the problem of sparse linear prediction analysis. The approach is based on our previous work for minimization of the weighted l_2-norm of the prediction error. The weighting of the l_2-norm is done in a way that less emphasis is given to the prediction error around the Glottal Closure Instants (GCI) as they are expected to attain the largest values of error and hence, the resulting cost function approaches the ideal l_0-norm cost function for sparse residual recovery. As such, the method requires knowledge of the GCIs. In this paper we use our recently developed GCI detection algorithm which is particularly suitable for this problem as it does not rely on residuals themselves for detection of GCIs. We show that our GCI detection algorithm provides slightly better sparsity properties in comparison to a recent powerful GCI detection algorithm. Moreover, as the computational cost of our GCI detection algorithm is quite low, the computational cost of the overall solution is considerably lower.

1 Introduction

It is generally desirable for voiced speech sounds that the residuals obtained by their Linear Prediction (LP) analysis (the prediction error) form a sparse time series that is almost zero all the time, except for few instants where considerably larger values of error may occur (the outliers). Such sparse representation is beneficial for coding applications [9,13] and also leads in a more accurate estimation of human vocal tract system [11,16].

Classical approaches for LP analysis of speech rely on minimization of l_2-norm of prediction error. As the l_2-norm is numerically highly sensitive to outliers [18], such minimum variance solution favors non-sparse solutions with many small non-zero entries rather than the sparse solutions having the fewest possible non-zero entries. A more suitable cost function is the l_1-norm of prediction error as it puts less emphasis on outliers. The l_1-norm minimization of residuals is already shown to be advantageous for sparse residual recovery with the use of convex programming tools with special care to avoid an unstable solution [5,10,12].

We have previously shown in [16] that the minimization of a weighted version of l_2-norm results in a more sparse solution with less computational burden.

T. Drugman and T. Dutoit (Eds.): NOLISP 2013, LNAI 7911, pp. 17–24, 2013.

In this approach, GCIs are considered as the points that have the potential of attaining largest norms of residuals and then a weighting function is constructed such that the prediction error is relaxed at those points. Consequently, the weighted l_2-norm objective function is minimized by the solution of normal equations of liner least squares problem. In [16] a powerful method called SEDREAMS [7] is employed for detection of GCIs and it is shown that the weighted l_2-norm minimization achieves better sparsity properties compared to l_1-norm minimization.

In continuation of our sparse weighted l_2-norm solution mentioned above, in this paper we employ our recently developed GCI detection algorithm [15,17] for construction of the weighting function. This GCI detection algorithm relies on a novel multi-scale non-linear signal processing approach called the Microcanonical Multiscale Formalism (MMF) and extracts GCIs directly from the speech signal without being based on any model of speech production. This makes it more suitable to be used for sparse residual recovery compared to SEDREAMS. Indeed, although SEDREAMS is shown to provide the best of performances compared to several state-of-the-art algorithms [7], the fact that it relies on residuals themselves for detection of GCIs, controverts its use for sparse residual recovery (SEDREAMS uses the classical minimum variance solution for calculation of LP residuals). We show that our GCI detection algorithm provides slightly better sparsity properties compared to SEDREAMS when used inside the weighted-l_2-norm solution. Moreover we show that the MMF-based solution is more efficient than SEDREAMS and hence is a better choice for keeping down the overall computational burden.

The paper is organized as follows. In section 2 we present the weighted l_2-norm minimization approach. We then briefly introduce in section 3, the MMF based GCI detection algorithm that we use in this paper. In section 4, the experimental results are presented and finally in section 5, we draw our conclusion and perspectives.

2 The Weighted l_2-Norm Solution

The ideal solution for sparse residual recovery in LP analysis is to directly minimize the number of non-zero elements of the residual vector, i.e. its cardinality or the so-called l_0-norm [4]. This minimization problem is however a N-P hard optimization problem [12]. The classical LP analysis technique on the other hand is very simple (minimization of l_2-norm of residuals), but can not provide the desired level of sparsity. This is due to the exaggerative effect of l_2-norm on larger values of error (the so-called outliers) [18]. Indeed, the minimizer puts its effort on lowering the value of these outliers, with the cost of more non-zero elements and hence the resulting residuals are not as sparse as desired. To reduce the exaggerative effect of l_2-norm on the outliers, one may replace it with l_1-norm which is less sensitive to larger values [4]. The l_1-norm minimization problem can be solved by by recasting the minimization problem into a linear program [3] and then using convex optimization tools [2]. Special care must be taken however, to avoid stability and computational issues for the case of speech signal [5,10].

We have shown in [16] that a simple minimization of the weighted version of l_2-norm cost function may lead to better sparsity properties, while avoiding stability issues. Indeed, the use of l_2-norm cost function preserves the computational efficiency while the weighting function is used to cope with its exaggerative effect on outliers (by careful down-weighting of the cost function at those points).

Formally, the linear prediction of the speech signal $x(n)$ with a set of K prediction coefficients a_k can be written as:

$$x(n) = \sum_{k=1}^{K} a_k x(n-k) + r(n) \tag{1}$$

The weighted l_2-norm solution is based on solving the following optimization problem:

$$\hat{\mathbf{a}} = \underset{\mathbf{a}}{\operatorname{argmin}} \sum_{k=1}^{N} w(k)(r(k)^2) \tag{2}$$

where $w(\cdot)$ is the weighting function. Once $w(\cdot)$ is properly defined, the solution to Eq. (2) is straight-forward. Indeed, setting the derivative of the cost function to zero results in a set of normal equations that can be easily solved as explained in [16].

The weighting function is constructed in a way that it de-emphasizes the exaggerative effect of l_2-norm on outliers. This is achieved by down-weighting the l_2-norm at the time instants where an outlier is expected to occur. Indeed, it is argued in [16] that the outliers of LP analysis are expected to coincide with GCIs. Hence, the weighting function is expected to provide the lowest weights at the GCI points and to give equal weights to the remaining points. To put a smoothly decaying down-weighting around GCI points and to have a controllable region of tolerance around them, a natural choice is to use a Gaussian-shape weighting function. The final weighting function is thus defined as:

$$w(n) = 1 - \sum_{k=1}^{N_{gci}} g(n - T_k) \tag{3}$$

where $T_k, k = 1 \cdots N_{gci}$ denotes the detected GCI points and $g(\cdot)$ is a Gaussian function ($g(x) = \kappa e^{(\frac{x}{\sigma})^2}$). The parameter σ allows the control of the width of the region of tolerance and κ allows the control of the amount of down-weighting on GCI locations. Overall, in minimizing the resulting weighted l_2-norm cost function (Eq. (2)), the minimizer is free to pick the largest residual values for the outliers and it concentrates on minimizing the error on the remaining points and hence, the sparsity is granted. It is noteworthy that a recent work (independently) proposed a similar weighted linear prediction which downgrades the contribution of the glottal source and, thus, leads to more accurate formant estimates [1]. This model does not use however GCI estimation.

3 The MMF Based GCI Detection Algorithm

We have introduced a robust GCI detection algorithm in [15,17] that is based on a novel multi-scale non-linear signal processing approach called the MMF. The MMF is centered around precise estimation of local quantities called the Singularity Exponents (SE) at every point in the signal domain. When correctly defined and estimated, these exponents alone can provide valuable information about the local dynamics of complex signals. The singularity exponent $h(n)$ for any given signal $x(n)$, can be estimated by evaluation of the power-law scaling behavior of a multi-scale functional Γ_r over a set of fine scales r:

$$\Gamma_r\left(x(n)\right) \propto r^{h(n)} + o\left(r^{h(n)}\right) \qquad r \to 0 \tag{4}$$

where $\Gamma_r(\cdot)$ can be any multi-scale functional complying with this power-law like the gradient-based measure introduced in [21]. The details about the choice of $\Gamma_r(\cdot)$ and the consequent estimation of $h(n)$ are provided in [21,15].

In MMF, a particular set of interest is the level set called the *Most Singular Manifold* (MSM) which comprises the points having the smallest SE values. It has been established that the critical transitions of a complex signal occurs at these points. This property has been successfully used in several signal processing applications [19,20,22]. In case of voiced speech sounds, we have shown in [15,17] that indeed the MSM coincides with the instants where the most significant excitations of the vocal tract occur (the GCIs). Consequently, we used this property to develop a simple GCI detection algorithm which is much faster than SEDREAMS and we showed that it has almost the same performance as the SEDREAMS algorithm in case of the clean speech. In case of noisy speech our MMF-based approach shows considerably higher accuracy in comparison to the SEDREAMS in presence of 14 different types of noise taken from different real-world acoustic environments.

In this paper we aim at using this MMF-based GCI detection algorithm inside the weighted l_2-norm solution of section 2 for sparse residual recovery. Indeed, the MMF-based algorithm is particularly suited for this problem as it extracts the GCIs exclusively using the singularity exponents $h(t)$ and as opposed to SEDREAMS, it does not rely on residuals themselves for GCI detection. Moreover, as the computational complexity of our MMF-based GCI detector is much less than SEDREAMS and hence, the overall computational effort for solution of Eq. (2) will be reduced. As such, this MMF-based GCI detector can be seen as a complement to the weighted l_2-norm solution of section 2 for sparse residual recovery: combined together, they form a unified efficient and closed-form solution for sparse LP analysis of speech.

4 Experimental Results

We perform an extensive set of experiments on 3000 utterances that are randomly selected from TIMIT database to compare the sparsity properties of the residuals obtained by four different LP approaches: the classical l_2-norm minimization, the l_1-norm minimization, weighted l_2-norm minimization using SEDREAMS for GCI detection and weighted l_2-norm minimization using our MMF-based GCI detector. Following [9], the utterances are downsampled to 8 KhZ and the prediction order of $K = 13$ is used. As for the l_1-norm minimization method, we use the publicly available l_1-magic toolbox [3] which uses the primal-dual interior points optimization [2]. For the weighted l_2-norm minimization, all the results presented in this section are obtained using the following set of parameters for $w(\cdot)$: $\kappa = 0.9$ and $\sigma = 50$. The choice of the parameters was obtained using a small development set (of few voiced frames) taken from the TIMIT database [8]. As for the SEDREAMS GCI detection algorithm [7] we use the implementation that is made available on-line by its author [6] (GLOAT toolbox).

Fig. 1 shows an example of the residuals obtained by all these different optimization strategies. It is clear that the weighted-l_2 and also l_1-norm criteria achieve higher level of sparsity compared to the classic l_2-norm criterion. Moreover, a closer look reveals that in this example the weighted-l_2-norm solution which uses the MMF based GCI detector shows better sparsity properties compared to the rest of optimization strategies.

To perform a more quantitative comparison, we use the kurtosis of residuals as a quantitative measure of the level of sparsity of the obtained residuals. The kurtosis is an appropriate measure of sparsity as it satisfies three of the most important properties that are intuitively expected from such a measure: scale invariance, rising tide and Robin Hood [14]. Kurtosis is a measure of peakedness of a distribution and higher values of kurtosis implies higher level of sparsity. Table 1 shows the kurtosis of the residuals obtained from the above-mentioned optimization strategies, averaged over the 3000 utterances from TIMIT database. It can be seen from table 1 that the highest value for the kurtosis is achieved by the weighted l_2-norm solution, when the MMF based approach is used for GCI detection.

Table 1. Quantitative comparison of sparsity level of different LP analysis strategies

Method	kurtosis on the whole sentence	kurtosis on voiced parts
l_2-norm	49.46	95.67
l_1-norm	67.01	114.93
weighted-l_2-norm+SEDREAMS GCIs	62.78	114.69
weighted-l_2-norm+MMF GCIs	66.23	120.62

In terms of computational efficiency we compare the computational processing times for the weighted l_2-norm solutions using SEDREAMS and MMF for GCI detection, in terms of the average empirical Relative Computation Time that is defined as:

$$RCT(\%) = 100.\frac{CPU\ time\ (s)}{Sound\ duration\ (s)} \tag{5}$$

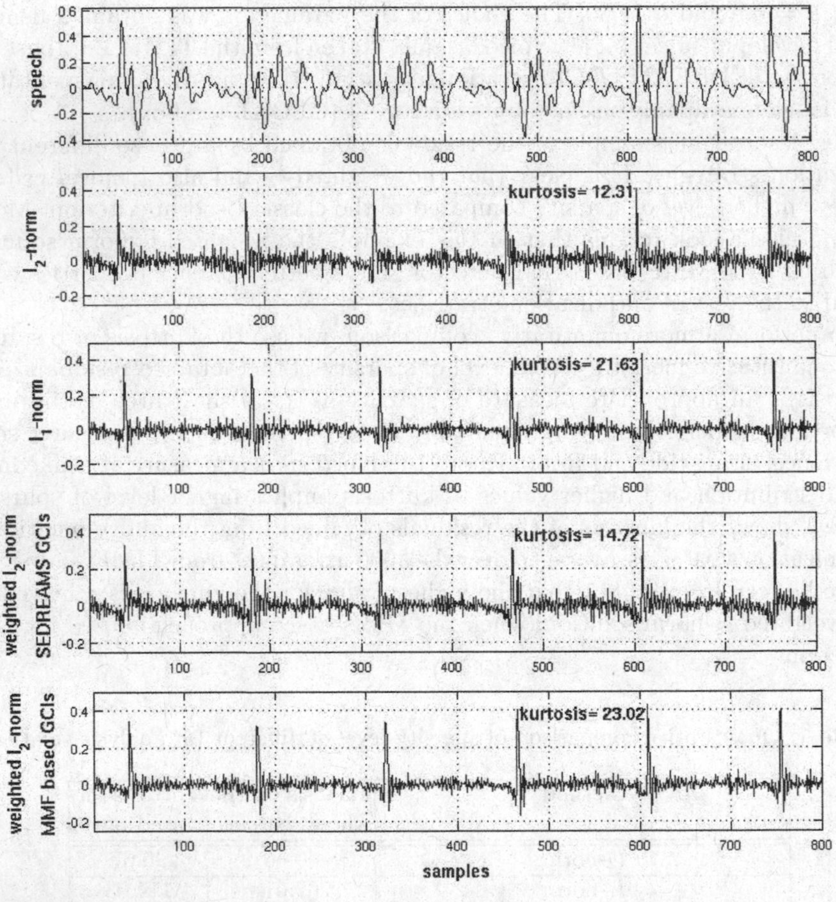

Fig. 1. The residuals of the LP analysis obtained from different optimization strategies for Fs=16 Khz, K = 26 and frame length of 25 msec

The results are reported in table 2 and it can be seen that the MMF based solution is indeed much faster than the one based on SEDREAMS. It must be noted that we have used the original implementation of SEDREAMS in the GLOAT toolbox [6] and not its fast implementation which should be about 4 times faster than the original one [7].

Table 2. Comparison of the average Relative Computation Time

Method	RCT (%)
weighted l_2-norm+SEDREAMS GCIs	46.97
weighted-l_2-norm+MMF GCIs	7.75

5 Conclusions

In continuation of our previous work for retrieval of sparse LP residuals using a weighted l_2-norm minimization [16], in this paper we introduced the use of our MMF based GCI detection algorithm for construction of the weighting function. Apart from having considerably lower computational cost, this GCI detection algorithm is particularly suited for sparse residual recovery as it does not rely on residuals themselves and extracts GCIs exclusively from geometric multi-scale measurements. As such, the MMF based GCI detection serves as a complement to our weighted-l_2-norm solution for sparse residual recovery. We showed that such a unified approach provide slightly better sparsity properties, while considerably reduces the overall computational burden of the algorithm. These results suggest further investigation of the potential of such a unified non-linear solution for speech analysis: performance in presence of noise, the accuracy of formant estimation, the quality of the synthesis when used inside parametric multipulse coders and etc. This indeed will be the subject of our future communications.

References

1. Alku, P., Pohjalainen, J., Vainio, M., Laukkanen, A., Story, B.: Improved formant frequency estimation from high-pitched vowels by downgrading the contribution of the glottal source with weighted linear prediction. In: INTERSPEECH (2012)
2. Boyd, S., Vandenberghe, L.: Convex Optimization. Cambridge University Press (2004)
3. Candès, E.J., Romberg, J.: l1-magic: Recovery of sparse signals via convex programming (2005)
4. Candès, E.J., Wakin, M.B.: Enhancing sparsity by reweighted l1 minimization. Journal of Fourier Analysis and Applications 14, 877–905 (2008)
5. Denoel, E., Solvay, J.P.: Linear prediction of speech with a least absolute error criterion. IEEE Transactions on Acoustics, Speech and Signal Processing 33, 1397–1403 (1985)
6. Drugman, T.: Gloat toolbox, `http://tcts.fpms.ac.be/drugman/`

7. Drugman, T., Thomas, M., Gudnason, J., Naylor, P., Dutoit, T.: Detection of glottal closure instants from speech signals: A quantitative review. IEEE Transactions on Audio, Speech, and Language Processing 20(3), 994–1006 (2012)
8. Garofolo, J.S., Lamel, L.F., Fisher, W.M., Fiscus, J.G., Pallett, D.S., Dahlgren, N.L., Zue, V.: DARPA TIMIT acoustic-phonetic continuous speech corpus. Tech. rep., U.S. Dept. of Commerce, NIST, Gaithersburg, MD (1993)
9. Giacobello, D.: Sparsity in Linear Predictive Coding of Speech. Ph.D. thesis, Multimedia Information and Signal Processing, Department of Electronic Systems, Aalborg University (2010)
10. Giacobello, D., Christensen, M.G., Dahl, J., Jensen, S.H., Moonen, M.: Sparse linear predictors for speech processing. In: Proceedings of the INTERSPEECH (2009)
11. Giacobello, D., Christensen, M.G., Murth, M.N., Jensen, S.H., Marc Moonen, F.: Sparse linear prediction and its applications to speech processing. IEEE Transactions on Audio, Speech and Language Processing 20, 1644–1657 (2012)
12. Giacobello, D., Christensen, M.G., Murthi, M.N., Jensen, S.H., Moonen, M.: Enhancing sparsity in linear prediction of speech by iteratively reweighted 1-norm minimization. In: Proceedings of the International Conference on Acoustics, Speech, and Signal Processing, ICASSP (2010)
13. Giacobello, D., Christensen, M., Murthi, M., Jensen, S., Moonen, M.: Retrieving sparse patterns using a compressed sensing framework: Applications to speech coding based on sparse linear prediction. IEEE Signal Processing Letters 17 (2010)
14. Hurley, N., Rickard, S.: Comparing measures of sparsity. IEEE Transactions on Information Theory 55, 4723–4740 (2009)
15. Khanagha, V.: Novel Multiscale methods for non-linear speech analysis, Ph.D. thesis, University of Bordeaux 1 (2013), `http://geostat.bordeaux.inria.fr/index.php/vahid-khanagha.html`
16. Khanagha, V., Daoudi, K.: An efficient solution to sparse linear prediction analysis of speech. EURASIP Journal on Audio, Speech, and Music Processing (2013)
17. Khanagha, V., Daoudi, K., Yahia, H.: A novel multiscale method for detection of glottal closure instants. Submitted to IEEE Transactions on Audio, Speech, and Language Processing (2013)
18. Meng, D., Zhao, Q., Xu, Z.: Improved robustness of sparse pca by l1-norm maximization. Pattern Recognition 45, 487–497 (2012)
19. Turiel, A., del Pozo, A.: Reconstructing images from their most singular fractal manifold. IEEE Transactions on Image Processing 11, 345–350 (2002)
20. Turiel, A., Parga, N.: The multi-fractal structure of contrast changes in natural images: from sharp edges to textures. Neural Computation 12, 763–793 (2000)
21. Turiel, A., Yahia, H., Pérez-Vicente, C.: Microcanonical multifractal formalism: a geometrical approach to multifractal systems. part 1: singularity analysis. Journal of Physics A: Mathematical and Theoretical 41, 015501 (2008)
22. Yahia, H., Sudre, J.: Garçon, V., Pottier, C.: High-resolution ocean dynamics from microcanonical formulations in non linear complex signal analysis. In: AGU Fall Meeting. American Geophysical Union, San Francisco (2011)

Gender Detection in Running Speech from Glottal and Vocal Tract Correlates

Cristina Muñoz-Mulas, Rafael Martínez-Olalla, Pedro Gómez-Vilda, Agustín Álvarez-Marquina, and Luis Miguel Mazaira-Fernández

Neuromorphic Speech Processing Lab, Centro de Tecnología Biomédica, Universidad Politécnica de Madrid, Campus de Montegancedo, s/n, 28223 Pozuelo de Alarcón, Madrid
ce.munoz@upm.es

Abstract. Gender detection from running speech is a very important objective to improve efficiency in tasks as speech or speaker recognition, among others. Traditionally gender detection has been focused on fundamental frequency (f0) and cepstral features derived from voiced segments of speech. The methodology presented here discards f0 as a valid feature because its estimation is complicate, or even impossible in unvoiced fragments, and its relevance in emotional speech or in strongly prosodic speech is not reliable. The approach followed consists in obtaining uncorrelated glottal and vocal tract components which are parameterized as mel-frequency coefficients. K-fold and cross-validation using QDA and GMM classifiers showed detection rates as large as 99.77 in a gender-balanced database of running speech from 340 speakers.

Keywords: speech processing, joint-process estimation, speaker's biometry, contextual speech information.

1 Introduction

Accurate gender detection from voice is a very important premise in many speech and voice analysis tasks, as automatic speech recognition (ASR), voice pathology detection (VPD), automatic speaker characterization (ASC) or speech synthesis (SS). It is well known that many applications improve substantially detection error trade-offs or classification and recognition rates if appropriate gender-oriented models are used, as inter-speaker variability is reduced. This is especially so in voice quality analysis for organic pathology detection [1]. For such pitch estimates were classically used as it was thought that pitch is a precise mark of gender, when actually it is not. It is true that pitch in modal phonation (that one produced under quiet and controlled conditions in sustained vowels as /a/ as more comfortably as possible) tends to distribute differently in male and female voices. But these conditions are not fulfilled in running speech, where pitch may be altered by prosody and emotion effects, or in singing. Voice pathology may alter also pitch, reducing the fundamental frequency (f0) in females or incrementing it in males, and phonation bifurcations may produce

T. Drugman and T. Dutoit (Eds.): NOLISP 2013, LNAI 7911, pp. 25–32, 2013.

drastic changes in pitch within an octave. Other factors maybe the interaction between the glottal formant and the first vocal tract formant, and the influence of telephone channels in affecting the fundamental frequency band. Therefore detecting gender based on a single feature as f0 may become rather unreliable having in mind the problems associated to f0 estimation in itself, especially if a wider description of biometric features as gender and age is involved. There are several gender detection techniques which are of interest to this study. A classical analysis is given in [2, 3], in which the authors investigate the relative role of fundamental frequency and formants in gender recognition experiments using mainly vowels. The results claimed 100% accuracy with a limited number of speakers (27 male and 25 female). In [4] gender detection is based on a combination of features derived only from the glottal source separated from vowel segments by inverse filtering and approximate reconstruction. The features used are f0, the instant of maximum glottal area (gap), the maximum derivative of the gap, the slope of the glottal flow spectrum, and the harmonic amplitude ratios. False classification rates are 5.3% for males and 4.1% for females on a database with 92 speakers (52 male and 40 female). Several inconveniences are found in all these approaches. The first one is to rely strongly on f0 estimates, having in mind that this is a complicate task, or to depend on estimates of the formants, which are also dependent on f0 and on peak tracking. These facts raise the question of providing gender detection based on the following premises: exclude f0 as feature if possible; step on robust features derived from vocal tract and glottal source estimates obtained from a source-filter separation technique granting orthogonal descriptions; use running speech similar to what can be found in real applications; test the methodology on a large database enough to grant statistical significance. The present approach is based on a careful reconstruction of the glottal source and resonant cavities using techniques derived from voice pathology studies [5]. The paper is organized as follows: in Section 2 a description of the methodology to produce statistically independent features for the vocal tract and the glottal source. In Section 3 the database used in the experiments is described and the experimental setup is commented. Section 4 is devoted to present and discuss gender detection results obtained using the methodology and database described. In section 5 conclusions are derived.

2 Present Approach

The model of speech production proposed by Fant is a very well know one to need any further explanation [6] (see Fig. 1). Its main interest is founded in the presence of an excitation which may be voiced or voiceless, modified by a time-varying filter representing the articulation organs (pharynx, oral and nasal cavities), usually modeled as a tube of irregular shape which may be approximated by a concatenation of time-varying cross-section tubes. In a first order approach the system is considered loss-less, and time variations are handled by means of adaptive algorithms which may cope with changes in the cross-section profile.

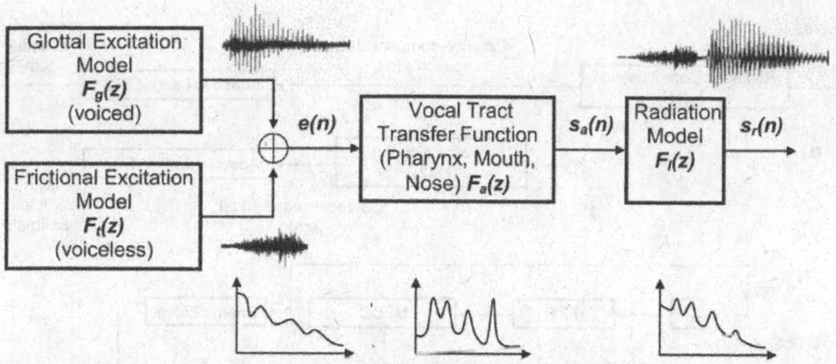

Fig. 1. Fant's source-filter model of speech production: the excitation signal e(n) may be produced by phonation (voicing) or by turbulent excitation (voiceless). The articulation organs (pharynx, vocal/nasal tracts) have a specific behavior in the frequency domain given as a set of resonances and anti-resonances (mid-bottom) which produce a pre-radiated speech signal $s_a(n)$. The radiation model changes the spectral tilt of produced speech $s_r(n)$.

The interest of the model resides in the possibility of obtaining features to describe separately the glottal source (in voiced sounds) and the vocal tract filter (both in voiced and in voiceless sounds), thus a descriptor of the human features behind the vocal tract will be available in any situation where speech is present. The glottal source in voiced sounds is affected by the length, mass and tension of the vocal folds, which are clearly differentiated by gender (longer length, higher mass and lower tension in adult males with respect to females). The vocal tract is also clearly differentiated accordingly with gender (overall length and pharyngeal cavity dimensions [7]), thus a second set of features may be added to those from the glottal source for detection purposes. Traditionally the separation of the source and filter have been carried out by inverse filtering using estimates of the vocal tract structure to remove the resonances introduced by its equivalent transfer function in speech spectra. This separation has taken into account source-system coupling effects mainly. In the present approach a joint-process estimation methodology is proposed to create orthogonal estimates of the glottal source and vocal tract impulse responses under second order statistics [8]. The combined joint-process estimator consists in a lattice adaptive filter and a ladder mirror filter, both using dynamic adaptation of weights to produce residual signals which may be shown to be uncorrelated under second order statistics (see Fig. 2). The source-filter separation method (a) consists in producing a first estimate of the inverse vocal tract transfer function $H_v(z)$, which is used to estimate a de-vocalized residual error $e_g(n)$. Classically this residual was considered useless [9] to be recently recognized as an important source of information on phonation characteristics [5, 9]. This residual is contrasted in a lattice-ladder joint-process estimator against the radiation-compensated speech $s_l(n)$ to produce two other estimates $s_g(n)$ and $s_v(n)$, corresponding to the glottal and tract components. These correlates present the property of being orthogonal under second-order statistics [8], and are used in (b) to produce mel-frequency estimates of the vocal and glottal power spectral densities. These vectors are aligned with estimates of pitch (f0), voiced/voiceless (v/u) and the log of the energy to define the final feature vector. One of the most relevant aspects of parameterization is to decide on the orders of mfcc sets of parameters for the vocal tract (k_v) and glottal source (k_g) in Fig. 2.

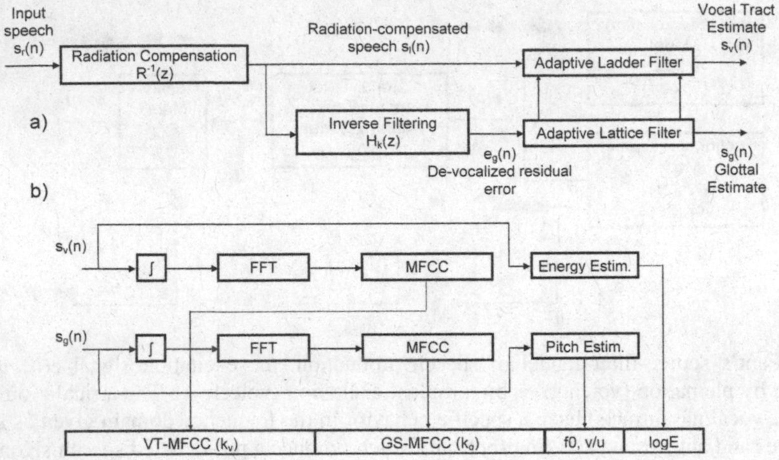

Fig. 2. Parameterization method: a) Lattice-Ladder Adaptive Joint-Process estimator to separate source and filter estimates $s_g(n)$ and $s_v(n)$; b) mel-frequency cepstral parameterization of glottal and tract components

There is not a clear criterion on this respect except considering the number of frequency channels to split spectra following mel scale. In general the region of interest of the vocal tract transfer function extends well to 8 kHz, whereas the relevant glottal information concentrates mainly in the band 0-5 kHz. Therefore a 20-band mfcc parameterization was used both to parameterize full speech and the vocal tract transfer function (k_v=20), whereas a 12-band mfcc parameterization was used for the glottal source (k_g=12), at a sampling rate of 16 kHz. This strategy creates a 55-dimmension feature vector. Examples of feature distributions from the database used, which will be described in section 3 are given in Fig. 3. Obviously not all the features will have the same relevance accordingly to gender detection criteria, therefore a study of parameter relevance would be mandatory. This is carried out using Fisher's metric according to:

$$F_m = \frac{\left(\bar{\xi} - \bar{\xi}_f\right)^2 n_f + \left(\bar{\xi} - \bar{\xi}_m\right)^2 n_m}{\mathrm{var}\left(\xi_f\right)\left(n_f - 1\right) + \mathrm{var}\left(\xi_m\right)\left(n_m - 1\right)} \qquad (1)$$

where ξ is the feature vector for the whole speaker's set, $\bar{\xi}_m$ and $\bar{\xi}_f$ are the respective average feature vectors for male and female speaker sets, and n_m and n_f are the respective number of speakers in each set. The list including the most relevant parameters in the feature set is given in Table 1. The analysis exposed in the table is very clarifying concerning feature selection: among the 14 first features by Fisher's metric the two most relevant ones are glottal source related (10 and 8); f0 is classified in third place, the following six ones are also glottal source related (11, 12, 7, 9, 1 and 6), the most relevant one derived from full speech is in position 10, and its Fisher's metric is almost four times lower than the first one.

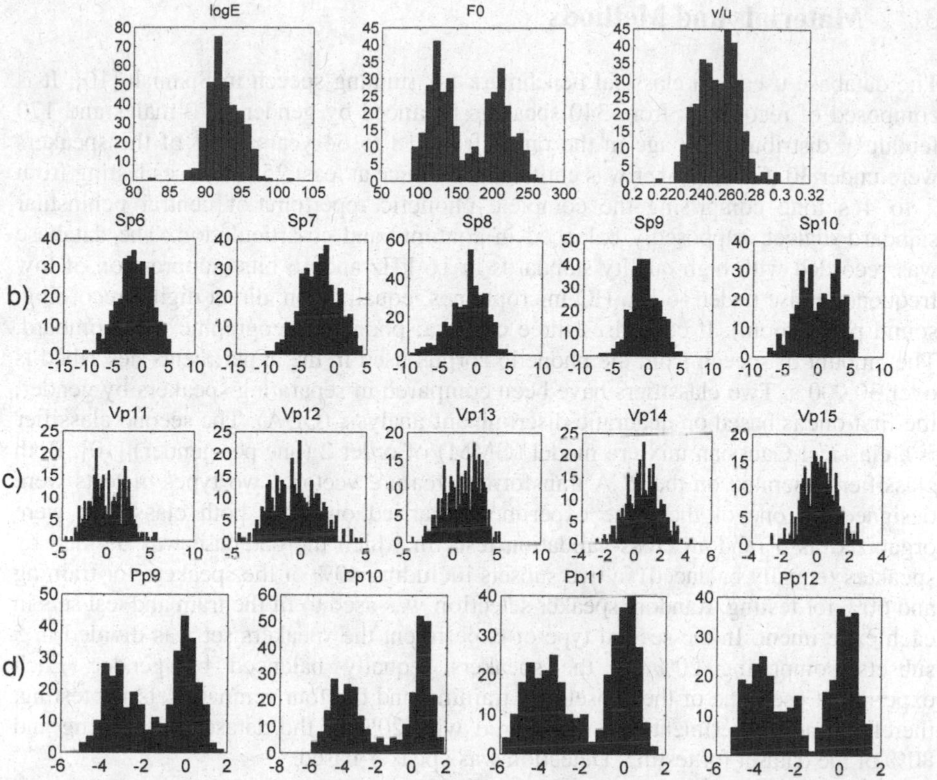

Fig. 3. Distribution histograms for some of the features estimated: a) energy, f0 and voiced/unvoiced; b) selected speech mfcc's (Sp); c) selected vocal tract mfcc's (Vp); d) selected glottal source mfcc's (Pp). Some distributions show clear gender bimodality (f0, Sp10, Vp11, Pp9, Pp10, Pp11, Pp12).

Table 1. Fisher's metric for a subset of estimated features

Order	Feature	Value	Order	Feature	Value
1	Pp10	2.0201	9	Pp6	0.7938
2	Pp8	1.6473	10	Sp10	0.5540
3	f0	1.4616	11	Vp13	0.5496
4	Pp11	1.4455	12	Vp11	0.5281
5	Pp12	1.2388	13	Pp5	0.4603
6	Pp7	1.2178	14	Sp13	0.3867
7	Pp9	0.9271	32	v/u	0.0563
8	Pp1	0.8136	49	logE	0.0019

The first feature from vocal tract is in position 11 (Vp13). Finally the feature voiced/unvoiced (v/u) and logE have been included as a reference in positions 32 and 49. These results do not clarify possible redundant relations among the different features, therefore in detection tasks instead of the original feature vector its PCA transformation has been used in the experiments.

3 Materials and Methods

The database used is a classical benchmark for running speech in Spanish [10]. It is composed of recordings from 340 speakers balanced by gender (170 males and 170 females), distributed by age in the range from 18 to 64 years. Half of the speakers were under 30. Each speaker was entitled to produce at least 25 sentences lasting from 2 to 4 s long comprising the complete phonetic repertoire of central peninsular standard dialect, supposedly balanced in contents and co-articulation. The database was recorded with high quality standards in 16 kHz and 16 bits (suppression of low frequency noise under 16 Hz, HQ microphones, equalization, direct digital recording, sound proof room). It comprises three corpora: phonetic, geographic and Lombard. The amount of speech from the phonetic corpus used in the experiments described is over 30,000 s. Two classifiers have been compared in separating speakers by gender, the first one is based on quadratic discriminant analysis (QDA). The second classifier is a classical Gaussian mixture model (GMM) of order 2 (one per gender) [10]. Both classifiers operated on the PCA transformed feature vector. Two types of tests were designed. In one of them the experiments carried out with both classifiers were organized as 5 random cross-validation tests in which the database was divided by speakers (equally balanced) in two subsets including 40% of the speakers for training and 60% for testing. Random speaker selection was used to fit the train and test sets in each experiment. In the second type of experiment the speakers set was divided in 5 subsets comprising 20% of the speakers, equally balanced by gender. Each experiment used one of the subsets for training and the four remnant sets for testing, therefore each experiment was configured with 20% of the dataset for training and 80% of the dataset for testing. Detection was speaker-based.

4 Results and Discussion

Blind clustering by MANOVA analysis was carried out to determine the relevance of each feature set. The results are given in Fig. 4 in terms of the first two canonical components from MANOVA ($c_2$vsc_1): (a) if speech mfcc's are used two main clusters are observed which are clearly separated with an overlapping region within dot lines (6 errors); (b) vocal tract mfcc's reduce the errors (4) but clusters are less separate; (c) glottal source mfcc's separate clusters better, but number of errors is larger (8); (d) if glottal pulse and vocal tract mfcc's are combined the separation between clusters improve and the number of errors is lower (3). In the detection experiments using QDA and GMM's reported in Table 2 the feature vector was configured in seven different ways: 20 speech-derived features only (S), 12 glottal source-derived features (GS), 20 vocal tract-derived features (VT), 32 speech and glottal source fused features (S+GS), 40 speech and vocal tract fused features (S+VT), 32 glottal source and vocal tract features (GS+VT) and 52 speech, glottal source and vocal tract fused features (S+GS+VT). The detection rates obtained in each task after averaging over the 5 experiments per trial are given in Table 2. These results confirm the first impression derived from MANOVA analysis: complementing speech features with glottal and vocal tract features outperform features from original speech only.

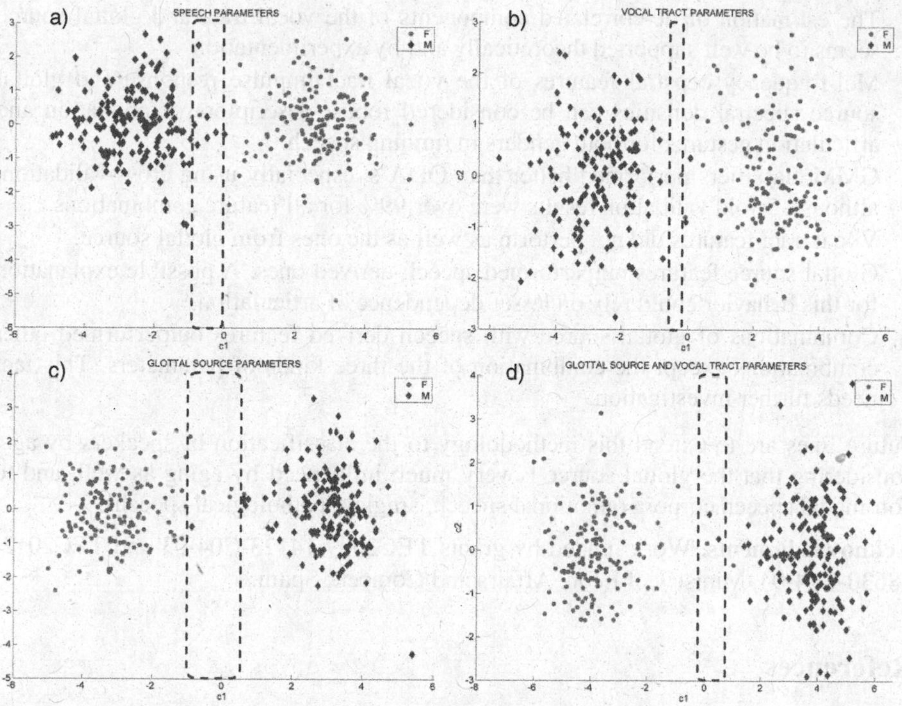

Fig. 4. Gender group separation after MANOVA analysis on different mfcc combinations from: a) original speech, 6 OS); b) vocal tract transfer function (TF), 4 OS; c) glottal source power spectral density (PSD), 8 OS; d) glottal source PSD and vocal tract TF; 3 OS. OS: overlapped subjects.

Table 2. Detection results: averages over 5 experiments

Av. Rel. Err.	S	GS	VT	S+GS	S+VT	GS+VT	S+GS+VT
QDA-xval	98.47	98.00	98.24	99.18	98.41	98.94	99.59
QDA-5 fold	96.08	96.08	96.08	98.53	98.53	98.53	99.41
GMM-xval	97.18	98.65	99.24	99.36	98.06	99.29	**99.77**
GMM-5 fold	99.18	99.41	99.35	99.41	99.47	98.94	99.59

5 Conclusions

First of all it must be stressed that f0, although estimated and put in comparison vs other features in Table 1 is not used in gender detection, as it may be inferred from the feature sets used in the experiments. The intention in proceeding so was two-fold, on one hand to avoid the problems found in accurate pitch estimation, on the other hand to avoid intra-speaker dispersion due to prosody and emotional factors (especially in male). Accordingly to the results this decision has shown to be crucial in obtaining reliable and robust results. From what has been exposed the following conclusions may be derived:

- The estimation of de-correlated components of the vocal tract and glottal source seems to be well supported theoretically and by experimentation.
- Mel-frequency cepstral features of the vocal tract impulse response and glottal source spectral densities can be considered robust descriptors of phonation and articulation gestures for both genders in running speech.
- GMM classifiers performed better than QDA's, especially using cross-validation, although 5-fold validation results were over 99% for all feature combinations.
- Vocal tract features did not perform as well as the ones from glottal source.
- Glottal source features outperformed speech-derived ones. A possible explanation for this behavior could rely on lesser dependence of articulation.
- Combinations of glottal source with speech derived features outperformed other combinations except the combination of the three kinds of parameters. This fact needs further investigation.

Future lines are to extend this methodology to the classification of speakers by age, considering that the glottal source is very much influenced by aging as well, and to non-modal speech corpora (emotional speech, singing, pathological speech).

Acknowledgments. Work funded by grants TEC2009-14123-C04-03 and TEC2012-38630-C04-04, Ministry of Econ. Affairs and Compet., Spain.

References

1. Fraile, R., Saenz-Lechon, N., Godino-Llorente, J.I., Osma-Ruiz, V., Fredouille, C.: Automatic detection of laryngeal pathologies in records of sustained vowels by means of mel-frequency cepstral coefficient parameters and differentiation of patients by sex. Folia Phoniatrica et Logopaedica 61, 146–152 (2009)
2. Wu, K., Childers, D.G.: Gender recognition from speech. Part I: Coarse analysis. J. Acoust. Soc. Am. 90(4), 1828–1840 (1990)
3. Childers, D.G., Wu, K.: Gender recognition from speech. Part II: Fine analysis. J. Acoust. Soc. Am. 90(4), 1841–1856 (1991)
4. Sorokin, V.N., Makarov, I.S.: Gender recognition from vocal source. Acoust. Phys. 54(4), 571–578 (2009)
5. Gómez, P., Fernández, R., Rodellar, V., Nieto, V., Álvarez, A., Mazaira, L.M., Martínez, R., Godino, J.I.: Glottal Source Biometrical Signature for Voice Pathology Detection. Speech Comm. 51, 759–781 (2009)
6. Fant, G.: Acoustic theory of speech production. Walter de Gruyter (1970)
7. Titze, I.: Principles of voice production. Prentice Hall, Englewood Cliffs (1994)
8. Manolakis, D., Ingle, V.K., Kogon, S.M.: Statistical and Adaptive Signal Processing. Artech House (2005)
9. Prasanna, S.R.M., Gudpa, C.S., Yegnanarayana, B.: Extraction of speaker-specific excitation information from linear prediction residual of speech. Speech Communication 48, 1243–1261 (2006)
10. Moreno, A., Poch, D., Bonafonte, A., Lleida, E., Llisterri, J., Mariño, J.B., Nadeu, C.: Albayzin Speech Database: Design of the Phonetic Corpus. In: Proc. Eurospeech 1993, vol. 1, pp. 653–656 (1993)
11. Reynolds, D., Rose, R.: Robust text-independent speaker identification using Gaussian mixture speaker models. IEEE Trans. SAP 3(1), 72–83 (1995)

An Efficient Method for Fundamental Frequency Determination of Noisy Speech

Mohamed Anouar Ben Messaoud[1,2], Aïcha Bouzid[1], and Noureddine Ellouze[1]

[1] Université de Tunis El Manar, Ecole Nationale d'Ingénieurs de Tunis, LR11ES17 Laboratoire du Signal, Images et Technologies de l'Information, 1002, Tunis Tunisie
[2] Université de Tunis El Manar, Faculté des Sciences de Tunis, 1002, Tunis Tunisie
{anouar.benmessaoud,bouzidacha}@yahoo.fr, n.ellouze@enit.rnu.tn

Abstract. In this paper, we present a fundamental frequency determination method dependent on the autocorrelation compression of the multi-scale product of speech signal. It is based on the multiplication of compressed copies of the original autocorrelation operated on the multi-scale product. The multi-scale product is based on realising the product of the speech wavelet transform coefficients at three successive dyadic scales. We use the quadratic spline wavelet function. We compress the autocorrelation of the multi-scale product a number of times by integer factors (downsampling). Hence, when the obtained functions are multiplied, we obtain a peak with a clear maximum corresponding to the fundamental frequency. We have evaluated our method on the Keele database. Experimental results show the effectiveness of our method presenting a good performance surpassing other algorithms. Besides, the proposed approach is robust in noisy environment.

Keywords: Speech, pitch estimation, multi-scale product, autocorrelation, compression analysis.

1 Introduction

The fundamental frequency extraction is one of the most crucial tasks in speech processing. Pitch is used for speech in many applications including determination of emotional characteristics of speech, speaker recognition systems, and aids to the handicapped. Because of its importance, many solutions to this problem have been proposed [1]. All of the proposed schemes have their limitations due to the wide range of applications, and operating environments. Thus various methods for pitch determination have been developed and a comprehensive review of these methods can be found in [2], [3]. However, due to the non-stationarity and quasi-periodicity of the speech signal, the development of more robust pitch determination algorithms still remains an open problem.

Most of the subsequent wavelet-based Pitch Detection Algorithms (PDAs) are originally inspired by the work presented by Kadambe and al [4].

There are two important issues which need to be improved in the PDAs. First, we show the efficacy of a PDA at the beginning of a vowel. Second, we obtain a robust PDA in a noisy environment.

T. Drugman and T. Dutoit (Eds.): NOLISP 2013, LNAI 7911, pp. 33–41, 2013.

We present an approach for estimation and detection of the pitch, extracted from speech signals, in this paper. Our proposed algorithm operates an autocorrelation compression on the voiced speech multi-scale product analysis. This analysis produces one peak corresponding to the fundamental frequency F_0.

The evaluation of the PDAs is an indispensable stage. Eventually, evaluating a pitch detection algorithm means simultaneously evaluating the Gross Pitch Error and the Root Mean Square Error.

The paper is presented as follows. After the introduction, we present our approach based on the multi-scale product analysis to provide the derived speech signal and the Autocorrelation Compression operated on the Multi-scale Product (ACMP) approach for the fundamental frequency estimation. Section 3 describes the pitch period estimation algorithm in clean and noisy voiced speech. In section 4, we give evaluation results and compare them with results of approaches for clean speech. Estimation results are also described for speech mixed with environmental noises at various SNR levels.

2 Proposed Approach

We propose an approach to estimate the fundamental frequency F_0 based on the Autocorrelation Compression (AC) of the voiced sound Multi-scale Product (MP). It can be decomposed into three essential stages, as shown in figure 1. The first stage consists of computing the product of the voiced speech wavelet transform coefficients (WTC) at successive scales. In accordance with the fast change of the instantaneous pitch, the wavelet used in this analysis is the quadratic spline function at scales $s_1=2^{-1}$, $s_2=2^0$ and $s_3=2^1$. It is a smooth function with property of derivative. The second stage consists of calculating the Autocorrelation Function (ACF) of the obtained signal. Indeed, the product is decomposed into frames of 512 samples with an overlapping of 50% points at a sampling frequency of 20 kHz. These two stages were described in our work reported by Ben Messaoud and al in [5]. The last stage consists of generating the functions obtained by the Autocorrelation compression and then multiplying them to provide a signal with a reinforced peak allowing an efficient estimation of the fundamental frequency value.

The product $p(n)$ of wavelet transforms coefficients of the function $f(n)$ at some successive dyadic scales is given as follows:

$$p(n)=\prod_{j=j_0}^{j=j_L} W_{2^j} f(n). \tag{1}$$

Where $W_{2^j} f(n)$ is the wavelet transform of the function f at scale 2^j.

For the second stage, the product $p(n)$ is split into frames of N length by multiplication with a hanning window $w[n]$:

$$p_w[n,i]=p[n]w[n-i\Delta n]. \tag{2}$$

Where i is the window index, and Δn the overlap.

Then, we calculate the short-term autocorrelation function of each weighted block $p_{wi}[n]$ as follows:

$$R_i(k)=\sum_{j=0}^{N-1} p_{wi}(j)p_{wi}(j+k)$$
$$ACF_i(k)=\frac{R_i(k)}{R_i(0)} \tag{3}$$

In the third stage, the Autocorrelation of the MP is compressed by integer factors (c = 1, 2, 3) and the obtained functions are multiplied. So the fundamental frequency F_0 became stronger.

The compression of each autocorrelation of the multi-scale product is described as follows:

$$ACMP_i(k)=\prod_{c=1}^{C-1}\left|\left(R_i(c*k)\right)\right| . \tag{4}$$

Where C is the number of harmonics to be considered.

The first peak in the original Autocorrelation Multi-scale Product (AMP) coincides with the second peak in the AMP compressed by a factor of two, which coincides with the third peak in the AMP compressed by a factor of three. Finally, we multiply to obtain one peak corresponding to pitch.

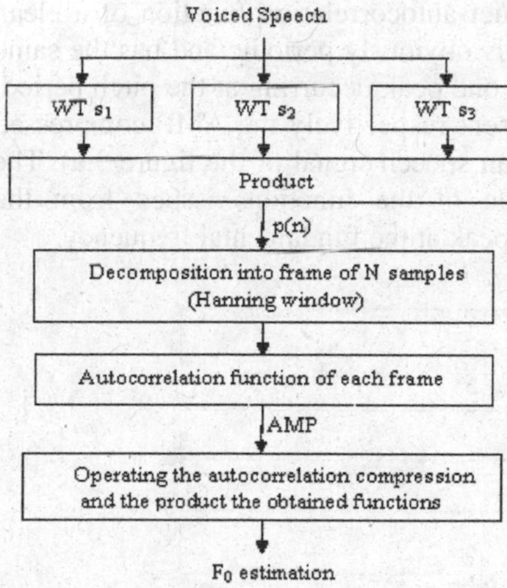

Fig. 1. Block diagram of the proposed approach for pitch estimation

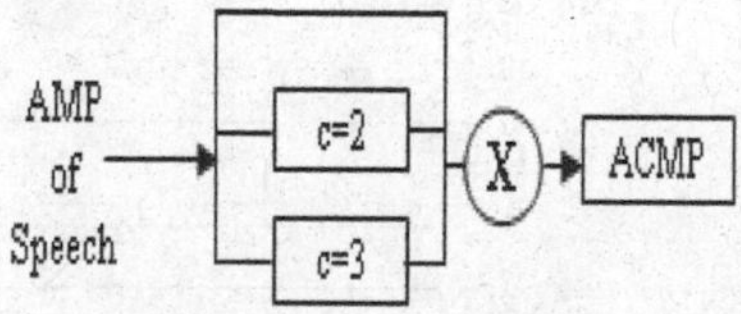

Fig. 2. Product of the compression of the speech AMP

The motivation for using the compression of the AMP is that for clean and noisy speech signals, multiplying the delay scale by integer factors should cause the peaks to coincide at F_0. Indeed the AMP of a voiced speech frame is zero between the peaks, the product of compression functions cancels out all the peaks falling between two harmonics of the F_0. Thus, in general, finding the largest peak reflecting the product of the shifted AMP would mean finding the F_0. The product of the functions issued from the compression of the AMP is presented in figure 2.

3 Pitch Estimation Algorithm

3.1 Pitch Estimation in Clean Voiced Speech

Figure 3 shows a clean voiced speech signal followed by its MP. The MP has a periodic structure and reveals extrema according to the glottal closure and opening instants.

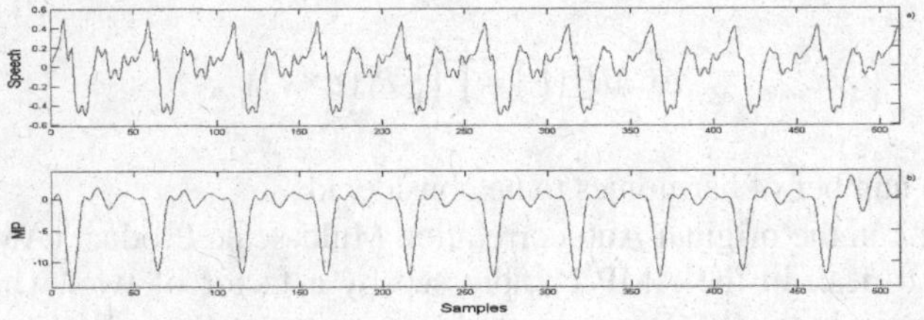

Fig. 3. a) Voiced clean speech. b) Its multi-scale product.

Figure 4.a) illustrates the multi-scale product autocorrelation function of a clean voiced speech signal. The calculated function is obviously periodic and has the same period as the MP. The obtained ACMP shows one peak occurring at the pitch period. The signals of the figures 4.b) and 4.c) represent respectively the AMP compressed with a factor c = 2 and c =3 of the voiced clean speech signal of the figure 3.a). The figure 4.d) corresponds to the multiplication of the functions issued from the compression of the AMP and shows one clear peak at the fundamental frequency.

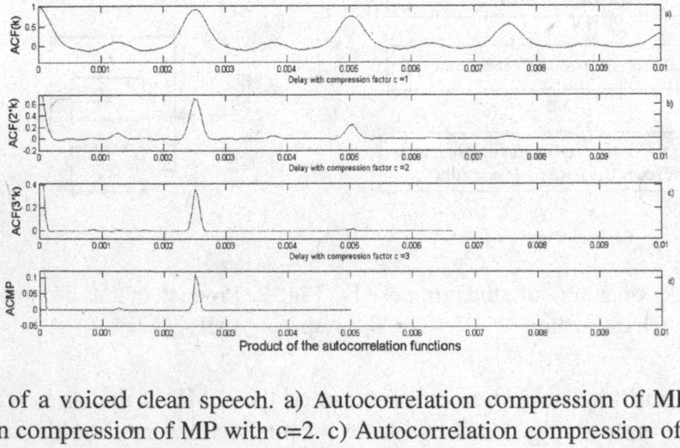

Fig. 4. ACMP of a voiced clean speech. a) Autocorrelation compression of MP with c=1. b) Autocorrelation compression of MP with c=2. c) Autocorrelation compression of MP with c=3. d) Autocorrelation functions multiplication.

Figure 5 treats the beginning of a voiced speech followed by its MP. Figure 6 shows the efficacy of the ACMP method for pitch estimation particularly at the beginning of a vowel. Signals represented in the figure 6.a), 6.b), 6.c) and 6.d) illustrate the compression of the autocorrelation multi-scale product of the speech depicted in 5.a).

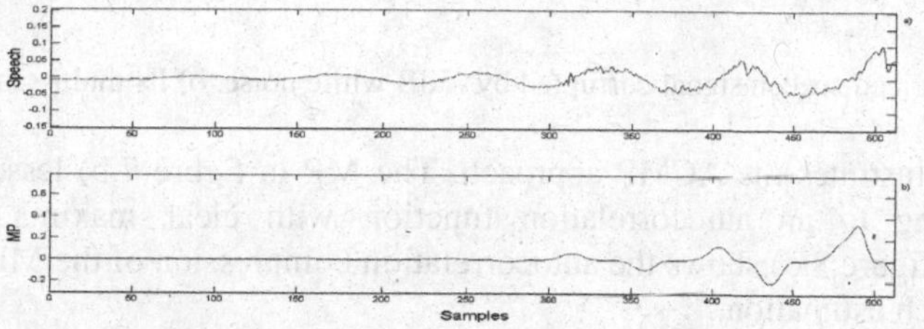

Fig. 5. a) The beginning of a vowel. b) Its multi-scale product.

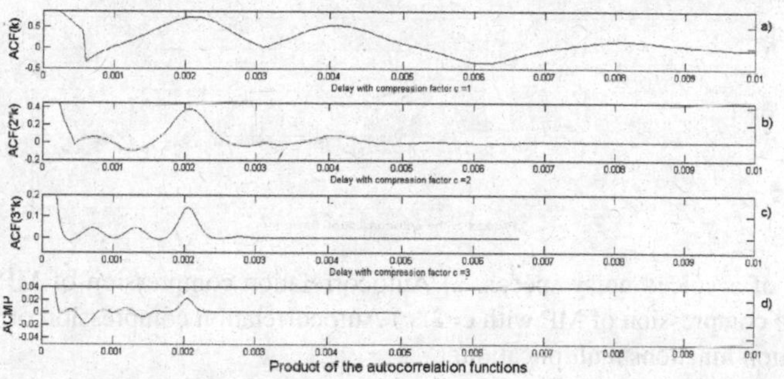

Fig. 6. ACMP of a vowel beginning. a) Autocorrelation compression of MP with c=1. b) Autocorrelation compression of MP with c=2. c) Autocorrelation compression of MP with c=3. d) Autocorrelation functions multiplication.

Figure 6 illustrates the efficacy of our approach for the fundamental frequency determination during a vowel onset. While the experimental results show that the other state of the art methods in literature give an F0 equals to zero at the beginning of vowel at this voiced region.

3.2 Pitch Estimation in a Noisy Environment

In this subsection, we try to show the robustness of our approach in the presence of the noise with high SNR levels.

Figure 7 depicts a noisy voiced speech signal with an SNR of -5 dB followed by its MP.

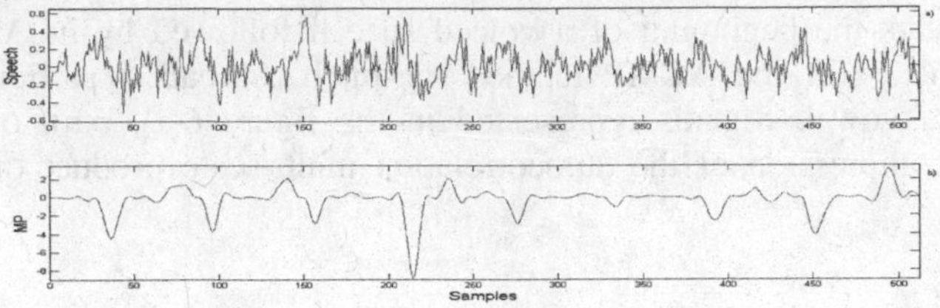

Fig. 7. a) Voiced speech signal corrupted by -5dB white noise. b) Its multi-scale product.

Figure 8 illustrates the ACMP approach. The MP in figure 7.b) lessens the noise effects leading to an autocorrelation function with clear maxima. The signal illustrated in figure 8.d) shows the autocorrelation compression of the MP with a peak giving the pitch estimation.

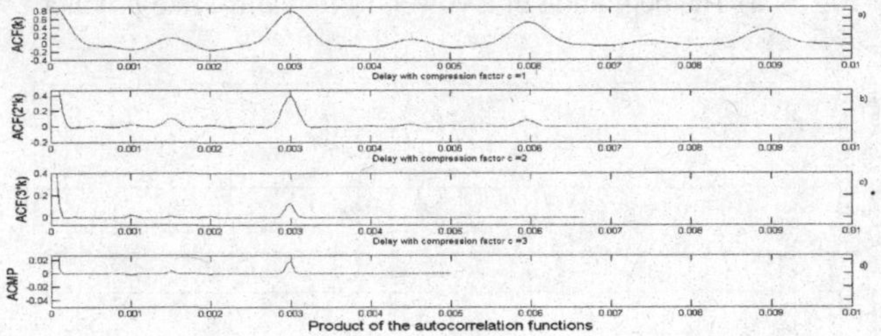

Fig. 8. ACMP of a voiced noisy speech. a) Autocorrelation compression of MP with c=1. b) Autocorrelation compression of MP with c=2. c) Autocorrelation compression of MP with c=3. d) Autocorrelation functions multiplication.

4 Results

4.1 Evaluation Databases

To evaluate the performance of our algorithm, we use the Keele pitch reference database [6]. The Keele database contains ten speakers sampling frequency of 20 kHz. It includes reference files containing a pitch estimation of 25.6 ms segments with 10 ms overlapping. The reference pitch estimation is based on a simultaneously recorded signal of a laryngograph.

We use common performance measures for comparing PDAs: The Gross Pitch Error (GPE) and the Root Mean Square Error (RMSE) [7]. The gross Pitch Error (GPE) is a standard error measure for the pitch tracking. It is defined as the percentage of estimated F_0 deviates from the referenced F_0 by more than 20% of voiced speech. The RMSE is defined as square root of the average squared estimation error with estimation errors which are smaller than the GPE threshold of 20 Hz. It should be noted that the pitch range of speech is 50 – 800 Hz.

4.2 Evaluation in a Clean Environment

For comparison, the four PDAs are based on the same reference database. The speech signal must be segmented into frames of 25.6 ms segments with 10 ms overlapping and is weighted by a Hanning window. The PDA's are only tested in the voiced frame.

Table 1 presents the evaluation results of the proposed approach (ACMP) for fundamental frequency determination in a clean environment and compared to the existed methods [8], [9], and [11].

Table 1. Pitch estimation Performance in a clean environment

Method	GPE (%)	RMSE (Hz)
ACMP	0.64	1.43
SWIPE'[8]	0.62	3.05
SMP [9]	0.75	2.41
NMF-PI [11]	0.93	2.84

The ACMP shows a reduced GPE rate of 0.64 % and the lowest RMSE of 1.43 Hz. It's obviously more accurate than the other methods.

4.3 Evaluation in a Noisy Environment

To test the robustness of our algorithm, we add various background noises (white, babble, and vehicle) at three SNR levels to the Keele database speech signals. For this, we use the noisex-92 database [10].

Table 2 presents the GPE of the ACMP, SMP, and NMF-PI methods in a noisy environment.

Table 2. Pitch estimation Performance of GPE in a noisy environment

		GPE (%)		
Type of noise	SNR level	ACMP	SMP [9]	NMF-PI [11]
White	5 dB	0.84	1.00	1.08
	0 dB	1.02	1.20	1.14
	-5 dB	1.09	1.40	1.32
Babble	5 dB	1.03	2.61	1.51
	0 dB	1.46	4.56	2.93
	-5 dB	1.67	7.62	5.10
Vehicle	5 dB	3.67	6.41	3.94
	0 dB	4.92	7.04	5.22
	-5 dB	5.80	8.98	8.74

As depicted in table 2, when the SNR level decreases, the ACMP algorithm remains robust even at -5dB.

Table 3 presents the RMSE of the ACMP, SMP and NMF-PI methods in a noisy environment.

Table 3. Pitch estimation Performance of RMSE in a noisy environment

Type of noise	SNR level	RMSE (Hz) ACMP	SMP [9]	NMF-PI [11]
White	5 dB	2.45	3.23	4.63
	0 dB	2.86	3.73	4.84
	-5 dB	3.57	4.67	4.95
Babble	5 dB	3.67	4.28	3.81
	0 dB	4.59	4.93	4.92
	-5 dB	5.21	6.38	6.53
Vehicle	5 dB	2.08	5.67	4.53
	0 dB	3.36	7.89	4.60
	-5 dB	5.09	11.57	6.28

As depicted in table 3, the ACMP method presents the lowest RMSE values showing its convenience for pitch estimation in hard situations.

5 Conclusion

In this paper, we presented a pitch estimation method that relies on the compression of the autocorrelation applied on the speech multi-scale product. The proposed approach can be recapitulated in three essential stages. First, we have constituted the product of the voiced speech WTC at three successive dyadic scales (The wavelet is the quadratic spline function with a support of 0.8 ms). The voiced speech MP has a periodic and clean structure that matches well with the speech signal singularities and lessens the noise effects. Second, we have calculated the autocorrelation function of each weighted frame. Third, we have operated the compression of the obtained autocorrelation with various scales and their product.

The experimental results show the robustness of our approach for noisy speech, and its efficacy for clean speech in comparison with state-of-the-art algorithms. Future work concerns the extension of the proposed approach to estimate F_0 in monophonic music.

References

1. Hess, W.J.: Pitch Determination of Speech Signals, pp. 373–383. Springer (1983)
2. Shahnaz, C., Wang, W.P., Ahmad, M.O.: A spectral Matching Method for Pitch Estimation from Noise-corrupted Speech. In: IEEE International Midwest Symposium on Circuits and Systems, pp. 1413–1416. IEEE Press, Taiwan (2009)
3. Chu, C., Alwan, A.: A SAFE: A Statistical Approach to F0 Estimation Under Clean and Noisy Conditions. IEEE Trans. Audio, Speech and Language Process. 20, 933–944 (2012)
4. Kadambe, S., Boudreaux-Bartels, G.F.: Application of the Wavelet Transform for Pitch Detection of Speech Signals. IEEE Trans. Information Theory 38, 917–924 (1992)

5. Ben Messaoud, M.A., Bouzid, A., Ellouze, N.: Autocorrelation of the Speech Multi-scale Product for Voicing Decision and Pitch Estimation. Springer Cognitive Computation 2, 151–159 (2010)
6. Meyer, G., Plante, F., Ainsworth, W.A.: A Pitch Extraction Reference Database. In: 4th European Conference on Speech Communication and Technology EUROSPEECH 1995, Madrid, pp. 837–840 (1995)
7. Rabiner, L., Cheng, M., Rosenberg, A., McGonegal, C.: A comparative performance study of several pitch detection algorithms. IEEE Trans. on Acoustic, Speech, and Signal. Process. 24, 399–418 (1976)
8. Camacho, A.: SWIPE: a Sawtooth Waveform Inspired Pitch Estimator for Speech and Music, Ph.D. dissertation, Dept. Elect. Eng., Florida Univ., USA (2007)
9. Ben Messaoud, M.A., Bouzid, A., Ellouze, N.: Using Multi-scale Product Spectrum for Single and Multi-pitch Estimation. IET Signal Process. Journal 5, 344–355 (2011)
10. Varga, A.: Assessment for Automatic Speech Recognition: II. Noisex-92: A Database and an Experiment to Study the Effect of Additive Noise on Speech Recognition Systems. Speech Communication 12, 247–251 (1993)
11. Joho, D., Bennewitz, M., Behnke, S.: Pitch Estimation Using Models of Voiced Speech on Three Levels. In: 4th IEEE International Conference on Acoustics, Speech and Signal Processing, ICASSP 2007, pp. 1077–1080. IEEE Press, Honolulu (2007)

Glottal Source Model Selection for Stationary Singing-Voice by Low-Band Envelope Matching

Fernando Villavicencio

Yamaha Corporation, Corporate Research & Development Center, 203
Matsunokijima, Iwata, Shizuoka, Japan

Abstract. In this paper a preliminary study on voice excitation modeling by single glottal shape parameter selection is presented. A strategy for direct model selection by matching derivative glottal source estimates with LF-based candidates driven by the Rd parameter is explored by means of two state-of-the-art similarity measures and a novel one considering spectral envelope information. An experimental study on synthetic singing-voice was carried out aiming to compare the performance of the different measures and to observe potential relations with respect to different voice characteristics (e.g. vocal effort, pitch range, amount of aperiodicities and aspiration noise). The results of this study allow us to claim competitive performance of the proposed strategy and suggest us preferable source modeling conditions for stationary singing-voice.

1 Introduction

The transformation of voice source characteristics represents a challenge of major interest in terms of expressive speech synthesis and voice quality control. A main task to achieve transformation is found in the modeling of the excitation (source) characteristics of the voice. However, a robust decomposition of the source and filter contributions represents a major challenge due to exisiting non-linear interactions limiting the robustness of an inverse filtering process.

Some works propose iterative and deterministic methods for voice decomposition such as [1] and [2] respectively. A recent strategy consists of approximating the glottal contribution by exhaustive search using the well-known LF model [3], [4]. Although the different techniques show promising results the performance is commonly sensitive to aspects of the voice that may significantly vary in continuous speech among individuals (e.g. first formant position, voice quality, voicing).

We aim to perform voice excitation modeling as an initial stage for future voice quality modification purposes on stationary singing-voice samples used for concatenative singing-voice synthesis. The controlled recording conditions (vocal effort, pitch, energy) of such signals allow us to delimit the analysis context of the main glottal source characteristics and to derive a simplified strategy to model them by selecting an approximative model.

Our study follows the works of [3] and [4] proposing derivative glottal signal modeling by selecting Liljencrants-Fant (LF) based models issued from a set of

T. Drugman and T. Dutoit (Eds.): NOLISP 2013, LNAI 7911, pp. 42–49, 2013.

glottal shape parameter (*Rd*) candidates. Furthermore, we propose a novel selection measure based on accurate spectral envelope information. This strategy, refered to as "normalized low-band envelope" (NLBE) is compared with the measures proposed in the referenced works based on phase and joint frequency-time information. An experimental study over a set of synthetic signals emulating the target singing samples was carried out seeking to observe the main relations between the signal's characteristics and the performance provided by the different selection measures.

This paper is structured as follows. In section 2 the proposed NLBE estimation is introduced. The synthetic data used for objective evaluation based on stationary singing-voice is described in section 3. In section 4 the results of the experimental study are reported. The paper ends at section 5 with conclusions and future work.

2 NLBE Glottal Source Model Selection

2.1 Rd Based Voice Quality Modeling

The Rd parameter allows us to quantify the characteristic trends of the LF model parameters (Ra, Rk, Rg) ranging from a tight, adducted vocal phonation $(Rd \approx 0.3)$ to a very breathy abducted one $(Rd \geq 2.7)$ [5]. Three main voice qualities are distinguished along this range: *pressed*, *modal* (or normal) and *breathy.* In [6] 0.8, 1.1 and 2.9 were found as approximative values of *Rd* for these voice qualities on baritono sung vowels. Similarly, our interest is focused on stationary singing preferably sung with modal voice. Accordingly, it can be expected that *Rd* estimates on the underlying glottal excitation are found close to the mentioned modal value keeping a slow and narrow variation over time. This principle was therefore considered in order to derive the glottal-model selection strategy described in the next section.

2.2 Normalized Low-Band Envelope Based Rd Estimation

One of the main features of the progress of the *Rd* parameter on the LF model is the variation of the spectral tilt of the resulting derivative glottal signal spectrum. Low *Rd* values produce flat-like spectra whereas higher ones show increasing slopes. Moreover, the low-frequency voiced band of voice source spectra is mainly explained by the glottal pulse contribution and studies have shown the importance of the difference between the two first harmonics $(H1 - H2)$ as one of the main indicators of variations on its characteristics [7].

We propose to measure the similiarity between *Rd*-modeled derivative glottal candidates and extracted ones by comparing their spectral envelope within a low-frequency band after normalization of the average energy. The spectral envelope is estimated pitch synchronous in a narrow-band basis (4 pulses) centered at the glottal closure instant. The envelope model correspond to the one described in [8] seeking to use accurate envelope information. Note that by following this strategy we aim to approximate the main glottal characteristics within a small *Rd* range rather than estimate accurate *Rd* values. Moreover, assuming a smooth variation of the vocal phonation a simple candidates selection is proposed by exclusively considering a small deviation of *Rd* between succesive epochs.

The method is described as follows. Let $S(f)$ be the narrow band spectrum of the speech frame $s(t)$ (4 periods) and $A_{vt}(f)$ the system representing its corresponding vocal tract transfer function. As usual, the derivative glottal signal $dg_e(t)$ is extracted by analysis filtering according to

$$DG_e(f) = S(f)/A_vt(f) \tag{1}$$

Following, a *Rd* candidate is used to generate an excitation sequence $dg_{rd}(t)$ of same length (*Rd* fixed, gain $Ee = 1$). The spectral envelopes $Edg_e(f)$ and $Edg_{rd}(f)$ are estimated from $dg_e(t)$ and $dg_{rd}(t)$ respectively using *optimal* True-Envelope estimation [8] in order to observe accurate $H1 - H2$ information.

The matching is limited to the low-band defined within the range $[f0, Mf0]$, where M represents a number of harmonics fully considered as voiced. The normalization gain G_{dB} is computed as the difference between the average energy of $Eg_e(f)$ and $Eg_{rd}(f)$ within the mentioned low-frequency band

$$G_{dB} = \frac{1}{K}\sum_{f=f0}^{Mf0} Edg_e(f) - \frac{1}{K}\sum_{f=f0}^{Mf0} Edg_{rd}(f) \tag{2}$$

note that G_{dB} represents an estimation for $dg_{rd}(t)$ of the actual gain Ee . The matching error is defined as the mean square error between the envelope of the extracted excitation and the one of the normalized *Rd* model, according to

$$Error_{nlbe} = \frac{1}{K}\sum_{f=f0}^{Mf0} (Eg_e(f) - [Eg_{rd}(f) + G_{dB}])^2 \tag{3}$$

where K represents the number of frequency bins within $[f0, Mf0]$. The corresponding Rd_{nlbe} value for $s(t)$ is selected following the candidate observing the smallest error.

For comparison, the *Mean Squared Phase* (MSP) measure described in [3] and the joint spectral-time cost function proposed by [4] (labeled as *SpecTime*) were also used as selection cost measures. Note that the harmonic phase information for MSP compuation was obtained from the closest DFT bin to the harmonic frequencies and that the DFT size N was set equal to the frame length. We note that a potential lack of precision of the harmonic information given the DFT size may limit the performance of the MSP and *SpecTime* measures.

3 Synthetic Data

3.1 "Emulating" Stationary Singing-Voice Samples

The synthetic data consist of short units (1 sec length) aiming to emulate stationary singing samples of individual vowels. To generate the LF-based pulses sequence a small sinusoidal modulation (5% of maximal deviation) over time was applied around the central values of $f0$ and Rd selected for test seeking to reproduce a smooth variation of the glottal excitation. The modulation of Ee was derived from that of Rd (double negative variation). These criteria follow the basic correlations between these features mentioned in [5]. An example of the resulting parameters evolution used for synthesis is shown in Figure 1.

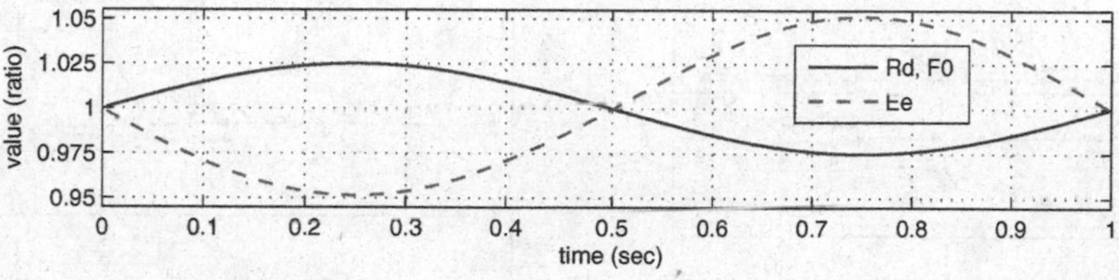

Fig. 1. Evolution of the sythesis LF parameters normalized by their average value

The vocal tract function (VTF) correspond to a *True-envelope* all-pole system [9] estimated after manual LF modeling on central segments of 5 stationary sung vowels of 6 singers (3 males, 3 females), resulting in 30 different VTFs of varying order ([83 – 170]). The original VTF information was kept unchanged for both synthesis and extraction purposes in order to exclusively compare the selection performance of the different measures. The *aspiration* (excitation) noise corresponds to the two-components modulated white-noise model proposed in [6]. The synthetic signals were generated by convolution of the filter and source parts after the sumation of the LF and noise contributions in an overlapp-add basis. Note that given the large filter orders it was applied a zero-padding to the source frames of the same frame length in order to ensure a reasonable underdamping on the synthesized waveforms. The samplerate was fixed to $44.1KHz$.

3.2 Aperiodicities Synthesis

Beyond the degree of aspiration noise other common excitation phenomena are $T0$ *aperiodicities* in the form of pitch and energy frame-to-frame variations (known commonly as *jitter* and *shimmer* respectively). The characteristic of these variations is random with reported maximal values of $\approx 2\%$ in pathological voices (e.g. *harsh, hoarse*) [10]. Although these phenomena mainly concerns non-modal voice it may be found in intended "modal" phonations of individuals with voices observing some natural degree of *roughness*. Following, shimmer and jitter were also considered in the synthesis framework and applied jointly as random frame-by-frame variations of Ee and $f0$.

3.3 Experiments

We aimed to evaluate the proposed modeling strategy using the different selection measures on a data set including varied filter and excitation characteristics.

Accordingly, 3 different pitch ranges corresponding to the musical notes $A2$, $G3$ and $F4$ ($110, 196, 350 Hz$) were considered to build the synthetic data seeking to explore a reasonable singing range. Moreover, several *Rd* ranges and amounts of aspiration noise and aperiodicities arbitrarily selected were also considered, resulting in about 750 different test signals.

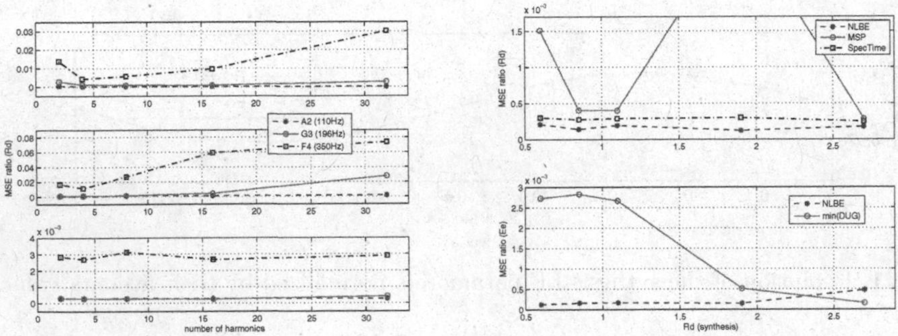

Fig. 2. *Rd* selection performance as a function of the low-band length (for matching) and the pitch range on a modal region ($Rd = 1.1$) for NLBE (left, top), MSP (left, middle) and *SpecTime* (left, bottom) selection cost measures. Evaluation over a set of *Rd* values (top, right) and estimation of the LF gain parameter *Ee* (bottom, right).

4 Results

The set of candidates Rd_c tested for *Rd* selection at each voice epoch consisted of the previous selected value and 2 neighbouring ones limited to a potential deviation Rd_{step} (arbitrarily set to 2.5%). We used this criterion instead of a fixed *Rd* step due to the non-linear evolution of the spectral envelope gaps observed along the *Rd* scale. The selection performance was quantified by means of the MSE ratio (normalized error) between the actual and selected *Rd* values according to the NLBE, MSP and *SpecTime* cost functions. Two *Ee* estimation strategies were also compared and evaluated similarly: a proposed one using the gain parameter G_{dB} of NLBE and the standard strategy consisting on a direct computation from the negative peak of the derivative glottal signal, labeled as min(DUG).

4.1 Effect of the Low-Band Length and the Rd Range

We were firstly interested to observe the performance on signals corresponding to a modal range ($Rd = 1.1$) in terms of the low-band length (number of harmonics) considered on the cost functions and the effect of the pitch range. The results are shown in Fig. 2 (left), note that for clarity a different axis scaling was applied on the plots. As expected, it can be seen the negative effect of increasing pitch on the *Rd* identification performance. A smaller fundamental period may represent a larger overlapping between pulses, and therefore, a larger mixing of the spectral information. In general, it was found that by using 4 harmonics it was already possible to achieve the lower error regions accross the different measures. NLBE provided the lowest average error on low-pitched data although all methods showed comparable performance and stability ($NLBE = 2.0e-4$, $MSP = 4.6e-4$, $SpecTime = 2.9e-4$). Accordingly, aiming to focus on preferable modeling conditions only the low-pitch ($A2$) data set and the 4 harmonics limit as low-band criterion were kept for the following experiments.

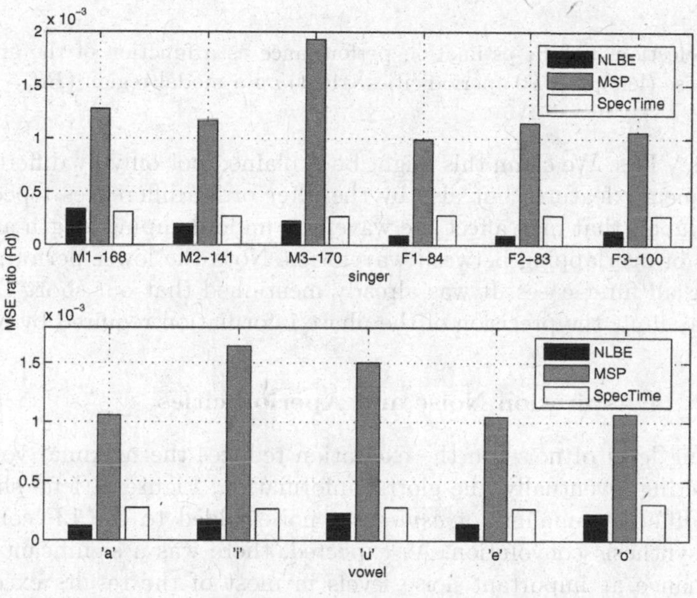

Fig. 3. *Rd* selection performance per singer (top) and vowel (bottom) case for synthetic data covering different *Rd* regions and single pitch range ($A2$)

In Fig. 2 (right) are also shown the results when using several *Rd* ranges on the synthetic signals. There was not a significant effect of the glottal shape (*Rd* range) on the selection performance besides an irregular evolution on the MSP selection (some values on the plot are out of range). NLBE and *SpecTime* showed higher and more stable performance. Concerning *Ee* estimation (bottom), there was some dependency of the direct computation with respect to *Rd*, showing maximal errors of about $\approx 5\%$ of the parameter value on low *Rd* signals.

4.2 Effect of the VTF Charateristics

Figure 3 shows the results of the previous experiment per singer (top) and vowel (bottom) case. The scores suggest some dependency of the performance accross

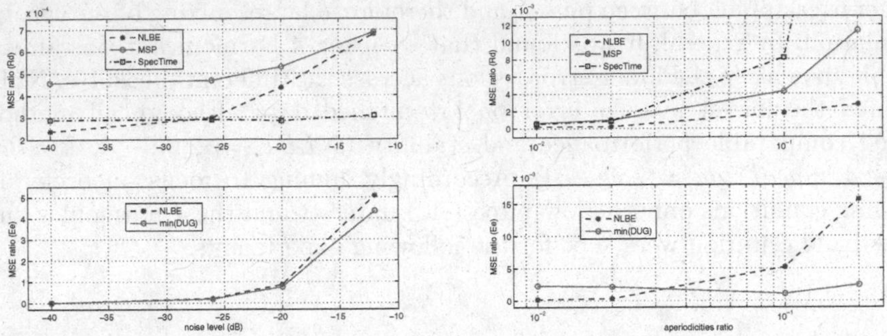

Fig. 4. *Rd* selection and *Ee* estimation performance as a function of the amount of aspiration noise (left) and $T0$ aperiodicities (right) on a modal region ($Rd = 1.1$)

the different VTFs. We claim this might be explained not only by differences on the low-frequency features but also by the filter order differences (specified at each singer label) that may affect the waveform underdamping length and thus, the amount of overlapping between waveforms. Note the lower performance of MSP among all filter cases. It was already mentioned that our short DFT size criterion may limit the precision of the phase information required by MSP.

4.3 Effect of Aspiration Noise and Aperiodicities

An increasing level of noise on the excitation reduces the maximal voiced frequency affecting, eventually, the glottal information. Figure 4 (left) shows the results for different amounts of *aspiration* noise added to the LF component before the synthesis convolution. As expected, there was a significant drop in the performance at important noise levels in most of the results excepting a surprising stability showed by the *Rd* selection from *SpecTime*. The results confirm the difficulties of modeling *aspirated* and *breathy* voices. Note however that reasonable scores could be keep until moderate amounts of noise ($\leq -25dB$).

Conversely, *SpecTime* was the most sensitive measure with respect to $T0$ aperiodicities, as shown in Figure 4 (right). The aperiodicities scale denotes the maximal deviation percentage related to the mean values of Ee and $f0$ applied frame-by-frame. In general, the drop in the performance might be explained by the degradation of the harmonic structure at the low-band due to the random variations of energy y frequency applied to the fundamental component. NLBE shows the best performane, however, all results, including Ee estimation seem to be robust enough to cover aperiodicities amounts reaching the mentioned levels of pathological voices ($\leq 2\%$). The results above this value might be mainly relevant to study some extreme vocal phonation cases.

5 Conclusions and Future Work

This paper presented an experimental comparison of methods for glottal model selection on a large synthetic set of stationary singing signals. The results showed evidence that a proposed selection strategy based on low-frequency spectral envelope matching provides comparable estimation performance to recent techniques based on phase, amplitude and time-domain information.

The experiments showed relations between different voice characteristics and the glottal selection performance, suggesting preferable source modeling conditions. Furthermore, studies should be done to extend the study to real singing-voice. The author is currently studying the perfomance of the overall direct glottal modeling strategy in a joint source-filter estimation framework.

References

1. Alku, P.: Glottal wave analysis with pitch synchronous iterative adaptive inverse filtering. Speech Communication 11, 109–118 (1992)
2. Drugman, T., Bozkurt, B., Dutoit, T.: Causal-anticausal decomposition of speech using complex cepstrum for glottal source estimation. Speech Communication 53, 855–866 (2011)
3. Degottex, G., Röbel, A., Rodet, X.: Joint estimate of shape and time-synchronization of a glottal source model by phase flatness. In: Proc. of ICASSP, Dallas, USA, pp. 5058–5061 (2010)
4. Kane, J., Yanushevskaya, I., Chasaide, A.N., Gobl, C.: Exploiting time and frequency domain measures for precise voice source parameterisation. In: Proc. of Speech Prosody, Shanghai, China, pp. 143–146 (May 2012)
5. Fant, G.: The lf-model revisited. transformations and frequency domain analysis. STL-QPSR Journal 36(2-3), 119–156 (1995)
6. Lu, H.-L.: Toward a High-Quality Singing-Voice Synthesizer with Vocal Texture Control, Ph.D. thesis, Stanford University (2002)
7. Henrich, N.: Etude de la source glottique en voix parlée et chantée, Ph.d. thesis, Université Paris 6, France (2001)
8. Röbel, A., Rodet, X.: Efficient spectral envelope estimation and its application to pitch shifting and envelope preservation. In: Proc. of DAFx, Spain (2005)
9. Villavicencio, F., Röbel, A., Rodet, X.: Improving lpc spectral envelope extraction of voiced speech by true-envelope estimation. In: Proc. of ICASSP (2006)
10. Kreiman, J., Gerratt, B.R.: Perception of aperiodicity in pathological voice. Journal of the Acoustical Society of America 117, 2201–2211 (2005)

Contribution to the Multipitch Estimation by Multi-scale Product Analysis

Jihen Zeremdini, Mohamed Anouar Ben Messaoud,
Aïcha Bouzid, and Noureddine Ellouze

University of Tunis El Manar, National School of Engineers of Tunis,
LR11ES17 Signal, Image and Information Technology Laboratory, 1002, Tunis, Tunisia
zeremdini_jihen@hotmail.fr,
{anouar.benmessaoud,bouzidacha,nourellouze}@yahoo.fr

Abstract. This paper describes a new multipitch estimation method. The proposed approach is based on the calculation of the autocorrelation function of the Multi-scale product of the composite signal and its filtered version by a comb filter. After analyzing the composite speech signal, the autocorrelation applied on the multi-scale product (MP) of the signal allows us to find the first pitch; it's the dominant one. After applying the comb filter, we substract the resulting signal from the original one. Then we apply the same analysis to the residue to obtain the pitch estimation of the intrusion. Besides, this method is applied and evaluated on the Cooke database. It's also compared to other well known algorithms. Experimental results show the robustness and the effectiveness of our approach.

Keywords: Multipitch Detection Method, Wavelet transform, Multi-scale product, Autocorrelation function, Comb Filter, Pitch.

1 Introduction

The problem of estimating multiple fundamental frequencies also called multipitch comes exclusively from mixing two voices; the dominant one is called the target speaker and the other is called the intrusion. The multipitch estimation is today at the heart of many applications related to the analysis of the speech signal. Strongly related to separation problems, it is found in the identification of musical notes for transcription of partitions or for separating speakers.

In this context, there are different methods to estimate the fundamental frequencies of composite signals which can be classified into two groups: joint and iterative. For iterative methods, we find essentially the cancellation approach proposed by De Cheveigné and Kawahara [1]. It allows the dominant frequency f_0 estimation. Then, from the residual signal, a second pitch is estimated. More than two pitches can be identified. Furthermore, the Gilbert and Payton [2] method is based on the probability distributions of the fundamental frequency and its harmonics using the signal power spectrum. The harmonic windowing function (HWF) dramatically improves the arrival time difference (TDOA) of the estimation over the standard cross correlation at a

T. Drugman and T. Dutoit (Eds.): NOLISP 2013, LNAI 7911, pp. 50–59, 2013.

low SNR. The pitch estimation part of the algorithm detects implicitly voiced regions and does not require prior knowledge of the voicing.

On the other hand, we cite the Spectral Multi-scale Product approach of Ben Messaoud and Bouzid [3]. This approach can be summarized in three steps: Firstly, it operates the multi-scale product of the composite signal. Secondly, it performs a short-term spectral analysis of the signal. Finally, it estimates successively multiple fundamental frequencies of the voiced frames of the composite speech signal using a comb filter. Besides, Huang and Wang [4] propose a MLW (Multi-Length Windows) method which can be summarized into two steps. The first step consists of determining the fundamental frequency; this is done by the short-term autocorrelation of the mixture. The estimation of the second fundamental frequency is based on multiple length windows (MLW) which act as an amplifier of the frequency with a range of amplified amplitudes and therefore, the peaks of harmonic mixing can be distinguished. Thus, the estimation of the second pitch in each frame becomes easier.

For joint methods, we note essentially the approach of Meddis and O'Mard [5] who simulate the auditory system by dividing the input signal into multichannel signals. For each channel, they filter the signal and calculate the autocorrelation function ACF. Then, they sum the ACF obtained and calculate a global autocorrelation function. Thus, the two fundamental frequencies are estimated. On the other hand, for Vishnubhotla [6], the studies are based on the AMDF function. His algorithm is defined as follows: First, it applies a filter bank to the composite signal. Subsequently, areas of silence are removed. The fundamental frequency is determined by a two-dimensional representation. For each channel, the authors propose to find a couple of delays for which the AMDF is minimal. And the AMDF-2D couples are integrated into an histogram. Then, the two fundamental frequencies are estimated by the temporal evolution of the histograms. Moreover, Stark, Wohlmayr and Pernkopf [7] present a fully probabilistic approach for the source filter based on a single channel speech separation (SCSS). In particular, they make the separation iteratively, where they consider the aspects of the source-controlled by a HMM factorial for estimating multiple frequencies. Then, these F_0s tracks are combined with the vocal tract filter model to form a speech dependent model. In addition, they introduce an approach for estimating a gain to allow the adaptation of an arbitrary level of the mixture in speech mixtures.

In this work, we extend the Autocorrelation MP (AMP) method proposed by Ben Messaoud and Bouzid for the voicing classification and the pitch estimation to the multipitch estimation [8].They proposed a technique based on the autocorrelation analysis of the MP speech to determine voiced frames with an estimation of the fundamental frequency. The first step consists of making the speech MP. Then, they decompose the obtained signal into overlapping frames. The second step consists of calculating the ACF of each frame extracted from the obtained signal. The third step consists of looking for the ACF maxima that are classified to make a voicing decision and then giving the fundamental frequency estimation for the voiced frames. In our work, the method is applied on voiced speech only. It gives a first estimation of the dominant fundamental frequency.

The present paper is organized as follows. The second section describes the proposed approach. The evaluation and the comparison of our approach are presented in the third and fourth section respectively. Section 5 concludes this work.

2 The Proposed Approach for Multipitch Estimation

Our approach for estimating the multiple fundamental frequencies is based on the autocorrelation of the speech MP (AMP). Estimating the fundamental frequencies is operated iteratively. First, the F_0 of the dominant speaker is detected. The dominant speaker's contribution is eliminated by the substraction of the comb filter composite signal from the original one. The comb filter is parameterized by the F_0 given in the first estimation.

2.1 Multi-scale Product (MP)

The multi-scale product (MP) is a technique for nonlinear signal processing based on the product of wavelet coefficients at some scales. This product for harmonic signals allows to filter the signals and to reduce some structures while showing simple periodic structures. Besides, it shows peaks at the transitions in the signal and has low values elsewhere. On the other hand, the proliferation of adjacent scales strengthens singularities and reduces noise [9].The MP of the signal f at scales s_j is described by the following equation:

$$p(n) = \prod_{j=1}^{l} W f(n, s_j) \qquad (1)$$

With Wf (n, s_j) represents the Wavelet Transform of f (n) at the scale s_j.

This is distinctly a non-linear function on the input time series f (n). The wavelet used in this MP analysis is the quadratic spline function with a support of 0.8 ms at scales 2, 2.5 and 3.

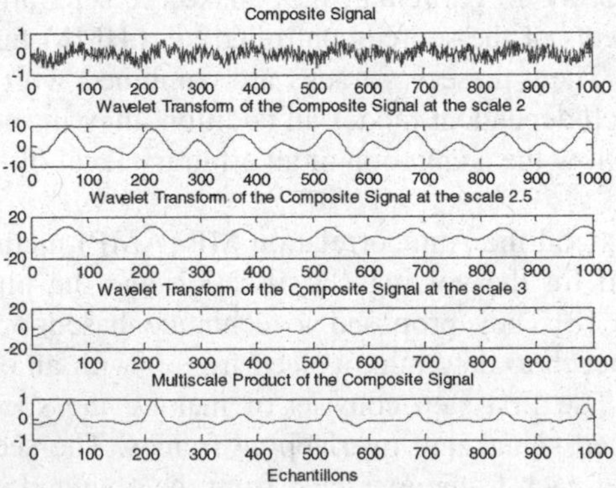

Fig. 1. Composite Signal (a male-a female from the Cooke database) followed by its Wavelet Transforms at scales 2, 2.5 and 3 and their MP

Figure 1 shows that the step edges are more observable by the product than by the WT. In fact, the speech MP has a periodic structure with more reinforced singularities marked by extrema.

2.2 Autocorrelation of the Speech MP (AMP)

The autocorrelation is a measure of the similarity between two waveforms as a function of a time-lag applied to one of them. It can detect regularities, profiles repeated in a signal as a periodic signal disturbed by noise, or the fundamental frequency of a signal which does not contain this fundamental, but implies it with its harmonics.

In this work, the product p[n] is divided into frames of N length by the multiplication with a sliding analysis Blackman window w[n] [8]:

$$P_{wi}[n] = p[n]\, w[n - iN/2] \tag{2}$$

Where i is the window index and N/2 is the overlap.

Then, we compute the autocorrelation function R_i for the time interval i of the multi-scale product P_{wi} as follows:

$$R_i(k) = \sum_{l=0}^{N-1} P_{wi}(l) P_{wi}(l+k) \tag{3}$$

The autocorrelation of the composite speech multi-scale product of signals permits to emphasize the dominant frequency as depicted in figures 2, 3 and 4.

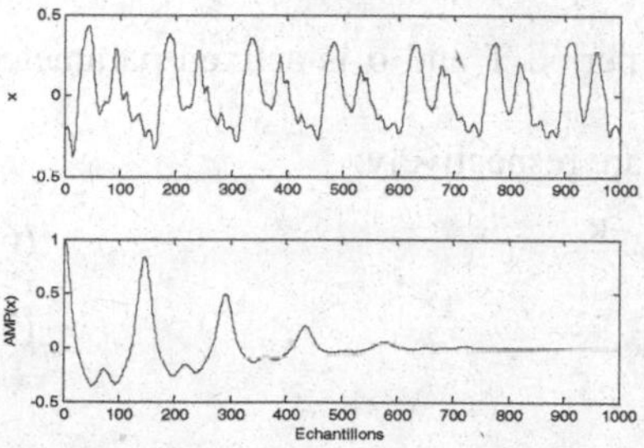

Fig. 2. Clean speech signal (a male voice from Cooke database) with fs=16 kHz, f_0=106.66 Hz and its AMP

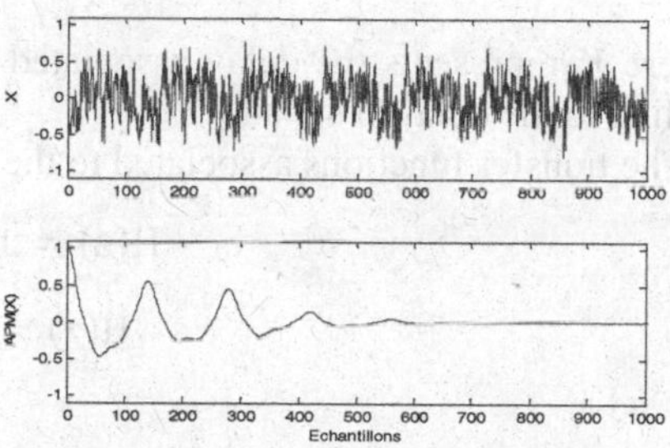

Fig. 3. Noisy speech signal (a male voice with a white noise from Cooke database) with SNR = - 4.07 dB, fs = 16 KHz and its AMP

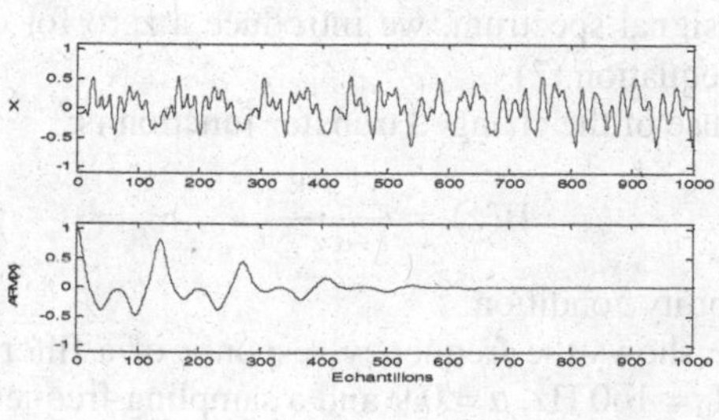

Fig. 4. Composite Speech signal (a male-a female from the Cooke database) with fs = 16 kHz and $f_{0Dominant}$ = 116.78 Hz and its AMP

Figure 2 depicts the case of a voiced speech signal. Its AMP shows a second pick corresponding to the pitch period. Figure 3 illustrates a male signal with additive noise having a high SNR level. The AMP eliminates the noise and shows the pitch period of the speech signal. Figure 4 represents the case of a mixed speech signals (a male voice with a female voice). The AMP of the composite signal shows the period estimation of the dominant speaker.

2.3 The Comb Filtering

A comb filter allows the addition of signal delayed version to itself causing constructive or destructive interferences. There are two types of comb filter: a filter with an anticipation and a filter with a feedback and this is according to the direction of the signal added to the original one. A periodic signal of a period T_0 has a spectrum composed of rays separated by the frequency $f_0 = 1/T_0$. Thus, the transfer function of a comb filter recovering the signal should be set to the harmonic frequencies of the signal. The following equations describe respectively a comb filter with finite impulse response (FIR) and a comb filter with infinite impulse response (IIR):

$$Y[n] = X[n] + \alpha X[n - K] \tag{4}$$

$$Y[n] = X[n] + \alpha Y[n - K] \tag{5}$$

Where K represents the delay associated to the period T and α is a fixed parameter applied to the delayed signal.

The transfer functions associated to the filters are respectively:

$$H(z) = 1 + \alpha z^{-k} \tag{6}$$

$$H(z) = \frac{1}{1 - \alpha z^{-k}} \tag{7}$$

We study and use the IIR comb filter modified by Mike Gainza, Eugene Coyle and Bob Lawlor [10] which ensures the cancellation of harmonics corresponding to the fundamental frequency and makes a plate bandwidth for the rest of the spectrum. In order to avoid, the alteration of the signal amplitude caused by IIR comb filter, and the deformation of the signal spectrum, we introduce a zero for each pole of the frequency response of the equation (7).

The frequency response of the changed transfer function is:

$$H(z) = \frac{1 - z^{-k}}{1 - \alpha z^{-k}} \tag{8}$$

With $0 < \alpha < 1$ is the stability condition.

The following figure shows the frequency response of a filter designed for a fundamental frequency of $f_0 = 160$ Hz, $\alpha = 0.9$ and a sampling frequency fs = 16 kHz.

Figure 5 represents the designed Comb Filter. We apply this comb filter on the composite signal tuned on the period already estimated. Then, we substract the resulting signal from the original one to obtain the residue which represents the intrusion.

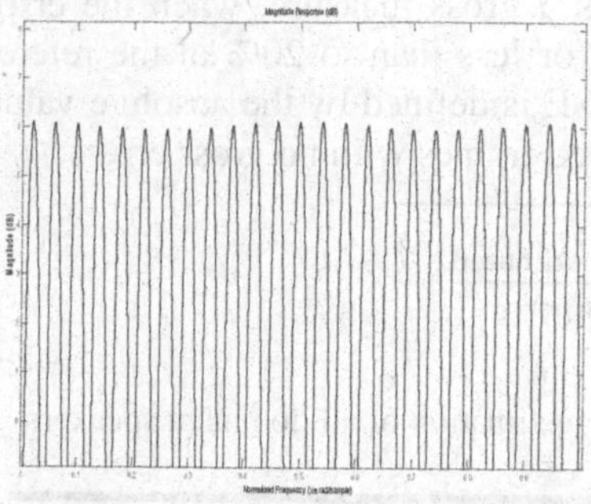

Fig. 5. IIR Comb Filter

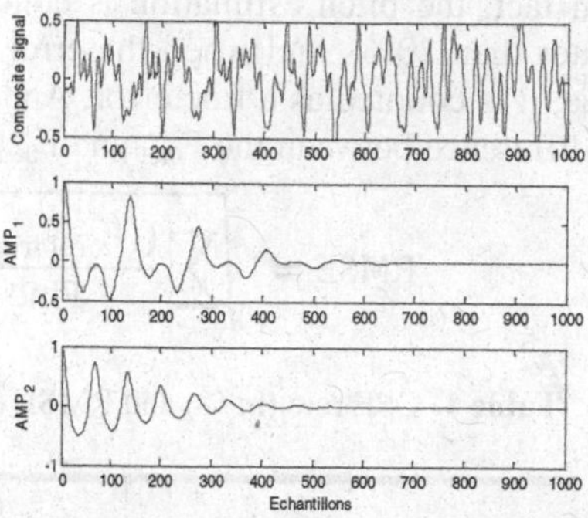

Fig. 6. Composite Signal (a male-a female from the Cooke database) followed by its AMP and the AMP of the residue of the filtered signal

Figure 6 shows respectively a composite speech signal (a male-a female from the Cooke database), its AMP which shows the dominant speaker fundamental frequency and the AMP of the residue of the filtered signal that brings up the fundamental frequency of the intrusion.

3 Evaluation

To evaluate the performance of our algorithm, we use the Cooke database [11]. This database is a collection of composite sounds obtained by mixing ten male voiced speech signals (V0, V1,..., V9) with ten other signals representing a variety of sounds.

The pronounced text is "Why are you all weary?". All signals are sampled at the frequency of 16 kHz. Interferences can be classified into three categories: 1) Interferences without pitch, this category consists of two different types of noise (N1: white noise and N2: impulse noise), 2) Interferences having a pitch quality (N0: pure frequency of 1 kHz, N3: cocktail party noise, N4: rock music, N5: siren and N6: ringtone) and 3) Speech interferences which contains three cases of speech intrusions (N7: speech signal uttered by a woman 1, N8: speech signal uttered by a man 2 and N9: speech signal uttered by a woman 2). The text of this category of interference corresponds to the sentence "Do not ask me to carry oily rag like that year".

For the evaluation, we compare the measurement of the reference pitch from the speech signal to that found by our approach for both the dominant speaker and the intrusion if it exists. The reference was not available in the Cooke database; it was obtained from the signal of the target directly using the AMP method. Like in all the conventionally work using the Cooke database, the pitch of the reference is calculated by the same method and is manually corrected.

Thus, we calculate, the gross pitch errors rate (GPE) and the standard deviation of the error (RMSE: Root Mean Square Error).

In fact, the pitch estimation is considered as a gross measure, when the error is greater than 20%. And when the error is equal or less than to 20% of the reference value, it is counted as a fine error. And the RMSE is defined by the absolute value of the difference between the F_{0ref} and F_{0est} for voiced frames with no gross errors:

$$\text{RMSE} = \sqrt{\sum \frac{((F_{0reference} - F_{0estimated})^2)}{\text{Fine error counter}}} \quad (9)$$

Table 1. GPE rate (in %) and RMSE (Hz) for f_0 estimation of all dominant speakers

	$\textbf{GPE}_{\textbf{Dominant}}$ (%)	$\textbf{RMSE}_{\textbf{Dominant}}$ (Hz)
Cooke database Category 1	0.06	0.23
Cooke database Category 2	0.63	0.39
Cooke database Category 3	1.63	0.76

Table 1 allows us to conclude that for the interferences without periodicity, the GPE rate is near to 0. And the RMSE has small values showing the accuracy of our approach. Even, in the difficult case when the intrusion corresponds to a speech signal, the GPE and the accuracy remain limited presenting the effectiveness of our method.

Table 2. GPE rate (in %) and RMSE (Hz) for f_0 estimation of all Intrusion speakers

	V_i (i=0..9)	
	$\textbf{GPE}_{\textbf{Intrusion\_ Average}}$ (%)	$\textbf{RMSE}_{\textbf{Intrusion\_ Average}}$ (Hz)
N7	35.11	28.11
N8	39.99	4.89
N9	12.02	1.67
Global	**29.04**	**11.56**

Table 2 shows that errors associated to intrusion are higher than those found in the case of the dominant speaker and this can be explained by the fact that the signal added to the original one consists of a speech signal which has a complex periodic structure.

Indeed, the intrusion N7 (woman 1) has a fundamental frequency multiple of the target pitch.

However, the intrusion N8 (man) is characterized by a relatively low pitch and close to the target. The values of the standard deviation for the intrusion are also higher than those obtained for the target, but remain satisfactory.

Our approach is not as efficient in the intrusion case as in the dominant one. But it remains, among the first approaches that have performed this type of evaluation.

4 Comparison

In this section, we compare our method with various algorithms SMP [3], Wu [12], Tolonen [13] and Gu [14] for estimating the pitch of the dominant speaker for various type of noise. The Wu, Gu and Tolonen evaluation are given in [12]. Wu uses frames of 256 samples and 512 samples against Gu and Tolonen use frames of 1024 samples with a step of 10 ms. And we use frames of 1024 samples. All these algorithms are applied on the Cooke database and evaluated by calculating the Gross Pitch Error (GPE). The following figure and table show considered estimation methods for the three categories of intrusion.

Table 3. GPE rate (in %) for the three Cooke database Categories for different methods

Method	GPE (%) Cooke database Category 1	GPE (%) Cooke database Category 2	GPE (%) Cooke database Category 3
APM	0.06	0.63	1.63
SPM [3]	0	0	0.08
Wu [12]	0	0.32	0.93
Gu [14]	0.36	2.10	4.28
Tolonen [13]	2.38	4.53	7.70

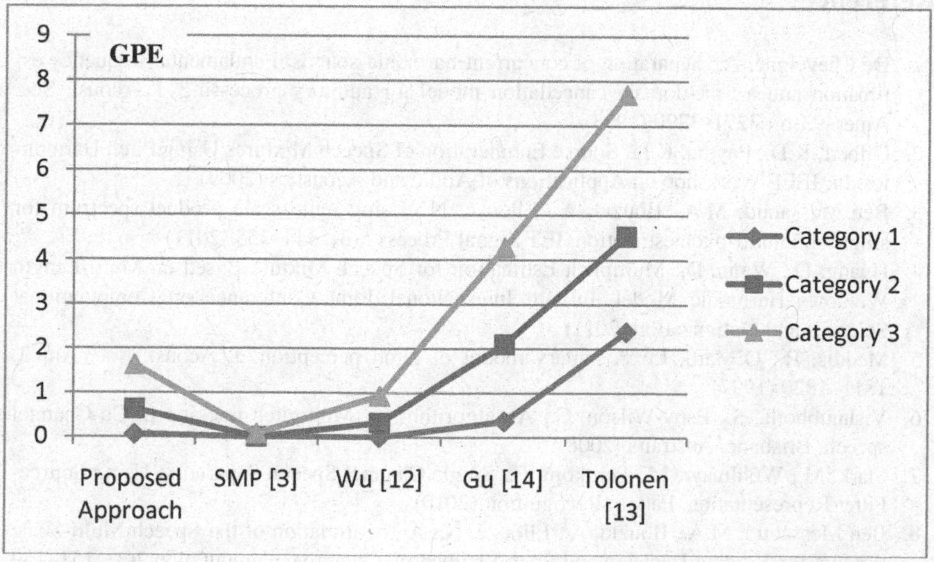

Fig. 7. Comparison of our approach with existing methods using Cooke database for Category 1, 2 and 3

The values given in table 3 are reported in figure 7.

We note that for the three categories of noise our proposed approach, the SMP and the Wu algorithms give the best results. The Tolonen method gives the worst results. This comparison shows the effectiveness and the robustness of our approach.

5 Conclusion

In this paper, we present a multipitch estimation method that relies on the autocorrelation analysis of the multi-scale product of a composite speech signal using a modified comb filter. The proposed approach can be summarized in three essential steps. First, we calculate the MP of the speech signal processed by multiplying the coefficients of the wavelet transform of the signal at the scales 2, 2.5 and 3 by using the quadratic spline wavelet. Second, we apply the autocorrelation to the MP weighted by the Blackman window. Thus, we determine the first fundamental frequency; it's that of the dominant speaker. Thirdly, we filter the composite signal by a comb filter keyed on the determined fundamental frequency f_0. Then, we substract the resulting signal from the original one to eliminate the harmonic component of the first speaker. The AMP of the residue allows the estimation of the intrusion fundamental frequency. The method is applied on the Cooke database for evaluation and comparison. We calculate the gross error rate (GPE) and the root mean square error (RMSE). The results obtained allow us to observe that our method gives good performance to estimate the F_0s of the dominant and the intrusion; however it is more reliable and powerful for the dominant estimation than the intrusion. Comparison with other state of the art algorithms confirms the efficiency and the accuracy of our approach.

References

1. De Cheveigné, A.: Separation of concurrent harmonic sounds: Fundamental frequency estimation and a time-domain cancellation model for auditory processing. J. Acoust. Soc. Amer. 93(6), 3271–3290 (1993)
2. Gilbert, K.D., Payton, K.L.: Source Enumeration of Speech Mixtures Using Pitch Harmonics. In: IEEE Workshop on Applications of Audio and Acoustics (2009)
3. Ben Messaoud, M.A., Bouzid, A., Ellouze, N.: Using multi-scale product spectrum for single and multi-pitch estimation. IET Signal Process 5(3), 344–355 (2011)
4. Huang, Q., Wang, D.: Multipitch Estimation for Speech Mixture Based on Multi-Length Windows Harmonic Model. In: 4th International Joint Conference on Computational Sciences and Optimization (2011)
5. Meddis, R., O'Mard, L.: A unitary model of pitch perception. J. Acoust. Soc. Am. 3, 1811–1820 (1997)
6. Vishnubhotla, S., Espy-Wilson, C.: An algorithm for Multipitch tracking in Co-Channel speech, Brisbane, Australia (2008)
7. Stark, M., Wohlmayr, M., Pernkopf, F.: Single Channel Speech Separation Using Source-Filter Representation. Pattern Recognition (2010)
8. Ben Messaoud, M.A., Bouzid, A., Ellouze, N.: Autocorrelation of the Speech Multi-Scale Product for Voicing Decision and Pitch Estimation. Cognitive Computation 2(3), 151–159 (2010)

9. Bouzid, A.: Contribution à la détection des instants d'ouverture et de fermeture de la glotte sur les signaux de parole voisée par transformée en ondelettes. Rapport de thèse de doctorat (2004)
10. Gainza, M., Lawlor, B., Coyle, E.: Multi pitch estimation by using modified IIR Comb Filters. In: 47th International Symposium ELMAR (2005)
11. Cooke, M.P.: Modeling auditory processing and organization. Doctoral thesis, Sheffield University, Sheffield, UK (1993)
12. Wu, M., Wang, D., Brown, G.J.: A multipitch tracking algorithm for noisy speech. IEEE Trans. Speech and Audio Process 11(3), 229–241 (2003)
13. Tolonen, T., Karjalainen, M.: A computationally efficient multipitch analysis model. IEEE Trans. Speech and Audio Process. 8(6), 708–716 (2000)
14. Gu, Y.H., Van Bokhoven, W.M.G.: Co-channel speech separation using frequency bin non-linear adaptive filter. In: Proc. Int. Conf. IEEE on Acoust. Speech and Signal Process, ICASSP 1991, pp. 949–952 (1991)

Speech Signals Parameterization Based on Auditory Filter Modeling

Youssef Zouhir and Kaïs Ouni

Unité de Recherche Systèmes Mécatroniques et Signaux,
École Supérieure de Technologie et d'Informatique, Université de Carthage, Tunisie
youssef.elc@gmail.com, kais.ouni@esti.rnu.tn

Abstract. This paper presents a parameterization technique of speech signal based on auditory filter modeling by the Gammachirp auditory filterbank (GcFB), which is designed to provide a spectrum reflecting the spectral properties of the cochlea filter, which is responsible of frequency analysis in the human auditory system. The center frequencies of the GcFB are based on the ERB-rate scale, with the bandwidth of the Gammachirp filter is measured in Equivalent Rectangular Bandwidth (ERB) of human auditory filters. Our parameterization approach gives interesting results vs. other standard techniques such as LPC (Linear Prediction Coefficients), PLP (Perceptual Linear Prediction), for recognition of isolated words of speech from the TIMIT database. The recognition system is implemented on HTK platform (Hidden Toolkit) based on the Hidden Markov Models with Gaussian Mixture observation continuous densities (HMM-GM).

Keywords: Auditory filter modeling, Speech signal paramerization, Speech recognition.

1 Introduction

The statistical modeling of speech is used in most of speech recognition applications. In fact, the statistical approach provides an appropriate framework to model speech variability in both time and frequency domains. The best models commonly used nowadays are based on the Hidden Markov Models with Gaussian Mixture continuous densities (HMM-GM). In this case speech signal is classically represented as a sequence of acoustic vectors computed in synchronous way. The most efficient representations are based on spectral methods taking into account certain knowledge of speech production and perception proprieties [1].

Popular speech analysis techniques is based on simplified vocal tract models such as Linear Prediction Coefficients (LPC), whereas other techniques based on perceptual model of auditory system such as Mel-Frequency Cepstral Coefficients (MFCC) [2], and Perceptual Linear Prediction (PLP) [3]. Our technique is based on cochlear filter modeling in order to have a close parametric representation of the ear.

In fact, an acoustic signal entering the ear induced a complex spatiotemporal pattern of displacements along the length of the basilar membrane (BM) of the cochlear

T. Drugman and T. Dutoit (Eds.): NOLISP 2013, LNAI 7911, pp. 60–66, 2013.

filter. These mechanical displacements at any given place of the BM can be viewed as the output signal of a band-pass filter whose frequency response has a resonance peak at frequency which is characteristic of the place [4]. Filters with a so-called gammatone impulse response are widely used for modeling of the cochlear filter [4.]

Recently, the auditory filter system is known to be level-dependent as evidenced by psychophysical data on masking, [5], [6]. The Gammachirp filter was proposed by Irino and Patterson is an extension of the gammatone filter with a frequency modulation term, or chirp term. Indeed, in the analytic Gammachirp, the level-dependency of the filter shape was introduced as the level-dependency of the chirp parameter. This filter provides a well-defined impulse response; it would appear to be an excellent candidate for an asymmetric, level dependent auditory filterbank. [7], [8], [5]

In this paper, we propose a parameterization technique based on the human auditory system characteristics and relying on the Gammachirp auditory Filterbank (GcFB). The filterbank has 34 filters with center frequencies equally spaced on the ERB-rate scale from 50 to 8 kHz, which gives a good approximation to the frequency selective behavior of the cochlea. The Model training and recognition were performed using speech recognition toolkit HTK.3.4.1 [9]. One Hidden Markov model (HMM) with five states and four Gaussian Mixtures per state were trained for each vocabulary word. The recognition performance of this approach was evaluated using the TIMIT database. The obtained evaluation results are compared to those of the standards techniques of parameterizations LPC and PLP.

This paper is organized as follows: It starts with, an auditory filter model in Section 2. Following this, section 3 gives the parameterization based an auditory filters modeling. The main results are presented in section 4. Finally, the major conclusions are summarized in section 5.

2 Auditory Filter Model

The objective of auditory modeling is to find a mathematical model which represents some perceptual aspects and physiological of the human auditory system [10]. In time-domain of auditory models, the spectral analysis performed by the basilar membrane is often simulated by the Gammachirp auditory filterbank [7], [6].

2.1 Gammachirp Auditory Filter

The Gammachirp auditory filter is widely used for auditory speech analysis. Irino and Patterson have developed a theoretically optimal auditory filter [5], [11], [12], [7], in which the complex impulse response of the Gammachirp, is given as

$$g_c(t) = at^{n-1} e^{-2\pi b ERB(f_0)t} e^{j2\pi f_0 t + jc\ln t + j\varphi} \tag{1}$$

Where time t>0, a is the amplitude, n and b are parameters defining the envelope of the gamma distribution, and f_0 is the asymptotic frequency [13]. ln(t) is the natural logarithm of time. c is a parameter for the frequency modulation or the chirp rate, φ is the initial phase, and ERB(f0) is the equivalent rectangular bandwidth of the auditory filter at f_0 [14], [15].

The bandwidth of the Gammachirp filter is set according to its equivalent rectangular bandwidth (ERB) of the human auditory filter. For auditory filter the ERB may be regarded as a measure of critical bandwidth [16], [14] and a good match with human data. The value of ERB at frequency f in Hz [15] is given by [16].

$$ERB(f) = 24.7 + 0.108 f \tag{2}$$

The Fourier magnitude spectrum of the gammachirp filter is:

$$|G_c(f)| = \frac{a|\Gamma(n+jc)|e^{c\theta}}{(2\pi)^n \left[(bERB(f_0))^2 + (f-f_0)^2\right]^{\frac{n}{2}}} \tag{3}$$

Where $$\theta = arctg\left(\frac{f-f_0}{bERB(f_0)}\right) \tag{4}$$

And $\Gamma(n+jc)$ is the complex gamma distribution.

2.2 Gammachirp Auditory Filterbank

The used Gammachirp auditory filterbank (GcFB) is composed by 34 Gammachirp filters with center frequencies equally spaced between 50 Hz and 8 kHz on the ERB-rate scale of Glasberg and Moore [14]. This is a warped frequency scale, similar to the critical band scale of the human auditory system, on which filter center frequencies are uniformly spaced according to their ERB bandwidth. The ERB-rate scale is an approximately logarithmic function relating frequency to the number of ERBs, ERBrate(f), which is given by [16].

$$ERBrate(f) = 21.4 \log_{10}\left(\frac{4.37 f}{1000} + 1\right) \tag{5}$$

The basilar membrane motion (BMM) produced by the GcFB in response of the waveform is presented in Fig.1 [17]. It is drawn as a set of lines, and each individual line is the output of one of the channels in the auditory filterbank [17]. As shown in Fig.1, the concentrations of activity in channels above 191 Hz show the resonances of the vocal tract which represents the 'formants' of the waveform.

Table 1. Used Gammachirp Parameters

Parameter	Value
n	4 (default)
b	1.019 (default)
c	2

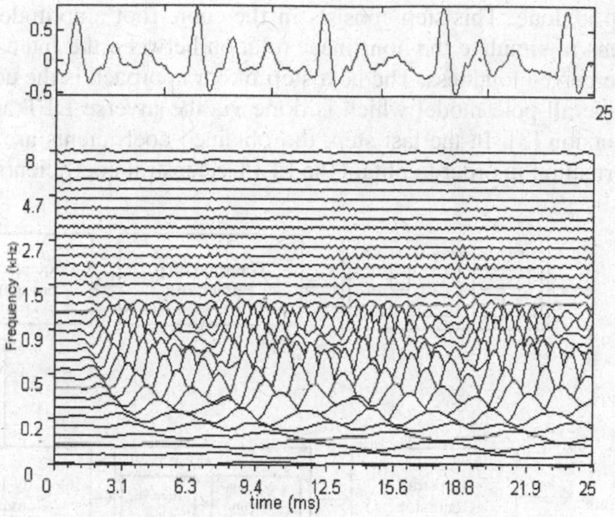

Fig. 1. The top panel shows the first 25ms -segment the waveform of the word 'ALL' extracted from TIMIT database. The bottom panel shows the Basilar membrane motion for the waveform produced by the GcFB.

3 Parameterization Based on Auditory Filter Modeling

The standard technique PLP analysis is based on an approximation of the basic psychophysical knowledge [3]. The proposed technique includes the use of a Gammachirp auditory filterbank for auditory spectral analysis.

3.1 The Standard PLP

The PLP technique is an LP-based analysis method that successfully incorporates a non-linear frequency scale and other known properties from the psychophysics of hearing. This technique uses three concepts from the psychophysics of hearing to extract an estimation of the auditory spectrum: the critical-band spectral resolution, the equal-loudness curve, and the intensity-loudness power law. The auditory spectrum is then approximated by an autoregressive all-pole model, followed by a cepstral parameterization. PLP analysis seems more consistent with human hearing, in comparison with conventional linear predictive analysis (LP) [3].

3.2 The PLPGc Technique

The proposed parameterization technique of speech signal, PLPGc (perceptual linear predictive Gammachirp) is illustrated in Fig. 2. After calculating the power spectrum of the windowed segment of speech signal, the result is passed to Gammachirp filterbank which is based on the cochlea filtering. The output is pre-emphasized by an equal loudness curve, which represents an approximation to the non-equal sensitivity of human auditory system at different frequencies. After that the Intensity loudness

Conversion step is done. This step consists in the cubic-root amplitude compression operation. It aims to simulate the non-linear relation between the intensity of speech signal and its perceived loudness. The next step of our approach is the computation of the autoregressive all-pole model which is done via the inverse DFT and the Levinson-Durbin recursion [3]. In the last step, the obtained coefficients are converted by cepstral transformation in order to obtain the PLPGc cepstral coefficients.

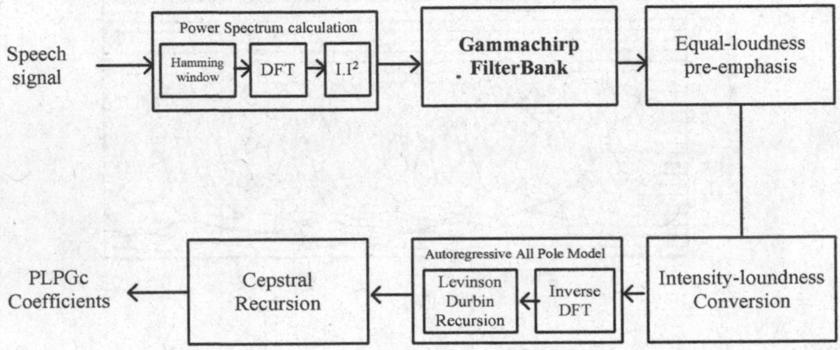

Fig. 2. Block diagram of the proposed technique PLPGc

4 Experimental Results

The proposed technique has been evaluated on the TIMIT database [18], composed of 9702 isolated words for the learning phase. For the recognition phase, we used 3525 isolated words. All words were extracted from TIMIT database. The signals of this database are sampled at 16 kHz.

The Hidden Markov Model Toolkit (HTK) [9], is a portable toolkit for building and manipulating Hidden Markov Models with continuous Mixture Gaussian densities (HMM_GM). HTK is primarily used for speech recognition. The HMM topology is a 1st -order 5-states HMM model. The observation probability distribution is a 4 Gaussian mixture density with diagonal covariance matrix. 12 static coefficients vectors were computed using 25 ms hamming window, shifted with 10 ms steps. The Gammachirp filter was applied using the parameters given in the table 1.

The tables 2, 3 and 4 represent the recognition rates of different techniques: PLPGc (proposed technique), LPC and PLP [3]. Every time we add one of the following parameter to the first 12 coefficients: Energy (E), the first differential coefficients (Δ) and second order differential coefficients (A).

For HMM, we used 4 Gaussian Mixture, with 5 states of observation.

We define the parameters below: HMM 4 GM: Hidden Markov Models with 4-Gaussian-Mixtures. H is the number of correct words, D is the number of deletions words, S is the number of substitutions words and N is the total number of words in the defining transcription files. The percentage number (%) is the recognition rate of words.

As reported in the table 2 we can observe that an improvement of 2.52% relative increase of recognition rate is achieved with the PLPGc proposed technique of parameterization over the baseline PLP method. In tests the energy was also added to the feature vector. It can be seen in table 3 that the recognition rate improves slightly, with the PLPGc technique compared with PLP method.

The dynamic properties (E+Δ+A) were computed so that the final parameterization vector for techniques consisted of 39 coefficients (12 coefficients of the technique +E+Δ+A). The table 4 shows a small increase of recognition rate for the PLPGc proposed technique of parameterization compared to this of the standard technique PLP. We also observed that the standard LPC technique generally decreases the recognition scores compared to PLP and PLPGc, as shown in tables 2, 3 and 4.

Table 2. Recognition rate obtained by parameterization techniques in their brut state

Technique	HMM 4 GM				
_brut	%	N	H	S	D
PLPGc	92.00	3525	3243	282	0
PLP	89.48	3525	3154	371	0
LPC	58.55	3525	2064	1461	0

Table 3. Recognition rate obtained by parameterization techniques combined with energy (_E)

Technique	HMM 4 GM				
_E	%	N	H	S	D
PLPGc	93.67	3525	3302	223	0
PLP	93.33	3525	3290	235	0
LPC	70.07	3525	2470	1055	0

Table 4. Recognition rate obtained by parameterization techniques combined with energy, differential coefficients first and second order (_E_Δ_A)

Technique	HMM 4 GM				
_E_ Δ_A	%	N	H	S	D
PLPGc	98.16	3525	3460	65	0
PLP	97.93	3525	3452	73	0
LPC	78.24	3525	2758	767	0

5 Conclusion

In this paper, we have proposed paramerization technique PLPGc of speech signals based on the auditory filter modeling which uses the Gammachirp auditory Filter-bank. Experimental results using the TIMIT database have shown that the PLPGc technique increases the recognition rate relatively according to conventional techniques such as PLP and LPC.

References

1. Frikha, M., Hamida, A.B.: A Comparitive Survey of ANN and Hybrid HMM/ANN Architectures for Robust Speech Recognition. American Journal of Intelligent Systems 2(1), 1–8 (2012)
2. Davis, S.B., Mermelstein, P.: Comparison of parametric representations for monosyllabic word recognition in continuously spoken sentences. IEEE Transactions on Acoustics, Speech and Signal Processing 28(4), 357–366 (1980)
3. Hermansky, H.: Perceptual linear predictive (PLP) analysis of speech. J. Acoust. Soc. Amer. 87(4), 1738–1752 (1990)
4. Ouni, K., Ellouze, N.: A Time-Frequency Analysis of Speech Based on Psychoacoustic Characteristics. In: Proceedings of the 17th International Congresses on Acoustics, ICA-ROME (2001)
5. Irino, T., Patterson, R.D.: A Dynamic Compressive Gammachirp Auditory Filterbank. IEEE Transactions on Audio, Speech, and Language Processing 14(6) (2006); author manuscript, available in PMC (2009)
6. Unokia, M., Irino, T., Glasberg, B., Moore, B.C.J., Patterson, R.D.: Comparison of the roex and gammachirp filters as representations of the auditory filter. J. Acoust. Soc. Am. 120(3), 1474–1492 (2006); available in PMC (2010)
7. Irino, T., Patterson, R.D.: A time-domain, level-dependent auditory filter: The Gammachirp. J. Acoust. Soc. Am. 101(1), 412–419 (1997)
8. Park, A.: Using Gammachirp filter for auditory analysis of speech. 18.327, Wavelets and Filter banks (2003)
9. Young, S., Evermann, G., Gales, M., Hain, T., Kershaw, D., Liu, X., Moore, G., Odell, J., Ollason, D., Povey, D., Valtchev, V., Woodland, P.: The HTK Book (for HTK Version 3.4.1). Cambridge University Engineering Department (2009)
10. Zoghlami, N., Lachiri, Z., Ellouze, N.: Speech Enhancement using Auditory Spectral Attenuation. In: Proceedings of the 17th European Signal Processing Conference, EUSIPCO, Glasgow, Scotland (2009)
11. Patterson, R.D., Unoki, M., Irino, T.: Extending the domain of center frequencies for the compressive gammachirp auditory filter. J. Acoust. Soc. Amer. 114(5), 1529–1542 (2003)
12. Irino, T., Patterson, R.D.: A compressive gammachirp auditory filter for both physiological and psychophysical data. J. Acoust. Soc. Am. 109(5), 2008–2022 (2001)
13. Irino, T., Patterson, U.M.: A time-domain, level-dependent auditory filter: An Analysis/Synthesis Auditory Filterbank Based on an IIR Gammachirp Filter. J. Acoust. Soc. Jpn (E) 20(5), 397–406 (1999)
14. Moore, B.C.J.: An Introduction to the Psychology of Hearing, 5th edn. Academic Press, London (2003)
15. Glasberg, B.R., Moore, B.C.J.: Derivation of auditory filter shapes from notched-noise data. Hearing Research 47, 103–138 (1990)
16. Wang, D.L., Brown, G.J.: Computational Auditory Scene Analysis: Principles, Algorithms, and Applications. IEEE Press / Wiley-Interscience (2006)
17. `http://www.acousticscale.org/wiki/index.php/AIM2006_Documentation`
18. The DARPA TIMIT Acoustic-Phonetic Continuous Speech Corpus (TIMIT) Training and Test Data and Speech Header Software NIST Speech Disc CD1-1.1 (1990)

Towards a Better Representation of the Envelope Modulation of Aspiration Noise

João P. Cabral and Julie Carson-Berndsen

School of Computer Science and Informatics, University College Dublin, Ireland

Abstract. The control over aspects of the glottal source signal is fundamental to correctly modify relevant voice characteristics, such as breathiness. This voice quality is strongly related to the characteristics of the glottal source signal produced at the glottis, mainly the shape of the glottal pulse and the aspiration noise. This type of noise results from the turbulence of air passing through the glottis and it can be represented by an amplitude modulated Gaussian noise, which depends on the glottal volume velocity and glottal area. However, the dependency between the glottal signal and the noise component is usually not taken into account for transforming breathiness. In this paper, we propose a method for modelling the aspiration noise which permits to adapt the aspiration noise to take into account its dependency with the glottal pulse shape, while producing high-quality speech. The envelope of the amplitude modulated noise is estimated from the speech signal pitch-synchronously and then it is parameterized by using a non-linear polynomial fitting algorithm. Finally, an asymmetric triangular window is obtained from the non-linear polynomial representation for obtaining a shape of the energy envelope of the noise closer to that of the glottal source. In the experiments for voice transformation, both the proposed aspiration noise model and an acoustic glottal source model are used to transform a modal voice into breathy. Results show that the aspiration noise model improves the voice quality transformation compared with an excitation using only the glottal model and an excitation that combines the glottal source model and a spectral representation of the noise component.

1 Introduction

For voice transformations, it is important to control parameters related to both the shape of the glottal source and the aspiration noise components of speech. One of the main characteristics of the aspiration noise is the time-modulation effect that shapes its energy envelope. It has been shown in the literature that this amplitude modulation depends on the glottal pulse waveform and that white Gaussian noise convolved with the glottal pulse waveform improves the speech quality compared with non-modulated noise or sinusoidal modulation [1].

The modulation envelope can be estimated from the noise component of speech and explicitly modified for voice transformation, e.g. by adequately resampling it for pitch modification [1]. Alternatively, the envelope can be represented by a parametric model which can be easily manipulated for pitch and

T. Drugman and T. Dutoit (Eds.): NOLISP 2013, LNAI 7911, pp. 67–74, 2013.

time-scale manipulations. For example, it can be represented by a Fourier series representation of the energy envelope [2] or a window that resembles the glottal source waveform, such as the symmetric Gaussian and triangular windows [3]. However, the aspiration noise may contain effects of the glottal source such as pulse asymmetry which cannot be represented and controlled using these models. This control is particularly important in voice quality transformations using a glottal source model to produce voiced speech, in which it is desirable to adapt the modulation envelope of the noise according to variations in the glottal pulse shape. The glottal model can also be used to represent the noise envelope, such as in [4], which overcomes the limitation of the previous models to adapt the envelope based on the glottal shape. However, this representation may not be accurate because the correlation between the glottal pulse shape and the amplitude modulation effect of the noise source is not well known.

The aspiration noise model proposed in this paper enables to control the modulation envelope relatively to the important glottal pulse shape characteristics and to estimate the envelope from the noise component of speech, which is expected to be more accurate than the envelope represented by an acoustic glottal model. Basically, it consists of representing the noise envelope estimated from the speech signal by an asymmetric triangular window, which allows for adjusting this asymmetry depending on the transformations of the glottal pulse shape parameters. The proposed noise model was developed in the scope of improving voice quality transformation using the analysis-synthesis method called Glottal Spectral Separation (GSS) [5], which incorporates the Liljencrants-Fant (LF) model of the glottal source [6]. In [7], the GSS method was implemented using a mixed excitation model to synthesise voiced speech, which is the combination of the LF-model with a noise signal in the frequency domain. However, this model does not represent the amplitude modulation of the noise in the time-domain, which is necessary for modelling aspiration noise effects. An experiment was conducted to show that the quality of breathiness produced by the GSS method can be improved by using the proposed aspiration noise model compared with the baseline spectral representation of the noise.

2 Glottal Spectral Separation

2.1 Speech Model

The speech signal $S(w)$ can be represented by $S(w) = D(w)E(w)V(w)$, where $D(w)$ is the Fourier Transform (FT) of an impulse train, $V(w)$ is the vocal tract transfer function and $E(w)$ represents the glottal flow derivative (incorporates the radiation component which is modelled by a differentiating filter).

In this work, the glottal flow derivative signal $E(w)$ was represented by the LF-model, i.e. $E_{LF}(w)$, which can be defined by five shape parameters: t_p, t_e, T_a, T_0, and E_e. The waveform starts at the instant of glottal opening, $t_o = 0$, and ends at the instant of abrupt glottal closure, t_e. The amplitude of maximum excitation, E_e, occurs at this discontinuity point. Finally, the transition region between this abrupt closure and the closed phase has duration T_a.

The LF-model can also be described by the voice quality parameters: open quotient $OQ = (t_e + T_a)/T_0$, speed quotient $SQ = t_p/(t_e - t_p)$, and the return quotient $RQ = T_a/T_0$. OQ measures the relative duration of the glottal pulse, SQ is related to the symmetry of the glottal pulse and RQ is mainly correlated with the spectral tilt characteristic of the glottal signal.

2.2 Analysis

During analysis, the first step of the GSS method is to estimate the LF-parameters from the speech signal, which was performed similarly to [5]. The main difference was that the glottal source derivative was estimated from speech using the Iterative Adaptive Inverse Filtering (IAIF) method [8], because it is more accurate than the original LPC inverse filtering technique with pre-emphasis. The LF-model parameters were calculated for each pitch cycle of the residual, which was delimited by contiguous epochs (estimates of t_e). Initial estimates of the LF-model parameters, with the exception of t_e, were obtained by performing direct measurements, as described in [5]. In order to obtain more accurate estimates of the parameters t_o, t_p and T_a, a non-linear optimisation algorithm (the Levenberg-Marquardt algorithm) was used to fit each period of the LF-model signal to a low-pass filtered version of the short-time residual signal. Afterwards, the estimated trajectories of the LF-parameters for each utterance were smoothed using the median function, in order to alleviate estimation errors.

The second step consists of removing the spectral effects of the source model from the speech signal, i.e. $H(w) = S(w)/|E_{LF}(w)|$, where $|E_{LF}(w)|$ is the amplitude spectrum of one period of the LF-model signal. Finally, the amplitude spectrum of the vocal tract filter is calculated by computing the spectral envelope of $|H(w)|$. This last operation is performed using the analysis method of the STRAIGHT vocoder [9], similarly to [5]. For unvoiced speech, the speech spectrum is represented by the spectral envelope of STRAIGHT.

2.3 Synthesis

Voiced speech is synthesised from the GSS parameters using the method described in [7], which consists of passing a mixed excitation model through the vocal tract filter defined by the spectral parameters. Instead, a white noise signal is used for unvoiced speech. The excitation is produced by mixing the LF-model signal with the noise using the aperiodicity parameters of STRAIGHT, which permit to derive weighting functions for the spectra of the two components.

3 Aspiration Noise Modelling

3.1 Asymmetric Triangular Window

The perceptual effect of aspiration noise can be reproduced by synthesising a noise burst with duration smaller than one pitch period and which is synchronised with the periodic component of the source (but out-of-phase), as demonstrated in [10]. A standard technique to synthesise the noise burst during one period is by shaping white noise with a symmetric triangular window [3]. Instead, we propose to model the modulation envelope by an asymmetric triangular window, which is expected to better represent the characteristics of the noise envelope (since the glottal pulse is also asymmetric and they are correlated).

Figure 1 shows an example of the asymmetric window for one pitch cycle. It is defined by its maximum n_{max}, the amplitude M at $n = n_{max}$ and the angles of the two linear curves to the horizontal axes, α and β. For pitch transpositions these angles are set to remain constant in order to preserve the shape of the envelope, while n_{max}, N_{op} and N_{cl} are expected to be scaled by the same factor as the pitch. In this case, the value of the amplitude M is calculated from the angles and desired durations N_{op} and N_{cl}.

For voice quality transformation using glottal parameters, the shape of the triangular window can also be adjusted to take into account the variations in the glottal pulse shape. For example, the durations of the window are equivalent to the opening and closing phases of the glottal pulse. That is, they are related to the LF-model parameters by $OQ = N_{op} + N_{cl}$ and $SQ = N_{cl}/(N_{op} - N_{cl})$.

During synthesis, a truncation of the triangular window may be required if its limit points extend behind the limits of the short-time signal.

3.2 Estimation of the Aspiration Noise

A common technique to estimate the aspiration noise, $N(w)$, is to perform spectral analysis to estimate the harmonic component, $H(w)$, of the speech signal, $X(w)$, and then obtain the noise component by spectral subtraction, $N(w) = X(w) - H(w)$. In this work, the spectral decomposition of the harmonic and stochastic components was performed using the UPC Voice Conversion Toolkit (it was available at `http://www.talp.upc.edu/talp/index.php/resources/tools`). Details about this implementation of the Harmonic/Stochastic Model (HSM) can be found in [11]. First, the harmonic component of the speech signal is calculated. Then, the resulting signal is subtracted from the speech signal to obtain the noise component of speech. This signal is assumed to contain the phase information related to the pitch-synchronism property of the aspiration noise, because the speech and harmonic signals are synchronised in phase. Finally, the noise is inverse filtered using the LPC model, similarly to [12], which has the effect of removing the vocal tract and radiation components from the speech signal to obtain an estimate of the aspiration noise. This operation relies on the assumption that the single zero of the radiation can be approximately modeled by several poles. The analysis method using the HSM also depends on the assumption that voiced speech is an harmonic signal, which may lead to inaccurate estimates of the aspiration noise. However, the estimated noise source seemed to have the synchronism and noise burst characteristics of the aspiration noise. For this reason, it was considered to be a good approximation of the aspiration noise for performing a preliminary test of the model using the asymmetric triangular window.

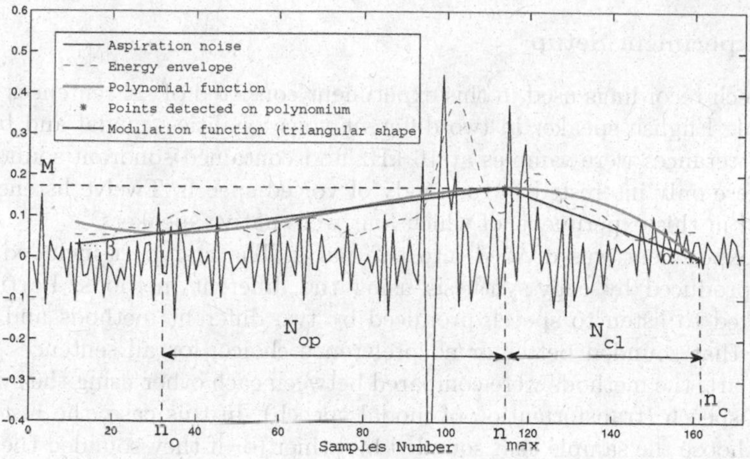

Fig. 1. One period of the aspiration noise signal (delimited by epochs) and the estimated envelope modulation functions

3.3 Estimation of the Noise Parameters

The aspiration noise signal is segmented by performing the same windowing operation as for the LF-model parameter estimation, i.e. the short-time signal is delimited by two consecutive epochs. The modulation function of the aspiration noise is estimated by using the Hilbert transform method of envelope detection. This is a common method for estimation of this function, e.g. [2,12].

The standard approach for estimation of the parameters of a symmetric triangular window representing the noise envelope is to measure them directly on the envelope. We use a preliminary step to this estimation which consists of performing a non-linear polynomial fitting algorithm on the estimated noise envelope, in order to improve the robustness of the analysis. In other words, the polynomial fitting produces a smoother curve which facilitates the estimation of the triangular window parameters. The polynomial order was chosen through visual inspection of the resulting polynomial functions. The fourth order gave the best results in terms of resembling the glottal pulse shapes.

Finally, the parameters of the triangular function are obtained by detecting three points on the polynomial curve: the two inflection points (local minima) and the maximum of that curve. These points are illustrated in Figure 1 by n_o, n_c, and n_{max} respectively. The angles α and β can then be calculated from these points using trigonometric functions. Figure 1 shows an example of the polynomial function fitted to the energy envelope of the noise and the resulting triangular representation, for a short-time noise signal (one period long). Note that this signal is delimited by two consecutive epochs which are an approximation of the glottal closure instants.

4 Perceptual Evaluation

4.1 Experiment Setup

The speech recordings used in this experiment consisted of six sentences spoken by a male English speaker in two different voice qualities: modal and breathy. These utterances were samples at 16 kHz and contained sonorant sounds only, as we were only interested in the study of voiced speech. Twelve listeners participated in this experiment, of which four were native speakers.

The experiment was divided into two parts. The first part included modal speech produced by copy-synthesis using the different methods. Participants were asked to listen to speech produced by two different methods and choose the one that sounded better or no preference choice, for all sentences. In the second part, the methods were compared between each other using the synthetic breathy speech (transformation of modal speech). In this case, the instruction was to choose the sample that sounded breathier (or if they sounded the same).

4.2 Methods

Three different versions of the GSS method for analysis-synthesis were used in this experiment. One baseline method (named GSS-LF) consists of synthesising speech using the LF-model to represent the voiced excitation. The other baseline, named GSS-LF-ST, synthesises speech using the LF-model and the aperiodicity measurements of STRAIGHT, as described in Section 2.3. Finally, the GSS-LF-NM consists of adding the speech synthesised with the LF-model to the noise component synthesised with the aspiration noise model described in Section 3.

4.3 Transformation of Voice Quality Parameters

The GSS method has been used in [5] to transform voice quality parameters of the LF-model. In this experiment two additional parameters are transformed: Harmonic-to-Noise Ratio (HNR) and the fundamental frequency F_0. Speech spoken with modal voice was transformed into breathy voice by transforming the mean values of F_0, OQ, SQ, RQ, and HNR However, the HNR was not transformed for the GSS-LF method because it does not have a noise component. The target values of the LF-model parameters for voice transformation were calculated from their measurements on modal speech and the variations of mean values of these parameters between the modal and breathy speech signals, as described in [5].

The HNR parameter was estimated in GSS-LF-NM by calculating the mean energy ratio between the harmonic and noise components of the HSM described in Section 3.2. For the GSS-LF-ST method, the mean HNR was calculated as the energy ratio between the periodic and noise components of speech synthesised by STRAIGHT. Note that the synthetic speech of STRAIGHT, as well as the recorded speech, were only used during analysis (not included in the stimuli).

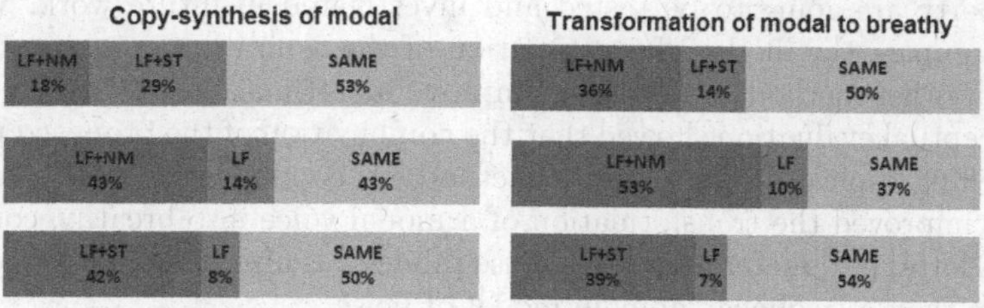

Fig. 2. Preference rates obtained in terms of: producing better sounding speech by copy-synthesis (left) and producing a breathier voice by transforming modal speech (right)

4.4 Results

Results of the copy-synthesis and transformation of modal into breathy experiments are shown in Figure 2 for the methods GSS-LF-NM, GSS-LF and GSS-LF-ST (represented by LF+NM, LF, and LF+ST respectively). Results from Friedman's ANOVA test indicate that the preference rates are statistically significant at 5% level ($p-value \leq 0.05$), with exception of the comparison between the GSS-LF-NM and GSS-LF-ST methods for copy-synthesis of modal voice.

The synthetic speech of the GSS-LF-NM method sounded significantly better than that of GSS-LF which indicates that the speech quality is improved by combining the LF-model excitation with the aspiration noise model proposed in this work. However, the effect of time-domain modulation of this model did not produce significant differences in speech quality compared with the frequency-domain model of noise.

The results of voice transformation show that the proposed GSS-LF-NM method was significantly better than the other two. This result supports the hypothesis that it is important to use a noise model that can accurately represent the amplitude modulation characteristic of the aspiration noise, for producing breathiness. Since the HNR parameter was transformed for both the GSS-LF-NM and GSS-LF-ST methods, it can be inferred that the effect of the time-domain modulation of the noise contributed to the better results compared with the frequency-domain model used as baseline.

5 Conclusions

This paper proposes a method to model the amplitude modulation of aspiration noise by fitting a fourth-order polynomial function to the energy envelope of the noise and parameterising the resulting curve using two linear functions, which represent a triangular shape. The proposed noise modelling technique is robust and is able to accurately represent the variations in the shape of the noise envelope. Another important property is that the shape characteristics of the triangular window can be controlled in order to take into account variations of voice quality properties of the glottal source signal. However, the benefits of this property are going to be tested and investigated in future work. We also plan to compare the method for estimation of the aspiration noise used in this work with other methods, in order to improve its estimation.

A perceptual evaluation showed that the combination of the proposed method for modelling aspiration noise and a method for controlling glottal source parameters improved the transformation of a modal voice into breathy, compared to using glottal parameter only. This noise model was also better for voice transformation than a frequency-domain model of noise.

Acknowledgments. This research is supported by the Science Foundation Ireland (Grant 07/CE/I1142) as part of the Centre for Next Generation Localisation (`www.cngl.ie`) at University College Dublin. The opinions, findings and conclusions, recommendations expressed in this material are those of the authors and do not necessarily reflect the views of Science Foundation Ireland.

References

1. Mehta, D., Quatieri, F.: Synthesis, analysis, and pitch modification of the breathy vowel. In: Proc. of IEEE WASPAA, pp. 1628–1639 (2005)
2. Pantazis, Y., Stylianou, Y.: Improving the modeling of the noise part in the harmonic plus noise model of speech. In: Proc. of ICASSP, pp. 4609–4612 (2008)
3. Stylianou, Y.: Harmonic plus Noise Models for Speech, combined with Statistical Methods, for Speech and Speaker Modification, PhD thesis, Ecole Nationale Supérieure des Télécommunications (1996)
4. Degottex, G., Roebel, A., Rodet, X., "Pitch transposition and breathiness modification using a glottal source model and its adapted vocal-tract filter", Proc. of ICASSP, 5128–5131, 2011.
5. Cabral, J.P., Renals, S., Richmond, K., Yamagishi, J.: Glottal Spectral Separation for Parametric Speech Synthesis. In: Proc. Interspeech, pp. 1829–1832 (2008)
6. Fant, G., Liljencrants, J., Lin, Q.: A four-parameter model of glottal flow. STL-QPSR 26(4), 1–13 (1985)
7. Cabral, J.P., Renals, S., Richmond, K., Yamagishi, J.: HMM-based speech synthesiser using the LF-model of the glottal source. In: Proc. of ICASSP (2011)
8. Alku, P., Vilkman, E., Laine, U.K.: Analysis of glottal waveform in different phonation types using the new IAIF method. In: Proc. of ICPhS, France, vol. 4, pp. 362–365 (1991)
9. Kawahara, H., Masuda-Katsuse, I., Cheveigné, A.: Restructuring speech representations using a pitch-adaptive time-frequency smoothing and an instantaneous-frequency-based f_0 extraction: Possible role of a repetitive structure in sounds. Speech Communication 27, 187–207 (1999)
10. Hermes, D.J.: Synthesis of breathy vowels: some research methods. Speech Communication 10, 497–502 (1991)
11. Erro, D., Moreno, A.: A Pitch-Asynchronous Simple Method for Speech Synthesis by Diphone Concatenation using the Deterministic plus Stochastic Model. In: SPECOM, Greece, pp. 321–324 (2005)
12. Mehta, D.: Aspiration noise during phonation: Synthesis, analysis, and pitch-scale modification, PhD Thesis, Massachussets Institute of Technology (2006)

Towards Physically Interpretable Parametric Voice Conversion Functions

Daniel Erro[1,2], Agustín Alonso[1], Luis Serrano[1], Eva Navas[1], and Inma Hernáez[1]

[1] AHOLAB, University of the Basque Country (UPV/EHU), Bilbao, Spain
[2] Basque Foundation for Science (IKERBASQUE), Bilbao, Spain
derro@aholab.ehu.es

Abstract. Typical voice conversion functions based on Gaussian mixture models are opaque in the sense that it is not straightforward to establish a link between the conversion parameters and their physical implications. Following the line of recent works, in this paper we study how physically meaningful constraints can be imposed to a system operating in the cepstral domain in order to get more informative conversion functions. The resulting method can be used to study the differences between source and target voices in terms of formant location in frequency, spectral tilt and amplitude in specific bands.

Keywords: voice conversion, Gaussian mixture models, frequency warping, amplitude scaling, spectral tilt.

1 Introduction

Voice conversion (VC) [1–16] is the technology that allows transforming the voice characteristics of a speaker (the source speaker) into those of another speaker (the target speaker) without altering the content of the transmitted message. The applications of VC include the personalization of artificial speaking devices, the transformation of voices in movie, music and computer game industries, and the real-time repair of pathological voices.

Among all possible voice characteristics, the timbre, which is closely related to the short-time spectral envelope, has attracted most of the attention of researchers. During the training phase, given a number of speech recordings from the two involved speakers, VC systems extract their corresponding acoustic information and then learn a mapping function to transform the source speaker's acoustic space into that of the target speaker. During the conversion phase, this function is applied to transform new input utterances from the source speaker. Various types of VC techniques have been studied in the literature: vector quantization and mapping codebooks [1], more sophisticated solutions based on fuzzy vector quantization [2], frequency warping transformations [3, 4], artificial neural networks [5], hidden Markov models [6], classification and regression trees [6], and Gaussian mixture model (GMM) based VC [7, 8, 9], which currently is the dominant technique.

Recently, the set of linear transforms characterizing the traditional GMM-based VC systems were replaced by a set of frequency warping (FW) plus amplitude scaling

T. Drugman and T. Dutoit (Eds.): NOLISP 2013, LNAI 7911, pp. 75–82, 2013.

(AS) transformations [10–13] to improve the quality and naturalness of the converted speech. FW+AS transformations have a clear physical meaning. FW is a nonlinear operation that maps the frequency axis of the source speaker's spectrum into that of the target speaker. Since it does not remove any detail of the source spectrum but just moves it to a different location in frequency, FW preserves well the quality of the converted speech. However, the conversion accuracy achieved via FW is moderate because it does not modify the relative amplitude of meaningful parts of the spectrum. For this reason, FW is complemented with AS to compensate for the differences in the amplitude axis, typically by means of smooth corrective filters.

In the works referenced above, particular signal representations were required for the specific FW+AS methods to be applicable, whereas current trends in speech synthesis technologies are pushing research towards methods that can be applied to well known parametric representations of speech. That is why it was shown in [14] that GMM-based FW+AS methods can be applied to a simple cepstral representation of speech, overcoming the need of specifically designed vocoders. In [15], the FW functions were constrained to be bilinear (BLFW), which led to a more elegant formulation of FW+AS in the cepstral domain with very few conversion parameters. The performance of BLFW+AS was found to be as good as that of the best existing GMM-based parametric VC methods [16].

Following the line of BLFW+AS, this paper goes one step beyond in making VC functions more understandable and controllable by users while reducing even more the number of involved conversion parameters. For this purpose, we suggest imposing constraints to the AS part of the VC function as it was done previously with the FW part. More specifically, we propose a new way of expressing the AS function as a combination of a spectral tilt related term and a set of smooth bandpass filters. We will show that the resulting VC functions are very informative in the sense that all their parameters can be interpreted from a physical point of view. Therefore, the method can be applied not only to synthesize high-quality converted voices but also to analyze the differences between the two involved voices.

The remainder of the paper is structured as follows. Section 2 contains a brief description of the BLFW+AS VC method. In section 3 we present the modified method and describe the corresponding automatic training procedures. The effectiveness of this method is experimentally shown and discussed in section 4. Finally, the conclusions of this work are summarized in section 5.

2 Description of BLFW+AS

In the cepstral domain, FW transformations are equivalent to multiplicative matrices [17] and AS can be implemented by means of additive cepstral terms. Given an input p-dimensional cepstral vector $\mathbf{x}$ and a GMM θ, the BLFW+AS operation proposed in [16] can be formulated mathematically as follows:

$$\mathbf{y} = \mathbf{W}_{\alpha(\mathbf{x},\theta)}\mathbf{x} + \mathbf{s}(\mathbf{x},\theta) \tag{1}$$

where $\mathbf{W}_\alpha$ is the matrix that implements the BLFW transform, which was proposed in [18]. $\mathbf{W}_\alpha$ can be expressed in terms of a single parameter α which will be referred to as the warping factor:

$$\mathbf{W}_\alpha = \begin{bmatrix} 1-\alpha^2 & 2\alpha-2\alpha^3 & \cdots \\ -\alpha+\alpha^3 & 1-4\alpha^2+3\alpha^4 & \cdots \\ \vdots & \vdots & \ddots \end{bmatrix} \quad (2)$$

In the original BLFW+AS implementation, both the current warping factor $\alpha(\mathbf{x}, \theta)$ and the AS vector $\mathbf{s}(\mathbf{x}, \theta)$ are obtained by means of a weighted combination of the individual contributions of each Gaussian acoustic class:

$$\alpha(\mathbf{x},\theta) = \sum_{k=1}^{m} p_k^{(\theta)}(\mathbf{x})\alpha_k, \quad \mathbf{s}(\mathbf{x},\theta) = \sum_{k=1}^{m} p_k^{(\theta)}(\mathbf{x})\mathbf{s}_k \quad (3)$$

where $p_k^{(\theta)}(\mathbf{x})$ denotes the probability that $\mathbf{x}$ belongs to the kth Gaussian mixture of θ. The elementary factors and vectors of the transformation, $\{\alpha_k\}$ and $\{\mathbf{s}_k\}$, result from a data-driven training procedure. Given a training set of N source-target vector pairs, $\{\mathbf{x}_n\}$ and $\{\mathbf{y}_n\}$, the training process is carried out sequentially in two steps. First, the warping factors are calculated by minimizing the error between the warped source vectors and the target vectors. An iterative algorithm was proposed in [15, 16] to train all the warping factors $\{\alpha_k\}$ simultaneously while dealing with the strongly nonlinear relationship between α and $\mathbf{W}_\alpha$ (we omit the details of this algorithm and encourage interested readers to refer to [15, 16]). Second, the differences between warped and target vectors are calculated for each of the N training pairs,

$$\mathbf{r}_n = \mathbf{y}_n - \mathbf{W}_{\alpha(\mathbf{x}_n,\theta)}\mathbf{x}_n, \quad n = 1 \ldots N \quad (4)$$

and then class-specific scaling vectors $\{\mathbf{s}_k\}$ are trained in such manner that these differences are maximally compensated. The least squares training algorithm proposed in [15, 16] is the following:

$$\underset{m\times p}{\mathbf{S}} = [\mathbf{s}_1 \ \ \mathbf{s}_2 \ \ \ldots \ \ \mathbf{s}_m]^{\mathrm{T}} = \arg\min_{\hat{\mathbf{S}}} \left\|\mathbf{R} - \mathbf{P}\hat{\mathbf{S}}\right\|^2 = \left(\mathbf{P}^{\mathrm{T}}\mathbf{P}\right)^{-1}\mathbf{P}^{\mathrm{T}}\mathbf{R} \quad (5)$$

where p is the vector dimension (equal to the cepstral order) and $\mathbf{P}$ and $\mathbf{R}$ are given by

$$\underset{N\times m}{\mathbf{P}} = \begin{bmatrix} p_1^{(\theta)}(\mathbf{x}_1) & p_2^{(\theta)}(\mathbf{x}_1) & \cdots & p_m^{(\theta)}(\mathbf{x}_1) \\ p_1^{(\theta)}(\mathbf{x}_2) & p_2^{(\theta)}(\mathbf{x}_2) & \cdots & p_m^{(\theta)}(\mathbf{x}_2) \\ \vdots & \vdots & \ddots & \vdots \\ p_1^{(\theta)}(\mathbf{x}_N) & p_2^{(\theta)}(\mathbf{x}_N) & \cdots & p_m^{(\theta)}(\mathbf{x}_N) \end{bmatrix}, \quad \underset{N\times p}{\mathbf{R}} = [\mathbf{r}_1 \ \ \mathbf{r}_2 \ \ \ldots \ \ \mathbf{r}_N]^{\mathrm{T}} \quad (6)$$

Although the resulting vectors $\{\mathbf{s}_k\}$ are optimal from a mathematical point of view, they are not informative in the sense that it is not straightforward to understand the information they convey. On the contrary, the meaning of the warping factors $\{\alpha_k\}$ is clear: positive values of α mean higher formant frequencies ($\alpha \approx 0.1$ for male to female conversion) and negative values mean lower formant frequencies. This informative transparency is partially due to the BL constraints imposed to the FW operation, which simplifies the warping curves and makes them dependent on a single meaningful parameter. At the same time, this helps increasing the robustness of the system. Inspired by this idea, in this paper we propose to constrain the AS vectors as well in order to get a new type of transformation which can be understood, intuitively manipulated and even used to analyze the differences between the source voice and the target voice.

3 BLFW + Constrained AS

The aim of AS is not making new formants appear in the converted spectrum, but just correcting the relative intensity of the already existing (warped-in-frequency) formants. Consequently, the spectral response of the AS filter represented by the elementary vectors $\{\mathbf{s}_k\}$ should be smooth by definition. In the original BLFW+AS system [16], this aspect was not taken into account explicitly. Smoothness was guaranteed simply by using a GMM with few acoustic classes, because intra-class averaging prevented sharp peaks in $\{\mathbf{r}_n\}$ from being transferred to $\{\mathbf{s}_k\}$. On the other hand, the fact that spectral tilt differences between the two involved speakers might explain a significant portion of $\{\mathbf{s}_k\}$ was neither taken into account in BLFW+AS. In our new proposal we force the AS frequency response to be formed by a weighted combination of a spectral tilt related term with 1 dB/decade slope and B smooth Hanning-like bands equally spaced in the Mel frequency scale. The AS elementary vectors $\{\mathbf{s}_k\}$ are now forced to be the result of the following combination:

$$\mathbf{s}_k = \tau_k \mathbf{t} + \sum_{j=1}^{B} \beta_{k,j} \mathbf{b}_j \ , \quad k = 1 \ldots m \tag{7}$$

where $\mathbf{t}$ and $\{\mathbf{b}_j\}$ are p-dimensional column vectors containing the cepstral representations of the tilt-related term and the B bands, respectively. These representations are constant and can be calculated numerically. This means that the shape of $\mathbf{s}_k$ depends exclusively on τ_k and $\{\beta_{k,j}\}$. Fig. 1 shows the involved spectral shapes reconstructed from their 24th-order Mel-cepstral parameterization ($p = 24$) for $f_s = 16$ kHz and $B = 9$. Thus, the value of τ_k coincides with the slope (dB/decade) by which the two involved voices differ at the kth acoustic class of model θ, whereas $\{\beta_{k,j}\}$ represent the exact amplitude (dB) of the complementary smooth amplitude correction envelope at equally spaced points in the Mel-frequency scale. Remarkably, the dimensionality of the resulting voice conversion function is reduced significantly because each amplitude scaling vector $\mathbf{s}_k$ is now given by 1+B weights. To prevent the tilt-related term from being diluted within the corrective bands, we propose the following two-step weight optimization during training. First we simultaneously optimize the weights of all the tilt-related terms by solving the corresponding least squares system:

$$\underset{m\times 1}{\boldsymbol{\tau}} = [\tau_1 \quad \tau_2 \quad \ldots \quad \tau_m]^{\mathrm{T}} = \arg\min_{\hat{\boldsymbol{\tau}}} \left\| \boldsymbol{\Gamma} - \mathbf{Q}\hat{\boldsymbol{\tau}} \right\|^2 = \left(\mathbf{Q}^{\mathrm{T}}\mathbf{Q}\right)^{-1} \mathbf{Q}^{\mathrm{T}} \boldsymbol{\Gamma} \tag{8}$$

where

$$\underset{Np\times m}{\mathbf{Q}} = \mathbf{P}\otimes\mathbf{t}\ ,\quad \underset{Np\times 1}{\boldsymbol{\Gamma}} = \left[\mathbf{r}_1^{\mathrm{T}}\ \ \mathbf{r}_2^{\mathrm{T}}\ \ \dots\ \ \mathbf{r}_N^{\mathrm{T}}\right]^{\mathrm{T}} \tag{9}$$

$\mathbf{P}$ and $\{\mathbf{r}_n\}$ are given by expressions (6) and (4) respectively, and $\otimes$ denotes the Kronecker product. Next, we update the residuals by subtracting the tilt-related terms and we determine the weights of the corrective bands for all the classes by solving another least squares system. This can be expressed mathematically as follows:

$$\begin{aligned}\underset{mB\times 1}{\boldsymbol{\beta}} &= \left[\beta_{1,1}\cdots\beta_{1,B}\ \ \beta_{2,1}\cdots\beta_{2,B}\ \ \cdots\ \ \beta_{m,1}\cdots\beta_{m,B}\right]^{\mathrm{T}} = \\ &= \arg\min_{\hat{\boldsymbol{\beta}}}\left\|\tilde{\boldsymbol{\Gamma}}-\tilde{\mathbf{Q}}\hat{\boldsymbol{\beta}}\right\|^2 = \left(\tilde{\mathbf{Q}}^{\mathrm{T}}\tilde{\mathbf{Q}}\right)^{-1}\tilde{\mathbf{Q}}^{\mathrm{T}}\tilde{\boldsymbol{\Gamma}}\end{aligned} \tag{10}$$

where

$$\underset{Np\times mB}{\tilde{\mathbf{Q}}} = \mathbf{P}\otimes\left[\mathbf{b}_1\ \ \mathbf{b}_2\ \ \dots\ \ \mathbf{b}_B\right]\ ,\quad \underset{Np\times 1}{\tilde{\boldsymbol{\Gamma}}} = \boldsymbol{\Gamma}-\mathbf{Q}\boldsymbol{\tau} \tag{11}$$

The efficiency of such operations can be increased by exploiting the properties of the Kronecker product.

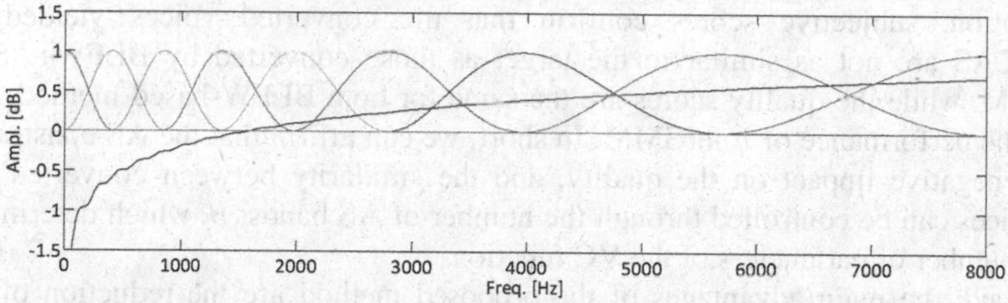

Fig. 1. Spectral shapes involved in constrained AS: tilt-related term (1dB/dec slope) and 9 Hanning-like bandpass filters, all reconstructed from a 24th-order Mel-cepstral representation

4 Study and Discussion

The speech data used in the experiments were taken from the CMU ARCTIC database [19]. Four speakers were selected from this database: two female speakers, *slt* and *clb*, and two male speakers, *bdl* and *rms*. 50 parallel training sentences per speaker were randomly selected for training and a different set of 50 sentences was separated for testing purposes. The remaining sentences of the database were simply discarded. We used the vocoder described in [20] to translate the speech signals into Mel-cepstral coefficients and to reconstruct the waveforms from the converted vectors. The order of the cepstral analysis was 24 (plus the 0th coefficient containing the energy, which does not take part in the conversion). The frame shift was set to 8ms. During conversion, the mean and variance of the source speaker's $\log f_0$ distribution were replaced by those of the target speaker by means of a linear transformation. In order to find the correspondence between the source and target cepstral vectors extracted from the parallel training utterances, we calculated a piecewise linear time warping function from the phoneme boundaries given by the available segmentation. Similarly as in [15, 16], the GMMs used in our experiments had 32 mixtures with full-covariance matrices.

Table 1 compares the proposed method with constrained AS (for $B = 9$ AS bands), labeled as BLFW+CAS, with BLFW+AS and also with a standard VC system based on joint-density GMMs (JointGMM) [8]. The comparison is made in terms of several measures: (i) the number of parameters in the VC function; (i) the average Mel-cepstral distortion (MCD) between converted and target vectors; (iii) the quotient between the variance of the converted Mel-cepstral coefficients and the variance of the target coefficients (VarQ); the mean opinion score and its 95% confidence interval for (iv) converted-to-target similarity (Sim. MOS) and for (v) converted speech quality (Qual. MOS), both calculated by averaging the individual opinion of 20 listeners on a 1-5 scale (1 = very bad, …, 5 = excellent). The objective and subjective scores were averaged over the different voice and gender combinations. Since the relative scores of JointGMM and BLFW+AS are consistent with those reported previously [15, 16], we focus our attention in BLFW+CAS. The proposed AS constraints produce a significant reduction of the number of parameters in the VC function, which results in a slight increment of MCD (slightly less accurate conversion) and VarQ (closer-to-natural variability) with respect to non-constrained AS. We verified that the objective performance of BLFW+CAS gets closer to that of BLFW+AS as B increases. For this configuration, subjective scores confirm that the converted voices yielded by BLFW+CAS are not as similar to the target as those converted by BLFW+AS or JointGMM, while the quality scores are the same for both BLFW-based methods, far beyond the performance of JointGMM. In short, we can affirm that the AS constraints have no negative impact on the quality, and the similarity between converted and target voices can be controlled through the number of AS bands, B, which determines also the number of parameters of the VC function.

This said, the main advantages of the proposed method are the reduction of the number of conversion parameters, which may increase the robustness of the system when few parallel training data are available (this aspect will be explored in future works), and the fact that it can be used as an analysis tool that helps rapidly visualizing the differences between source and target voices. To illustrate this second aspect, Table 2 displays the parameters of VC functions corresponding to two different voice pairs. For the sake of simplicity, only the voiced frames were considered during training and one single acoustic class was assumed. The first example involves two very different voices, *bdl* and *slt*. The parameters in Table 2 reveal that in order to recreate *slt* from *bdl* we have to move the formants towards higher frequencies ($\alpha \approx 0.1$), then apply a negative slope of ~5.5dB/dec, and finally apply local amplitude corrections with high contrasts mainly in mid-high frequencies. The voices in the second example, *slt* and *clb*, are perceptually close according to informal listenings. Table 2 confirms that the only remarkable differences are the spectral tilt and the energy at some high-frequency bands. Beyond these illustrative examples, in a general case with multiple classes, BLFW+CAS can also be used to observe the evolution of the instantaneous parameters over time. In future works we will use this tool to study the acoustic differences between emotional styles and between normal and Lombard speech.

Table 1. Objective and subjective comparison between several GMM-based VC techniques

Method	#Params.	MCD (dB)	VarQ	Sim. MOS	Qual. MOS
JointGMM	32 × 600	5.02	0.36	3.46 ± 0.17	2.01 ± 0.13
BLFW+AS	32 × 25	5.65	0.87	3.41 ± 0.18	3.15 ± 0.15
BLFW+CAS	32 × 11	5.88	0.92	3.15 ± 0.19	3.15 ± 0.16

Table 2. Parameters of the VC function for two different voice pairs

Voices	α (FW)	τ (tilt)	$\{\beta_j\}_{j=1...9}$ (bands)
bdl → *slt*	0.098	-5.56	{4.8, -4.2, 0.4, 0.8, 1.8, 1.6, -7.4, 8.9, -3.4}
slt → *clb*	-0.015	-3.85	{1.0, -2.4, -0.4, -0.1, 1.0, 1.9, 3.3, -7.3, 3.0}

5 Conclusions

We have shown that GMM-based voice conversion functions operating in the cepstral domain can be designed in such manner that relevant information about the physical differences between voices – relative location of the formants in frequency, relative spectral tilt and relative amplitude in specific frequency bands – becomes available. Therefore, the resulting system can be used as an automatic analysis tool. Regarding the performance of the conversion method itself, we have observed that the number of amplitude correction has to be adjusted to control the trade-off between conversion accuracy and dimensionality of the conversion function. Future works will at studying this trade-off in more depth, at studying the robustness of the described method against training data scarcity, and also at applying it to analyze the differences between speaking styles and emotions.

Acknowledgements. This work has been partially supported by the Spanish Ministry of Economy and Competitiveness (SpeechTech4All project, TEC2012-38939-C03-03) and the Basque Government (Ber2tek project, IE12-333).

References

1. Abe, M., Nakamura, S., Shikano, K., Kuwabara, H.: Voice conversion through vector quantization. In: Proc. IEEE ICASSP, pp. 655–658 (1988)
2. Arslan, L.M.: Speaker transformation algorithm using segmental codebooks (STASC). Speech Commun. 28(3), 211–226 (1999)

3. Valbret, H., Moulines, E., Tubach, J.P.: Voice transformation using PSOLA technique. Speech Commun. 1, 145–148 (1992)
4. Sündermann, D., Ney, H.: VTLN-based voice conversion. In: Proc. ISSPIT, pp. 556–559 (2003)
5. Narendranath, M., Murthy, H.A., Rajendran, S., Yegnanarayana, B.: Transformation of formants for voice conversion using artificial neural networks. Speech Commun. 16(2), 207–216 (1995)
6. Duxans, H., Bonafonte, A., Kain, A., van Santen, J.: Including dynamic and phonetic information in voice conversion systems. In: Proc. ICSLP, pp. 1193–1196 (2004)
7. Stylianou, Y., Cappé, O., Moulines, E.: Continuous probabilistic transform for voice conversion. IEEE Trans. Speech and Audio Process. 6, 131–142 (1998)
8. Kain, A.: High resolution voice transformation, Ph.D. thesis, Oregon Health & Science University (2001)
9. Toda, T., Black, A.W., Tokuda, K.: Voice conversion based on maximum-likelihood estimation of spectral parameter trajectory. IEEE Trans. Audio, Speech, Lang. Process. 15(8), 2222–2235 (2007)
10. Toda, T., Saruwatari, H., Shikano, K.: Voice conversion algorithm based on Gaussian mixture model with dynamic frequency warping of STRAIGHT spectrum. In: Proc. IEEE ICASSP, pp. 841–844 (2001)
11. Erro, D., Moreno, A., Bonafonte, A.: Voice conversion based on weighted frequency warping. IEEE Trans. Audio, Speech, Lang. Process. 18(5), 922–931 (2010)
12. Tamura, M., Morita, M., Kagoshima, T., Akamine, M.: One sentence voice adaptation using GMM-based frequency-warping and shift with a sub-band basis spectrum model. In: Proc. IEEE ICASSP, pp. 5124–5127 (2011)
13. Godoy, E., Rosec, O., Chonavel, T.: Voice conversion using dynamic frequency warping with amplitude scaling, for parallel or nonparallel corpora. IEEE Trans. Audio, Speech, Lang. Process. 20(4), 1313–1323 (2012)
14. Zorilă, T.-C., Erro, D., Hernaez, I.: Improving the Quality of Standard GMM-Based Voice Conversion Systems by Considering Physically Motivated Linear Transformations. In: Torre Toledano, D., Ortega Giménez, A., Teixeira, A., González Rodríguez, J., Hernández Gómez, L., San Segundo Hernández, R., Ramos Castro, D. (eds.) IberSPEECH 2012. CCIS, vol. 328, pp. 30–39. Springer, Heidelberg (2012)
15. Erro, D., Navas, E., Hernaez, I.: Iterative MMSE Estimation of Vocal Tract Length Normalization Factors for Voice Transformation. In: Proc. Interspeech, pp. 86–89 (2012)
16. Erro, D., Navas, E., Hernaez, I.: Parametric Voice Conversion based on Bilinear Frequency Warping plus Amplitude Scaling. IEEE Trans. Audio, Speech, and Lang. Process. 21(3), 556–566 (2013)
17. Pitz, M., Ney, H.: Vocal tract normalization equals linear transformation in cepstral space. IEEE Trans. Speech and Audio Process. 13(5), 930–944 (2005)
18. McDonough, J., Byrne, W.: Speaker adaptation with all-pass transforms. In: Proc. IEEE ICASSP, pp. 757–760 (1999)
19. CMU ARCTIC speech synthesis databases, `http://festvox.org/cmu_arctic/`
20. Erro, D., Sainz, I., Navas, E., Hernaez, I.: HNM-based MFCC+F0 extractor applied to statistical speech synthesis. In: Proc. IEEE ICASSP, pp. 4728–4731 (2011)

Reduced Search Space Frame Alignment Based on Kullback-Leibler Divergence for Voice Conversion

Abdoreza Sabzi Shahrebabaki, Jamal Amini, Hamid Sheikhzadeh, Mostafa Ghorbandoost, and Neda Faraji

Multimedia Signal Processing Research Laboratory (MSPRL),
Electrical Eng. Dept., Amirkabir University of Technology, Hafez Ave., Tehran
{rezasabzi,jamal.amini,hsheikh,m.ghorbandoost,nfaraji}@aut.ac.ir

Abstract. A new text independent voice conversion based on Kullback-Leibler divergence (KLD) is proposed. This method only uses acoustic information and does not require any linguistic or phonetic information. The KLD is used to find reliable correspondence between the source and target GMM clusters and to reduce the search space for alignment of source and target frames. Subjective evaluation results show that the proposed method can achieve the same performance as parallel voice conversion methods.

Keywords: KLD, GMM, Nearest neighbour.

1 Introduction

Voice conversion (VC) involves modifying the speech signal of a speaker (source speaker) so that it sounds like it had been pronounced by a different speaker (target speaker). Conventional VC methods use a parallel corpus, but in recent years non-parallel methods have also been developed. Some of these non-parallel methods use statistical approaches to adapt a conversion function obtained by a parallel corpus [1, 2]. Other methods use various alignment techniques for pairing source and target vectors. In [3], the source and target vectors are clustered separately and then these two separate sets of clusters are paired based on the nearest frequency warped spectra of the cluster centroids. In this method, the quality of converted speech is reduced in comparison with parallel methods. Alternatively, a hidden Markov model (HMM) based speech recognizer is employed in [4] to label all the source and target frames. Then the labeled source and target sequences are aligned and associated to each other. This method needs a labeled database and cannot be applied to cross lingual VC. Other methods use text to speech (TTS) systems to generate parallel sentences from source and target speakers [5]. In these methods the database size must be large to provide high-quality synthesized speech, and also they need phonetically labeled database. An alignment method based on unit selection is proposed in [6], using dynamic programming to find the sequence of target frames for a given sequence of source

T. Drugman and T. Dutoit (Eds.): NOLISP 2013, LNAI 7911, pp. 83–88, 2013.

frames, minimizing a cost function. This method requires a large database for the unit selection. However, as the size of database increases the associated source and target frames become more similar with each other, leading to a VC system that cannot model the target speaker well enough. Finally, another alignment method named INCA uses an iterative method for performing the alignment in two steps: a nearest neighbour search step and a conversion step to refine the alignment [7]. This method is computationally expensive, and also the euclidean distance between source and target frames with different acoustic space (especially in cross gender VC) is not a good criteria.

2 Voice Conversion Based on GMM

In recent years, many leading methods of spectral voice conversion have been based on a statistical method that uses Gaussian Mixture Model (GMM) [11] for conversion. In this method, joint combination of time aligned source features x and target features y are used for training the GMM model and extracting the parameters $\sum_{m=1}^{M} \mathcal{N}(\alpha_m, \mu_m^z, \Sigma_m^{zz})$ of the variable $z = [x^T\ y^T]^T$. The estimated mean and covariance matrices are

$$\mu_m^z = \begin{bmatrix} \mu_m^x \\ \mu_m^y \end{bmatrix}, \Sigma_m^{zz} = \begin{bmatrix} \Sigma_m^{xx} & \Sigma_m^{xy} \\ \Sigma_m^{yx} & \Sigma_m^{yy} \end{bmatrix} \tag{1}$$

From the MMSE estimation perspective, the conversion function is determined by the following equation:

$$\hat{y} = E(y_t|x_t) = \int P(y_t|x_t, \lambda) y_t dy_t, \tag{2}$$

where the parameter λ is the parameters of GMM that trained with EM algorithm, and $\int P(y_t|x_t, \lambda)$ is the conditional probability density function of y_t given x_t which modelled by a GMM as follows:

$$P(y_t|x_t, \lambda) = \sum_{m=1}^{M} P(m|x_t, \lambda) P(y_t|x_t, m, \lambda) \tag{3}$$

$$P(m|x_t, \lambda) = \frac{\alpha_m \mathcal{N}(x_t; \mu_m^x, \Sigma_m^{xx})}{\sum_{k=1}^{M} \alpha_k \mathcal{N}(x_t; \mu_k^x, \Sigma_k^{xx})} \tag{4}$$

$$P(y_t|x_t, m, \lambda) = \mathcal{N}(y_t; \mu_m^{(y|x_t)}, \Sigma_m^{(y|x_t)}), \tag{5}$$

$$\mu_m^{(y|x_t)} = \mu_m^y + \Sigma_m^{yx} \Sigma_m^{xx-1} (x_t - \mu_m^x) \tag{6}$$

$$\Sigma_m^{(y|x_t)} = \Sigma_m^{yy} - \Sigma_m^{yx} \Sigma_m^{xx-1} \Sigma_m^{xy} \tag{7}$$

Therefore, equation (2) is rewritten as follows:

$$\hat{y}_t = \sum_{m=1}^{M} P(m|x_t, \lambda) \mu_m^{(y|x_t)} \tag{8}$$

3 Proposed Method

A novel non-parallel VC method is proposed based on Kullback-Leibler divergence (KLD) [8] for finding the corresponding clusters between the source and target spaces. The use of KLD for finding the corresponding clusters is justified as it uses only acoustic features, reducing the search space for finding the nearest neighbours between source and target spaces and also needs no iteration compared to the INCA method of [7]. Let $s = [s_1, \ldots, s_{T_s}]$ and $t = [t_1, \ldots, t_{T_t}]$ be the sequences of voiced frames of source and target speaker, in which T_s and T_t are the lengths of the voiced frames of source and target, respectively. First, both source and target frames are clustered separately by an EM algorithm employing Gaussian mixture models (GMMs), and then the corresponding clusters between source and target spaces are obtained by a symmetric KLD defined as

$$\begin{aligned} D(s(x), t(x)) &= \frac{1}{2}(D(s(x)||t(x)) + D(t(x)||s(x))) \\ &= \frac{1}{2}(\int s(x) log \frac{s(x)}{t(x)} dx + \int t(x) log \frac{t(x)}{s(x)} dx) \end{aligned} \quad (9)$$

where $s(x)$ and $t(x)$ are the probability density of source and target speakers with mean vectors μ_s, μ_t and covariance matrices Σ_s, Σ_t respectively. In the GMM VC method, the probability density functions are assumed to be Gaussian, so Equation 9 can be simplified as

$$\begin{aligned} D((s(x)||t(x))) = \frac{1}{2}\{ &log \frac{|\Sigma_t|}{|\Sigma_s|} + tr(\Sigma_t^{-1} \Sigma_s) - d \\ &+ (\mu_s - \mu_t)^T \Sigma_t^{-1} (\mu_s - \mu_t), \} \end{aligned} \quad (10)$$

where d is the dimension of the covariance matrix. By calculating the KLD between source clusters and target clusters, a $M \times M$ divergence matrix is obtained. To find the corresponding clusters, first the minimum entry in the divergence matrix is found, specifying the first pair of corresponding clusters. Then all the elements in the corresponding row and column of the minimum entry are set aside from the divergence matrix and the minimum of the remaining elements of the divergence matrix is found again. This procedure repeated to find the total of M corresponding source and target clusters. This method is evaluated on the parallel VC method. Figure 1 shows the divergence matrix and arrangement of the corresponding clusters, for a parallel VC system with $M = 8$ mixtures. As the figure depicts, the minimum value of KLD occurs between the 6th mixtures of the source and target spaces. After removing the 6th row and column of the matrix, the next minimum divergence belongs to the 7th mixtures of the source and target spaces. This scheme is continued until the M corresponding clusters are found. After finding the corresponding GMM clusters, alignment between source and target frames has to be implemented. We first calculate the nearest neighbour distance between the dynamic vectors (defined as the concatenation of the frame with its two side neighbours as in Equations 11 12) and then the

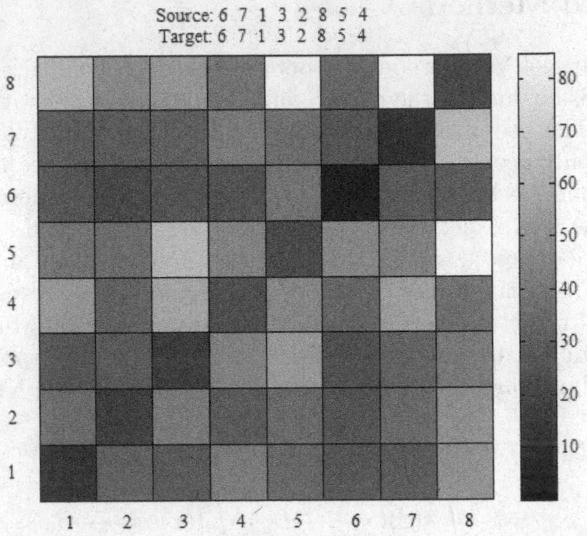

Fig. 1. Divergence matrix between distributions of the source and target acoustic spaces modelled by GMM with 8 mixtures

minimum of these distances is found, specifying the frame alignment. The alignment method is based on the two following equations

$$s2t(k) = \arg\min_j \left([s_{k-1}; s_k; s_{k+1}], [t_{j-1}; t_j; t_{j+1}]\right), \tag{11}$$

$$t2s(k) = \arg\min_j \left([t_{k-1}; t_k; t_{k+1}], [s_{j-1}; s_j; s_{j+1}]\right). \tag{12}$$

After finding the entire nearest neighbours, all the corresponding pairs of the source and target frames for which $s2t(k)$ and $t2s(k)$ entries are the same are removed from the training set because these aligned frames are similar to each other containing no useful information for conversion.After frame alignment, employing the same GMM clusters obtained in the alignment step, the GMM conversion method presented in [11] is used for non-parallel VC.

4 Experimental Results

We evaluate our proposed method using the CMU Arctic database. One female and two male speakers were chosen to evaluate the performance. A total of 200 sentences were selected for each speaker from which 150 sentences were used for training and the other 50 sentences were employed for testing. MFCCs of order 24 were extracted every 15ms from the STRAIGHT spectrum [9]. The speech waveform were synthesized by first converting the MFCCs back to the spectrum envelope based on the method of [10] and then using the STRAIGHT synthesis method [9]. The number of Gaussian mixtures is set to 16. A preference test was performed for comparing the proposed method with a parallel system trained using the method of [11]. Ten listeners participated in the experiments and were asked to give their preference to each sentence. The comparison results (Figure 2) show that the quality of the proposed non-parallel VC method approximately reached that of the parallel system. Furthermore, a MOS test was conducted to evaluate the overall performance. Table 1 exhibits the scores of the proposed method and the parallel method, clearly showing the efficiency of the proposed method since it has reached the results of the parallel method.

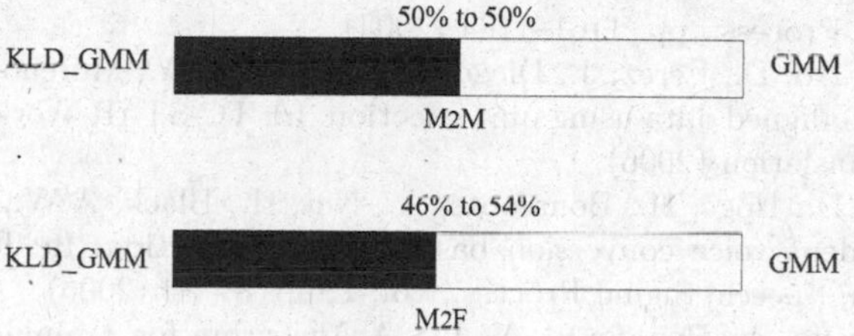

Fig. 2. Preference test, 'KLD-GMM' denotes the proposed non-parallel method and 'GMM' denotes the parallel method

Table 1. Similarity test at 95% confidence interval, 'KLD-GMM' denotes nonparallel method and 'GMM' denotes the parallel method

Test	MOS	
	KLD-GMM	GMM
M2M (male to male)	3.8±0.3	3.8±0.4
M2F (male to female)	2.6±0.35	2.8±0.3

5 Conclusion

A novel non-parallel VC method is presented. The proposed method employs KLD for developing a new cluster alignment technique in GMM-based VC. The KLD-GMM is computationally simple, since it reduces the search space for alignment of source and target frames. Moreover, by initially finding a reliable correspondence between the source and target clusters, this method does not need any iteration to refine the alignment of frames. Results of the preference and MOS tests demonstrate that KLD-GMM method achieves almost the same performance as the state-of-the-art parallel GMM approach.

Acknowledgments. We thank Dr. H. Kawahara for providing us with the STRAIGHT analysis/synthesis program.

References

1. Mouchtaris, A., Van der Spiegel, J., Mueller, P.: Nonparallel training for voice conversion based on a parameter adaptation approach. IEEE Trans. Audio, Speech and Lang. Process. 14(3), 952–963 (2006)
2. Lee, C.H., Wu, C.H.: MAP-based adaptation for speech conversion using adaptation data selection and non-parallel training. In: Proc. Int. Conf. Spoken Lang. Process., pp. 2446–2449 (2006)
3. Sündermann, D., Bonafonte, A., Ney, H., Höge, H.: A first step to- wards text-independent voice conversion. In: Proc. Int. Conf. Spoken Lang. Process., pp. 1173–1176 (2004)
4. Ye, H., Young, S.: Voice conversion for unknown speakers. In: Proc. Int. Conf. Spoken Lang. Process., pp. 1161–1164 (2004)
5. Duxans, H., Erro, D., Pérez, J., Diego, F., Bonafonte, A., Moreno, A.: Voice conversion of non-aligned data using unit selection. In: TC-STAR Workshop on Speech to Speech Translation (2006)
6. Sündermann, D., Höge, H., Bonafonte, A., Ney, H., Black, A.W., Narayanan, S.: Text-independent voice conversion based on unit selection. In: Proc. IEEE Int. Conf. Acoust., Speech, Signal Process., vol. 1, pp. 81–84 (2006)
7. Erro, D., Moreno, A., Bonafonte, A.: INCA Algorithm for Training Voice Conversion Systems From Nonparallel Corpora. IEEE Trans. Audio, Speech, and Lang. Process. 18(5), 944–953 (2010)
8. Kullback, S., Leibler, R.A.: On Information and Sufficiency. Annals of Math. Statistics 22(1), 79–86 (1951)
9. Kawahara, H., Masuda-Katsuse, I., de Cheveigné, A.: Restructuring speech representations using a pitch adaptive time-frequency smoothing and instantaneous frequency based f0 extraction: Possible role of a repetitive structure in sounds. Speech Commun. 27, 187–207 (1999)
10. Chazan, D., Hoory, R., Cohen, G., Zibulski, M.: Speech reconstruction from Mel frequency cepstral coefficients and pitch frequency. In: Proc. ICASSP, pp. 1299–1302 (2000)
11. Kain, A., Macon, M.W.: Spectral voice conversion for text-to-speech synthesis. In: Proc. ICASSP, Seattle, WA, pp. 285–288 (May 1998)

Average Voice Modeling Based on Unbiased Decision Trees

Fahimeh Bahmaninezhad, Soheil Khorram, and Hossein Sameti

Speech Processing Lab., Department of Computer Engineering,
Sharif University of Technology, Tehran, Iran

Abstract. Speaker adaptive speech synthesis based on Hidden Semi-Markov Model (HSMM) has been demonstrated to be dramatically effective in the presence of confined amount of speech data. However, we could intensify this effectiveness by training the average voice model appropriately. Hence, this study presents a new method for training the average voice model. This method guarantees that data from every speaker contributes to all the leaves of decision tree. We considered this fact that small training data and highly diverse contexts of training speakers are considered as disadvantages which degrade the quality of average voice model impressively, and further influence the adapted model and synthetic speech unfavorably. The proposed method takes such difficulties into account in order to train a tailored average voice model with high quality. Consequently, as the experiments indicate, the proposed method outweighs the conventional one not only in the quality of synthetic speech but also in similarity to the natural voice. Our experiments show that the proposed method increases the CMOS test score by 0.6 to the conventional one.

1 Introduction

The prevalent HSMM-based synthesis system, so-called speaker-dependent [1], employs one specific speaker's speech data for training the statistical model; later, the achieved model is used for synthesizing speech. This approach lacks acceptable quality when the training data is limited; therefore, for the sake of building a new voice naturally, collecting and preparing a tailored database is an essential task which leads to excessive waste of time and cost. On the contrary, speaker adaptive framework results in high quality output compared with the former one [2, 3] in small databases. The superiority of speaker adaptive system over speaker-dependent one is confirmed in [3, 4]. In fact, speaker adaptive system benefits from available multi-speaker corpus in order to compensate the restriction of target speaker's speech data. Hence, we proceed to make improvements in speaker adaptive framework.

Speaker adaptive synthesis system trains *average voice model* using multi-speaker speech database. Average voice model is a collection of speaker independent synthesis units. Thereafter, the adapted model is obtained by transforming the average voice model through adaptation algorithms and target speaker's speech data. Finally, synthetic speech is generated from the adapted model.

T. Drugman and T. Dutoit (Eds.): NOLISP 2013, LNAI 7911, pp. 89–96, 2013.

In contrast to popular misconception, diverse contexts between different training speakers result in improper speaker adaptive synthesizer. In other words, if the set of sentences pertaining to a person in the train database are positively different from others regarding their context then the average voice model will have tendency toward a specific gender or speaker. Moreover, small amount of training data causes such drawbacks too [5]. Therefore, adapting the average voice model and synthesizing speech would affect the synthetic speech destructively.

In [3] the author presented a new technique for context clustering to solve the above-mentioned problem; however, this new method does not ensure the identical contribution of every speaker to every leaf of decision tree in context clustering. Thus, it is highly probable to have leaves with great domination of a specific gender or speaker.

In this study, we recommend another option to conflict the tendency of average voice model toward a little proportion of database. The proposed method guarantees equal participation of each speaker in every leaf of decision tree in context clustering, which in its own turn results in high quality synthesized speech in contrast to the conventional speaker adaptive synthesis system.

The rest of this paper is structured as follows. Section 2 describes the conventional speaker adaptive synthesis system. Our proposed system is introduced in Section 3. Experimental conditions and results are presented in Section 4, and concluding remarks and our plans for the future work are mentioned in the final section.

2 Speaker Adaptive HSMM-Based Speech Synthesis System

Many papers, such as [3, 6, 7], describe the conventional speaker adaptive HSMM-based speech synthesis system in detail. Here, we merely investigate the structure of this system generally. The schema depicted in Fig. 1 represents the main parts of the speaker adaptive system, namely training, adaptation, and synthesis.

Based on Fig. 1 speaker adaptive system and the well-known speaker-dependent approach [1] have two major disparities, 1) in speaker adaptive system, training data comprises speech from multiple speakers, contrary to one speaker used in the speaker-dependent system; 2) the adaptation phase must be carried out in speaker adaptive system between training and synthesis steps to construct the specific target speaker's model.

In the training phase of speaker adaptive framework, spectral and excitation parameters are first extracted for each frame; then, a speaker-independent context-dependent [8, 9] multi-space-distribution HSMM [10] is modeled employing a set of training data collected from different speakers. The trained model of this step is a statistical model called *average voice model.*

Afterwards in adaptation step, the average voice model is transformed and adapted to the target speaker employing adaptation data and adaptation algorithms [11–15]. Finally, the output speech is synthesized through the adapted model in synthesis phase.

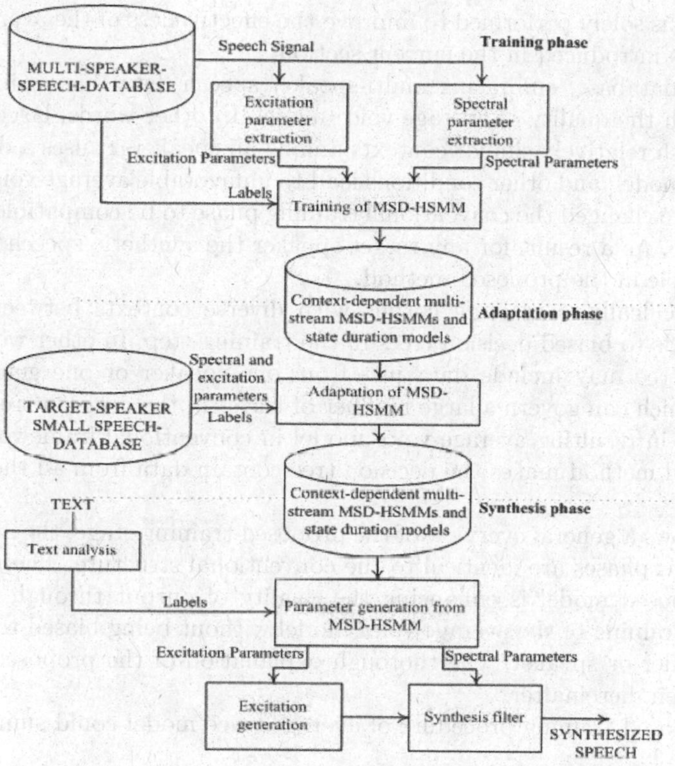

Fig. 1. Overview of speaker adaptive speech synthesis system [3]

All in all, the significant importance of speaker adaptive system is the necessity of very limited adaptation data. This effectiveness originates from the presence of rich and large training dataset. However, achieving a decent synthetic speech requires a high quality average voice model which is remarkably affected by the training data.

When the training corpus is small and embraces diversity among speakers' contexts we expect notable degradation in the quality of average voice model. Therefore, in such situations the widely-used decision-tree-based context clustering in training step causes an extreme reduction in the quality since average voice model would be biased toward just a limited section of database. In the next section we propose a new approach for training the average voice model which remarkably enhances the quality of average model.

3 Proposed Average Voice Model Training

In general, the average voice model affects the resulting adapted model and synthetic speech impressively; therefore, more favorable output will be synthesized if the average voice model is trained exactly and efficiently. Accordingly, our contribution is solely performed to improve the effectiveness of the average voice model and is introduced in the current section.

Training database, embracing multi-speaker speech data, has a direct relationship with the quality of average voice model. In other words, large training database with relatively similar contexts among all speakers causes a decent average voice model; and other conditions lead to unfavorable average voice model. Therefore, we changed the conventional training phase to be compatible with every database. As a result, for any target speaker the synthetic speech would be more desirable in the proposed method.

More specifically, a training corpus with diverse contexts between various speakers leads to biased decision trees in the training step. In other words, each leaf of the tree may include data just from one speaker or one gender. This tendency which can govern a large number of leaves in the decision tree leads to degradation in resulting average voice model in conventional framework. Thus, the proposed method makes the decision tree contain data from all the training speakers.

Fig. 2 shows a general overview of the proposed training stage; the adaptation and synthesis phases are identical to the conventional structure. The main goal of this proposed model is enhancing the quality of output through the exact and better training of the average voice model without being biased toward any specific gender or speaker. The thorough explanation of the proposed training phase is given, hereinafter.

The proposed training procedure of average voice model could summarize as follows:

1) A speaker-dependent model is trained for each speaker in the training database [1].

2) A list of all contexts, i.e. the union of all speakers' contexts, is prepared.

3) For each speaker, the model of all contexts (full-context list), listed in the preceding step, are determined. We use the decision trees resulting from pre-trained speaker-dependent models to establish each context model.

4) The general model of every context in the full-context list is achieved by averaging among each speaker's model; in other words, expectation of means and variances among every speaker's model for a particular context leads to the mean and variance of general model for that specific context.

5) The achieved full-context general model is clustered by utilizing decision-tree-based context clustering. This clustered model is our proposed average voice model, and it is not biased toward a minor section of database anymore.

Eventually, we transformed this proposed average model to a specific model for the target speaker; this transformation employs adaptation algorithms and we have utilized Maximum Likelihood Linear Regression (MLLR) algorithm [12] and Maximum A Posteriori (MAP) estimation [14, 15] for this purpose. In the

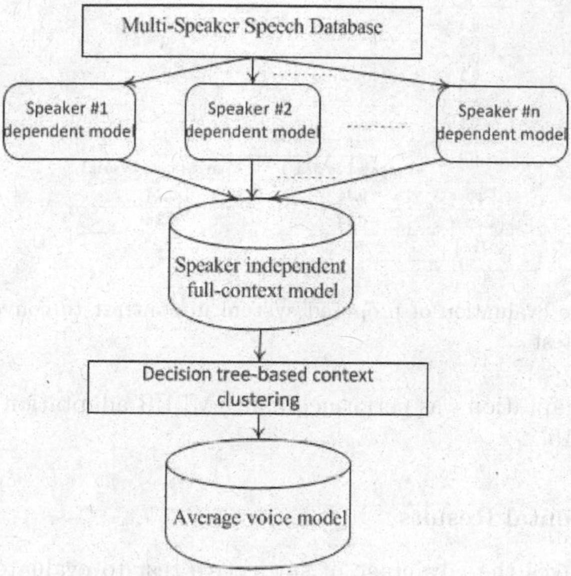

Fig. 2. Proposed method for training the average voice model

end, the favorable synthetic speech for the target speaker is resulted by applying the synthesis phase on the adapted model. These two steps are exactly alike those of conventional adaptation system [3].

4 Experiments

4.1 Experimental Conditions

A Persian speech database, named FARsi Speech DATabase (FARSDAT) [16], is adopted to evaluate the proposed method. Several steps were carried out on FARSDAT to prepare it for the purpose of speaker adaptive speech synthesis. These steps in addition to FARSDAT characteristics were reported in our previous work [4].

The sampling rate of speech signals was 16 kHz, and they were windowed by a 25-ms Blackman window with a 5-ms shift. The feature vector embraced mel-cepstral coefficients (mcep), bandpass aperiodicity (bap), and fundamental frequency (log-F0) that were extracted by STRAIGHT [17]. In addition, 5-state left-to-right context-dependent HSMMs without skip paths were used. The synthesis units were modeled by considering segmental and supra-segmental contextual features; they are partly introduced in [4].

Four male and four female speakers' speech data, constituting the training corpus, were arbitrarily selected from FARSDAT to conduct the experiments, and a male speaker's speech data was selected for adaptation data. Training and adaptation data respectively consist of about 360 and 50 minutes. Moreover, it should be noted that there is not any overlap between training and adaptation

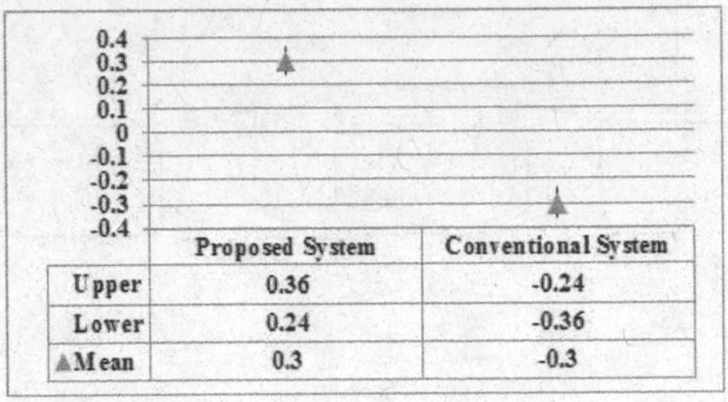

Fig. 3. Subjective evaluation of proposed system in contrast to conventional system based on CMOS test

data; and the adaptation was performed using MLLR adaptation [12] and MAP estimation [14, 15].

4.2 Experimental Results

This research takes the advantage of subjective test to evaluate the proposed method through two experiments. In both experiments, ten subjects were presented with seven synthesized speech. It is worthwhile to state that, seven test utterances were randomly chosen from 18 synthesized speech sentences which were contained in neither the training nor the adaptation datasets.

Subjective Evaluation of Proposed Method in Contrast to Conventional One. We determined the preference of proposed system over the conventional one regarding their voice characteristics by Comparison Category Rating (CCR) test [18] based on Comparison Mean Opinion Score (CMOS) scale in this experiment. Subjects were presented with a pair of synthetic speech from proposed and conventional system in random order and asked which one sounded better.

The results in Fig. 3 illustrate the priority of proposed speaker adaptive system. The figure shows the score with 95% confidence interval of the test. This enhancement in the quality of synthesized speech is the consequence of better training of average voice model; it also indicates the remarkable effect of average voice model on the synthetic speech.

Subjective Evaluation of Synthesized Speech versus Natural Speech. We examined the quality as well as the similarity of the synthetic speech to the target speaker's voice in current experiment; for this reason, we conducted Mean Opinion Score (MOS) test. Subjects scored the quality of synthetic speech generated from conventional and proposed system in the first test (Fig. 4). Additionally, they scored the similarity of speech synthesized from both systems to the original natural voice in the second test (Fig. 5).

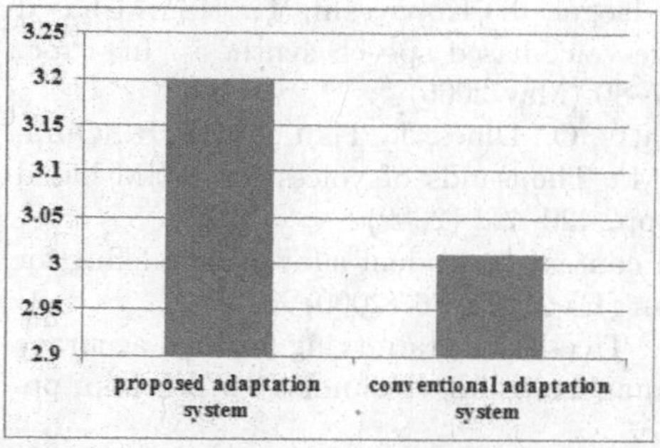

Fig. 4. Evaluation of quality

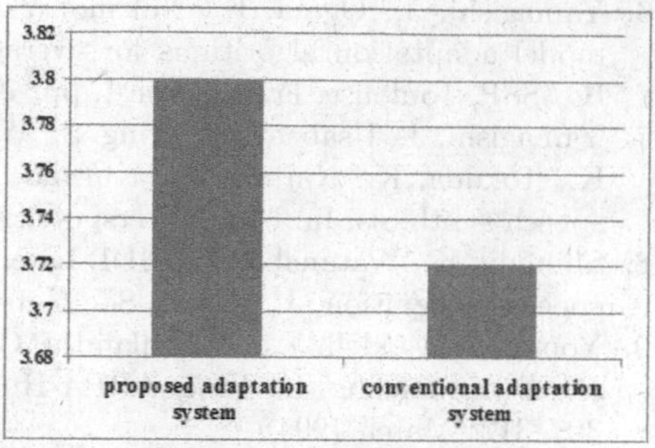

Fig. 5. Evaluation of similarity

As Fig. 4 shows the proposed system synthesizes speech with higher quality compared with the conventional one. Additionally, in Fig. 5 it is obvious that the speech synthesized from proposed system is more similar to the natural speech than that from conventional system.

5 Conclusion

In this research we proposed a new method for training the average voice model in speaker adaptive framework. The recommended system is more desirable against the conventional system when the training dataset is small or when speakers' contexts are very different. The subjective evaluations confirm the remarkable effect of the proposed average voice modeling on the quality of synthetic speech; therefore, the new output is more similar to the target speaker's voice and has higher quality in comparison with the conventional synthetic speech.

References

1. Zen, H., Tokuda, K., Masuko, T., Kobayashi, T., Kitamura, T.: Hidden semi-Markov model based speech synthesis. In: Proc. ICSLP, vol. 2, pp. 1397–1400 (October 2004)
2. Yamagishi, J., Tamura, M., Masuko, T., Tokuda, K., Kobayashi, T.: A training method of average voice model for HMM-based speech synthesis. IEICE Trans. Fundamentals E86-A(8), 1956–1963 (2003)
3. Yamagishi, J.: Average-voice-based speech synthesis. Ph.D. thesis, Tokyo Institute of Technology (2006)
4. Bahmaninezhad, F., Sameti, H., Khorram, S.: HMM-based persian speech synthesis using limited adaptation data. In: 11th International Conference on Signal Processing (ICSP 2012), October 21-25. IEEE (2012)
5. Yamagishi, J., Masuko, T., Tokuda, K., Kobayashi, T.: A training method for average voice model based on shared decision tree context clustering and speaker adaptive training. In: Proceedings of the 2003 IEEE International Conference on Acoustics, Speech, and Signal Processing (ICASSP 2003), vol. 1, IEEE (April 2003)

6. Yamagishi, J., Ogata, K., Nakano, Y., Isogai, J., Kobayashi, T.: HSMM-based model adaptation algorithms for average-voice-based speech synthesis. In: Proc. ICASSP, Toulouse, France, vol. I, pp. 77–80 (May 2006)
7. Yamagishi, J., Usabaev, B., King, S., Watts, O., Dines, J., Tian, J., Hu, R., Oura, K., Tokuda, K., Karhila, R., Kurimo, M.: Thousands of voices for HMM-based speech synthesis. In: Proc. Interspeech, pp. 420–423 (2009)
8. Shinoda, K., Watanabe, T.: MDL-based context-dependent subword modeling for speech recognition. J. Acoust. Soc. Japan (E) 21, 79–86 (2000)
9. Young, S.J., Odell, J.J., Woodland, P.C.: Tree-based state tying for high accuracy acoustic modeling. In: Proc. ARPA Human Language Technology Workshop, pp. 307–312 (March 1994)
10. Tokuda, K., Masuko, T., Miyazaki, N., Kobayashi, T.: Multi-Space Probability Distribution HMM. IEICE Transaction on Information and Systems E85-D(3), 455–464 (2002)
11. Yamagishi, J., Kobayashi, T., Nakano, Y., Ogata, K., Isogai, J.: Analysis of speaker adaptation algorithms for HMM-based speech synthesis and a constrained SMAPLR adaptation algorithm. IEEE Trans. Audio, Speech, Lang. Process. 17(1), 66–83 (2009)
12. Leggetter, C.J., Woodland, P.C.: Maximum likelihood linear regression for speaker adaptation of continuous density hidden Markov models. Computer Speech and Language 9(2), 171–185 (1995)
13. Tamura, M., Masuko, T., Tokuda, K., Kobayashi, T.: Adaptation of pitch and spectrum for HMM-based speech synthesis using MLLR. In: Proc. ICASSP, pp. 805–808 (May 2001)
14. Lee, C.H., Lin, C.H., Juang, B.H.: A Study on Speaker Adaptation of the Parameters of Continuous Density Hidden Markov Models. IEEE Trans. Acoust., Speech, Signal Processing 39(4), 806–814 (1992)
15. Tsurumi, Y., Nakagawa, S.: An Unsupervised Speaker Adaptation Method for Continuous Parameter HMM by Maximum a Posteriori Probability Estimation. In: Proc. ICSLP 1994, S09-1.1, pp. 431–434 (1994)
16. Bijankhan, M., Sheikhzadegan, J., Roohani, M.R., Samareh, Y., Lucas, C., Tebiani, M.: The Speech Database of Farsi Spoken Language. In: Proc. 5th Australian Int. Conf. Speech Science and Technology (SST 1994), pp. 826–831 (1994)
17. Kawahara, H., Masuda-Katsuse, I., de Cheveign, A.: Restructuring Speech Representations Using a Pitch-Adaptive Time-Frequency Smoothing and an Instantaneous-Frequency-based F0 Extraction: Possible Role of a Repetitive Structure in Sounds. Speech Communication 27(3-4), 187–207 (1999)
18. Recommendation ITU-U p.800, Methods for subjective determination of transmission quality. In: International Telecommunication Union (August 1996)

Non-linear Pitch Modification in Voice Conversion Using Artificial Neural Networks

Bajibabu Bollepalli, Jonas Beskow, and Joakim Gustafson

Department of Speech, Music and Hearing, KTH, Sweden

Abstract. Majority of the current voice conversion methods do not focus on the modelling local variations of pitch contour, but only on linear modification of the pitch values, based on means and standard deviations. However, a significant amount of speaker related information is also present in pitch contour. In this paper we propose a non-linear pitch modification method for mapping the pitch contours of the source speaker according to the target speaker pitch contours. This work is done within the framework of Artificial Neural Networks (ANNs) based voice conversion. The pitch contours are represented with Discrete Cosine Transform (DCT) coefficients at the segmental level. The results evaluated using subjective and objective measures confirm that the proposed method performed better in mimicking the target speaker's speaking style when compared to the linear modification method.

1 Introduction

The aim of a *voice conversion* system is to transform the utterance of an arbitrary speaker, referred to as source speaker, to sound as if spoken by a specific speaker, referred to as target speaker. Listeners perceive the source speaker's speech as if uttered by the target speaker. Voice conversion can also be referred to as *voice transformation* or *voice morphing*. Since past two decades voice conversion has been an active research topic in the area of speech synthesis [1], [2], [3], [4]. Applications like text-to-speech (TTS), speech-to-speech translation, mimicry generation and human-machine interaction systems are greatly benefited by having a voice conversion module.

In the literature, majority of voice conversion techniques focused mainly on the modification of short-term spectral features [5], [6]. However, prosodic features, such as pitch contour and speaking rhythm, also contain important cues of speaker identity. In [8] it was shown that pure prosody alone can be used, to an extent, to recognize speakers that are familiar to us. To build a good quality voice conversion system, it needs to modify the prosodic features along with the spectral features. The pitch contour is one of the most important prosodic features related to speaker identity.

The most common method for pitch contour transform is:

$$log(f_0^t) = \frac{log(f_0^s) - \mu^s_{logf_0}}{\sigma^s_{logf_0}} * \sigma^t_{logf_0} + \mu^t_{logf_0} \quad (1)$$

T. Drugman and T. Dutoit (Eds.): NOLISP 2013, LNAI 7911, pp. 97–103, 2013.

where f_0^s, f_0^t represent the pitch values at frame level, and $\mu^s_{log f_0}$, $\sigma^s_{log f_0}$, $\mu^t_{log f_0}$, and $\sigma^t_{log f_0}$ represent the mean and standard deviation of the pitch values in log domain for the source and target speakers, respectively. In this paper, we refer to this method as linear transformation. The local shapes of the pitch contour segments are not modelled and transformed in the linear transformation method. To capture the local dynamics of the pitch contour, we proposed a non-linear transformation method using artificial neural networks (ANNs). The pitch contours over the voiced segments are represented by their discrete cosine transform (DCT) coefficients.

There are some studies which have used the DCT for parametric representation of pitch contour and its modelling [9], [10], [11]. In [9], it is shown that the use of DCT for analysis and synthesis of pitch contours is beneficial. In [10], DCT is used to model the pitch contours of syllables for conversion of neutral speech into expressive speech using Gaussian mixture models (GMM). In [11], DCT representation is used for modelling and transformation of prosodic information in a voice conversion system using a code book generated by classification and regression trees (CART) methods. The work presented in this paper is different from [11] in the following aspects:

1. The proposed method does not use any linguistic information for pitch contour modification.
2. The proposed method uses ANNs to model the non-linear mapping between the pitch contours of source and target speakers.
3. The proposed method, represents the pitch contour of a voiced segment using two sets of parameters. One set represents the statistics, and another set represents the fine variations of a pitch contour.

This paper is organised as follows: Section 2 describes the database, feature extraction and parametrization of the pitch contour. Section 3, outlines the ANN based voice conversion system. The experimental results obtained using both subjective and objective tests are presented in Section 4. Section 5 gives a summary of the work.

2 Database and Feature Extraction

The experiments are carried out on the CMU ARCTIC database consisting of utterances recorded by seven speakers. Each speaker has recorded a set of 1132 phonetically balanced utterances, same for all speakers. ARCTIC database contains the utterances of SLT (US Female), CLB (US Female), BDL (US Male), RMS (US Male), JMK (Canadian Male), AWB (Scottish Male), and KSP (Indian Male).

To extract the features from a given speech signal we used a high quality analysis tool called STRAIGHT vocoder [12]. The features were extracted for every 5ms of speech. Features are: 1) mel-cepstral coefficients (MCEPs), 2)band aperiodicity coefficients (BAPs) and 3) fundamental frequency (pitch contour). All these three features were used for voice conversion. Section 2.1 explains about the parametrization of pitch contour.

2.1 Parametrization of Pitch Contour

The proposed pitch contour model is defined on a voiced segment basis. For voiced speech, the pitch contour varies slowly and continuously over time. It is therefore well modelled by using DCT, an orthogonal transform. One advantage of DCT representation is that the mean square error between two linearly time-aligned pitch contours can be simply estimated from the mean square error between coefficients. The following steps explains the parametrization of a pitch contour:

1. Derive the pitch contours from the utterances spoken by the source speaker.
2. Segment the pitch contour with respect to the voiced segments present in the utterance.
3. Consider only if the duration of each voiced segment is $\geq$ 50ms. If the duration is less than 50ms then use the linear transformation to transform the pitch values.
4. Map the pitch contour of each voiced segment onto equivalent rectangular bandwidth (ERB) scale [7] using Equation 2.

$$F0_{ERB} = \log_{10}(0.00437 * F0 + 1) \tag{2}$$

5. Compute the DCT coefficients for each voiced segment using Equation 3.

$$c_n = \sum_{i=0}^{M-1} F0(i)\cos(\frac{\pi}{M}n(i+\frac{1}{2})) \tag{3}$$

where pitch contour $F0$ of length M is decomposed into N DCT coefficients $[c_0, c_1, c_2, c_3, ...c_{N-1}]$. The first coefficient represents the mean value and remaining DCT coefficients represents the variations in pitch contour such as those due to syllable stress.

6. Each segment is represented by two sets of parameters. They are

$$F0_{shape} = [c_1, c_2, c_3, ...c_{N-1}] \text{ and } F0_{limits} = [c_0, var_{F0}, max_{F0}, min_{F0}, log(dur)] \tag{4}$$

Where $F0_{shape}$ and $F0_{limits}$ represents the local variations and the constraints in a pitch contour. $[c_0, c_1, c_2, c_3, ...c_{N-1}]$ are the DCT coefficients and var_{F0}, max_{F0}, min_{F0}, and $log(dur)$ are variance, maximum value, minimum value, and logrithm of duration of a pitch contour, respectively.

3 Voice Conversion Using ANNs

Figure 3, shows the block diagram of both training and transformation process in a voice conversion system. In this work, we used the parallel utterances to build a mapping function between source and target speakers. Even though both speakers speak the same utterances they still differ in the durations. To align

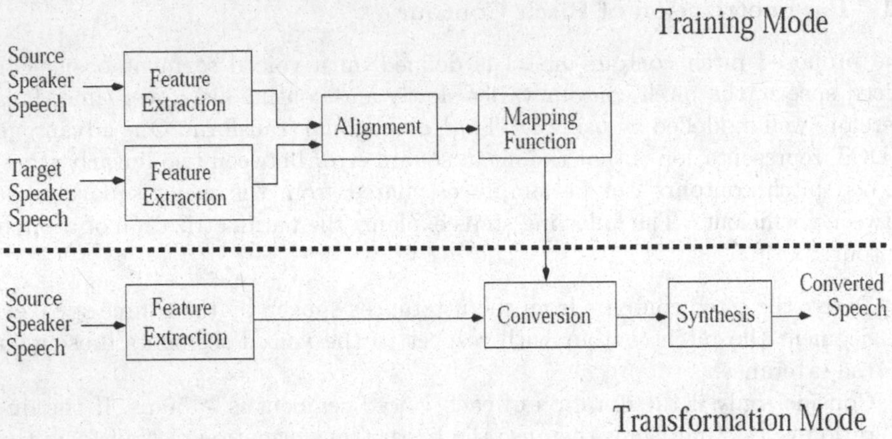

Fig. 1. A block diagram of voice conversion system

the feature vectors of source speaker with respect to target speaker we use the dynamic time warping (DTW) method. It enables us to build a mapping function at frame-level.

For mapping the acoustic features between the source and target speakers, various models have been explored in literature. These models are specific to the kind of features used for mapping. For instance, GMMs [3], vector quantization (VQ) [1] and ANNs [4] are widely used for mapping the vocal tract characteristics. The changes in the vocal tract shape for different speakers are highly non-linear, therefore to model these non-linearities, it is required to capture the non-linear relations present in the patterns. Hence, to capture the non-linear relations between acoustic features, we use a neural network based model (multi-layer feed forward neural networks) for mapping the MCEPs, BAPs and pitch contour coefficients.

During the process of training, acoustic features of the source and target speakers are given as input-output to the network. The network learns from these two data sets and tries to capture a non-linear mapping function based on minimum mean square error. A generalized back propagation learning [13] is used to adjust the weights of the neural network so as to minimize the mean squared error between the desired and the actual output values. Selection of initial weights, architectures of ANNs, learning rate, momentum and number of iterations are some of the optimization parameters in training. Once the training is complete, we get a weight matrix that represents the mapping function between the acoustic features of the given source and target speakers. Such a weight matrix can be used to predict acoustic features of the target speaker from acoustic features of the source speaker.

Different network structures can be possible by varying the number of hidden layers and the number of nodes in each of the hidden layer. In [14] it is shown that four layer network is optimal for mapping the vocal tract characteristics of the source speaker to the target speaker. Therefore, we consider the four layer

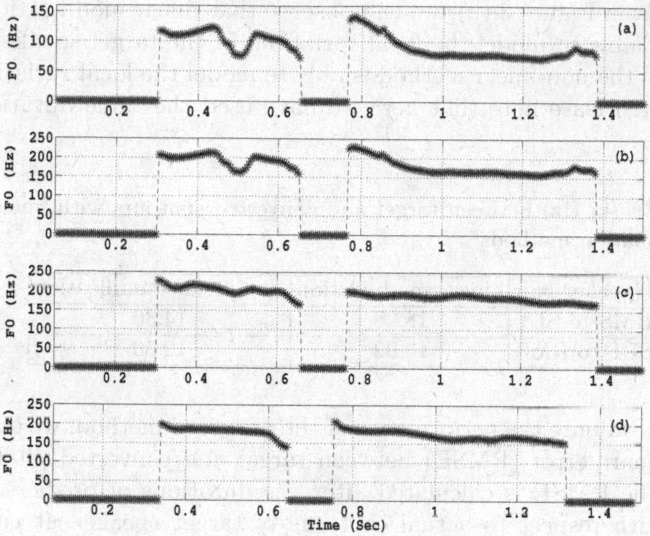

Fig. 2. Conversion of pitch contour from source speaker to target speaker. (a) original source speaker pitch contour, (b) linear modification of source speaker pitch contour, (c) non-linear modification of source speaker pitch contour and (d) original target speaker pitch contour.

networks with architectures $40L-80N-80N-40L$, $21L-42N-42N-21L$, $9L-18N-18N-9L$ and $5L-10N-10N-5L$ for mapping the features MCEPs, BAPs, $F0_{shape}$ and $F0_{limits}$, respectively. The first and fourth layers are input-output layers with linear units (L) and have the same dimension as that of input-output acoustic features. The second layer (first-hidden layer) and third layer (second-hidden layer) have non-linear nodes (N), which help in capturing the non-linear relationship that may exist between the input-output features.

4 Experiments and Results

As described in Section 2, from ARCTIC database we picked one male speaker (RMS) and one female speaker (SLT) for our experiments. For each speaker, we considered 80 parallel utterances for training and a separate set of 32 utterances for testing. We extracted acoustic features, MCEPs of dimension 40, BAPs of dimension 21, and 10 DCT coefficients for every 5ms of speech. Given these features for training, they are aligned using dynamic time warping to obtain paired feature vectors as explained in Section 3. We build a separate mapping function for spectral, band aperiodicity and pitch contour transformations. After the mapping functions are trained, we use the test sentences of the source speaker to predict the acoustic features of the target speaker. The pitch contour is constructed back by using the IDCT on predicted features. An instance of converted pitch contour from source speaker (RMS) to target speaker (SLT) is illustrated in Figure 3. From Figure 3.(b), we can observe that linear modification of pitch contour is not able to model the local variations of the target speaker, whereas in Figure 3.(c) the non-linear method is able to model the local variations of the target speaker. Please note that here we have used the same durations of the source speaker.

Table 1. RMSE (in Hz) between target and converted contours with linear and non-linear transformation methods

Speaker pair	Linear modification	Non-linear modification
RMS-to-SLT	18.28	14.36
SLT-to-RMS	15.92	12.50

In order to evaluate the performance of the proposed method, we estimate the root mean square error (RMSE) between target and converted pitch contours of test set. The RMSE is calculated after the durations of predicted contours normalized with respect to actual contours of target speaker. It can be seen from Table 1 that the non-linear transformation method performed better than linear method.

Table 2. Speaker similarity score

Speaker pair	Linear modification	Non-linear modification
RMS-to-SLT	3	3.3
SLT-to-RMS	2.55	3.1

An informal perceptual test was also conducted with 10 transformed speech signals randomly chosen for both conversion pair and presented to 10 listeners. We have used the STRAIGHT vocoder to synthesize the transformed speech signals. The subjects were asked to compare similarity of the transformed speech signals with respect to original target speaker speech signals. The ratings were given on a scale of 1-5, with 5 for excellent match and 1 for not-at-all match. The scores are shown in Table 2. It can be observed from Table 2, that non-linear modification performs better than linear modification in perceptual tests as well.

5 Conclusion

A non-linear pitch modification method was proposed for mapping the pitch contours of the source speaker according to the target speaker pitch contours. In this method, pitch contour was compressed to a few coefficients using DCT. A four layer ANN model was used for modelling the non-linear patterns of a pitch contour between the source and target speaker. The results showed that both objective and subjective scores gave very clear preference for the proposed method in mimicking the target speaker's speaking style when compared to the linear modification method.

References

1. Abe, M., Nakamura, S., Shikano, K., Kuwabara, H.: Voice conversion through vector quantization. In: Proc. of ICASSP, New York, USA, pp. 655–658 (April 1988)
2. Stylianou, Y., Cappe, O., Moulines, E.: Continuous probabilistic transform for voice conversion. IEEE Transactions on Speech and Audio Processing 6(2), 131–142 (1998)
3. Ohtani, Y., Toda, T., Saruwatari, H., Shikano, K.: Maximum likelihood voice conversion based on GMM with STRAIGHT mixed excitation. In: Proc. of INTERSPEECH, Pittsburgh, USA, pp. 2266–2269 (September 2006)
4. Bollepalli, B., Black, A.W., Prahallad, K.: Modeling a noisy-channel for voice conversion using articulatory features. In: Proc. of INTERSPEECH, Portland, USA (August 2012)
5. Dutoit, T., Holzapfel, A., Jottrand, M., Moinet, A., Perez, J., Stylianou, Y.: Towards a voice conversion system based on frame selection. In: Proc. of ICASSP, pp. 513–516 (2007)
6. Stylianou, Y.: Voice transformation: A survey. In: Proc. of ICASSP, pp. 3585–3588 (2009)
7. Smith, J.O., Abel, J.S.: Bark and ERB bilinear transforms. IEEE Transactions on Speech and Audio Processing 7(6), 697–708 (1999)
8. Helander, E., Nurminen, J.: On the importance of pure prosody in the perception of speaker identity. In: Proc. of INTERSPEECH, pp. 2665–2668 (2007)
9. Teutenberg, J., Watson, C., Riddle, P.: Modeling and synthesizing F0 contours with the discrete cosine transform. In: Proc. of ICASSP, pp. 3973–3976 (2008)
10. Veaux, C., Rodet, X.: Intonation conversion from neutral to expressive speech. In: INTERSPEECH, pp. 2765–2768 (2011)
11. Helander, E., Nurminen, J.: A Novel method for prosody prediction in voice conversion. In: Proc. of ICASSP, pp. IV-509–IV-512 (2007)
12. Kawahara, H., Masuda-Katsuse, I., Cheveigne, A.: Restructuring speech representations using a pitch-adaptive time-frequency smoothing and an instantaneous-frequency-based F0 extraction: Possible role of a repetitive structure in sounds. Speech Communication 27, 187–207 (1999)
13. Haykin, S.: Neural networks: A comprehensive foundation. Prentice-Hall Inc., NJ (1999)
14. Desai, S., Black, A.W., Yegnanarayana, B., Prahallad, K.: Spectral mapping using artificial neural networks for voice conversion. IEEE Trans. Audio, Speech and Language Processing 18(5), 954–964 (2010)

Analysis and Quantification of Acoustic Artefacts in Tracheoesophageal Speech

Thomas Drugman[1], Myriam Rijckaert[2], George Lawson[2], and Marc Remacle[2]

[1] TCTS Lab., University of Mons, Belgium
[2] Ontolaryngology Service, Mont-Godinne Hospital, University of Louvain, Belgium

Abstract. After total laryngectomy, the placement of a tracheoesophageal (TE) puncture offers the possibility to gain a new voice. However, the produced TE speech is known to have a lower quality and intelligibility. The goal of this paper is to identify and quantify the acoustic artefacts in TE speech. The advantage of this study is twofold. First, the proposed measures can be used by speech therapists in voice rehabilitation sessions to assess the voice of the patient, to follow up his/her evolution and to design tailored exercises. Secondly, these artefacts have to be quantified and taken into account in synthesis methods aiming at enhancing TE speech. Four categories of acoustic artefacts are identified in this work: a lower periodicity and regularity of the phonation, and the presence of high-frequency and gargling noises. Each artefact is studied and compared to normal laryngeal speech recorded either for speech synthesis purpose or by elderly people. Results quantify the importance of each of these artefacts, and show a large disparity between TE patients.

1 Introduction

Patients having undergone Total Laryngectomy (TL) cannot produce speech sounds in a conventional manner because their vocal folds have been removed. Gaining a new voice is then the major goal of the post surgery process. There are currently three options for voice restoration after TL: tracheoesophageal speech, electrolaryngeal speech and esophageal speech. In this article, we focus on the analysis of tracheoesophageal (TE) speech. Indeed, it has been shown in several studies that TE puncture leads to superior voice rehabilitation capabilities compared to the two other approaches [1], [2].

After TL, the patient's larynx has been removed and the esophagus and trachea are separated. A hole called tracheostoma is created in the patient's neck to allow breathing. In TE speech, a surgical fistula (TE puncture) is created in the wall separating the trachea and esophagus, allowing the placement of a phonatory prosthesis. Thanks to this prosthesis, an airflow passes from the trachea to the esophagus and further to the vocal tract cavities. For some patients, this airflow generates the vibration of residual organs called the pharyngoesophageal

T. Drugman and T. Dutoit (Eds.): NOLISP 2013, LNAI 7911, pp. 104–111, 2013.

(PE) segment. When patients are able control this neovibrator (also sometimes referred to as neoglottis), they can produce voiced sounds but with a lower level of periodicity. Therefore, although TE speech allows to recover a mode of communication way, it suffers from a clear diminution of naturalness and intelligibility in the produced voice. Besides, the individuality/personnality of the speaker is often lost (this is particularly true for female patients). These conclusions hold even in a more pronunced way for esophageal and electrolaryngeal speech.

The perception of TE speech has been evaluated in the literature [1], [2]. Its acceptability and intelligibility have been compared in [1] to those of both laryngeal and esophageal speech. As expected, it has been shown that both aspects are degraded with regard to laryngeal speech. Nonetheless, TE speech turns out to be more acceptable than good esophageal speech while they have a comparable level of intelligibility. In [2], Singer et al. investigated the intelligibility of alaryngeal speech during the first year after TL. It was noticed that patients with a TE puncture had the best results in intelligibility. Authors also emphasized the considerable improvement within the first year, and the importance for the patient to attend rehabilitation sessions.

TE speech has also been studied from an acoustic point of view. In [3], TE speech is analyzed using frequency, intensity and duration features. It is shown that, based on these characteristics, TE speech is more similar to normal speech than is esophageal speech, and that it is more intense than both other types of speech. The acoustic study led in [1] revealed that most of the differences between normal and laryngeal speech lies in the fundamental frequency of the speech signal. An acoustic signal typing system based on a visual inspection of a narrow-band spectrogram was proposed in [4]. According to this visualization, the user can classify TE speech from a given patient into one of four pre-defined categories. Authors also show the link of this classification with some acoustic features (standard deviation of F0, jitter, proportion of voiced speech and the band energy difference). In [5], the acoustic differences between TE and esophageal speech are studied based on the following measures: intensity, maximum phonation time, F0, jitter, shimmer, and Harmonic-to-Noise Ratio (HNR).

Finally, several approaches have targeted the resynthesis of an enhanced version of TE speech, in order to improve its quality and intelligibility. In [6], Qi et al. resynthesized female TE words with a synthetic glottal waveform and with smoothed and raised F0. It was shown that the replacement of the glottal waveform and F0 smoothing alone produced most significant enhancement, while increasing the average F0 led to less dramatic improvement. The speech repair system proposed in [7] resynthesizes TE speech using a synthetic glottal waveform, reduces its jitter and shimmer and applies a spectral smoothing and tilt correction algorithm. A subjective assessment reveals a reduction of the perceived breathiness and harshness of the voice. The solution described in [8] interestingly focuses on the speech reconstruction from whispered voice, and proposes a modified version of the CELP vocoder. Unfortunately, authors only report an improvement compared to electrolaryngeal speech, and no comparative results are given for TE speech.

The goal of this paper is to analyze and quantify the acoustic artefacts exhibited in TE speech. The applicability of this study is two-fold. First, the proposed acoustic features allow an objective assessment of the quality of the patient's voice through several dimensions. This information can be used by speech therapists for multiple purposes: *i)* to focus on specific aspects of the voice (as highlighted by the proposed assessment), *ii)* to compare various voice rehabilitation approaches, *iii)* to keep a follow-up of the patient. Secondly, the knowledge of these artefacts is of paramount importance for speaking aid systems aiming at resynthesizing an enhanced version of TE speech. Indeed, in order to improve the naturalness and intelligibility of TE speech, developed methods have to integrate procedures to alleviate such artefacts.

As aforementioned, some studies in the literature have already reported an acoustic analysis/assessment of TE speech [1], [3], [4], [5]. Nonetheless, these studies generally suffer from several drawbacks which we try to overcome in this paper. First, possible artefacts have never been categorized and the assessment is generally based only on periodicity-related measures. Secondly, the acoustic analysis either requires a manual inspection of signals or is based on the use of available automatic tools in a *black box* way. These latter tools have generally been designed for normal laryngeal speech, have a low robustness and are therefore not suited for the analysis of TE speech. Besides, most of the measures are derived from the F0 information whose estimation is problematic if the analysis tools are not appropriate. Third, studies generally involve a limited number of TE patients, or are only based on sustained vowels. In this paper, we target an automatic analysis led on read speech from a sufficiently large number of patients with a TE puncture. Artefacts are categorized and robust automatic methods for their acoustic characterization are proposed.

The paper is structured as follows. First, the database used throughout all our analyses is described in Section 2. The various acoustic artefacts in TE speech are presented in Section 3. In that section, each artefact is specifically analyzed, with regard to normal laryngeal speech, and the obtained results are discussed. Finally, Section 4 concludes the paper.

2 Database

The database we used throughout our experiments consists of three sets: *TTS*, *Control* and *TE*. In the first set, we considered recordings collected at the Language Technologies Institute at Carnegie Mellon University with the goal of developing unit selection Text-To-Speech (TTS) synthesizers. More precisely, we used data from 7 speakers (5M, 2F) of the CMU ARCTIC corpus [9], with 30 utterances per speaker. This set is used as a reference of normophonic high-quality voices recorded in studio conditions. The two other datasets were acquired by speech therapists at the hospital with a high-quality handheld recorder (Olympus LS-5) with an external lapel microphone (Olympus ME-52W) designed for noise cancellation. Subjects were asked to read a phonetically-balanced text of 10 sentences. The *TE* set consists of recordings from 23 patients (19M, 4F) having undergone a total laryngectomy and with a TE puncture. They are aged between 52 and 82 years (mean = 64.5). The time elapsed between the prosthesis placement and recordings varies between 3 months and 10 years (mean = 715 days). In the *Control* set, speech therapists recorded 12 speakers (6M, 6F) from a similar age (range= 51-72, mean=60 years) who never suffered from any voice pathology. They are here used as a comparison point for the *TE* set (same recording conditions, same age). Note that the data from the 3 sets were resampled at 16 kHz.

3 Acoustic Artefacts in Tracheoesophageal Speech

After a careful listening, we identified four main types of artefacts in TE speech. In the following, these artefacts are analyzed and quantified based on an automatic acoustic study. Since a reliable automatic estimation of the voiced segments in TE speech is a yet unsolved issue, our approach is driven as follows:

- The analysis is performed on segments with speech activity, regardless of a voicing criterion. These segments are identified as those with a total loudness exceeding by more than 25 dB the minimum loudness in the utterance.
- The extraction of acoustic information targets robust features being as independent from F0 as possible.
- To avoid the possible detrimental effects due to some spurious values, each speaker is characterized by the median of the extracted acoustic features.

The artefacts are now studied based on this methodolody.

3.1 Periodicity of the Speech Signal

The periodicity of the TE speech signal has been observed the literature to be less periodic, with pitch values comparable to those in normal speech [4]. Nonetheless, these results were obtained either from a manual input with a visual inspection of spectrograms, or from an automatic analysis using the Praat toolkit as a *black box*. However the two pitch tracking methods available in Praat (AC and CC) have been shown to have a poor robustness [10]. It is therefore not surprising to find spurious F0 values up to more than 400 Hz [5], which is irrealistic in TE speech. As a consequence, some of these results using F0-derived measures are sometimes suspicious and should be taken with caution.

In this work, the periodicity analysis relies on the Summation of the Residual Harmonics (SRH, [10]) method which was shown to clearly outperform state-of-the-art approaches for robust pitch tracking. This technique provides estimates of two periodicity characteristics: SRH values which quantify the level of periodicity in the signal, and the pitch values. As suggested in [10], the binary voicing decision is taken by applying a threshold of 0.07 to SRH values. This allows us to define the voiced proportion as the percentage of frames recognized as voiced according to this criterion. The distributions of these 3 measures for the 3 datasets are presented in Figure 1 under the form of boxplots. It is quantitatively confirmed that TE speech is much less periodic than normal speech, with SRH values significantly lower (except for one single speaker). We noticed that patients with a TE prosthesis were able to produce voiced speech with a proportion varying from 36 to 93% (median: 77%), with the exception of two patients who almost always spoke with whispered speech. Finally, TE patients were observed to use lower fundamental frequencies (median: 99 Hz) regardless of the gender, with a large variety across patients. For example, while one male patient produced pitch contours around 30 Hz, another used F0 values at about 160 Hz. Note that these results were confirmed by a manual inspection of the signals. Finally, it can be observed that the periodicity in the *Control* set was found to be lower than in the *TTS* set. This decrease is due to aging, as known from the literature [11].

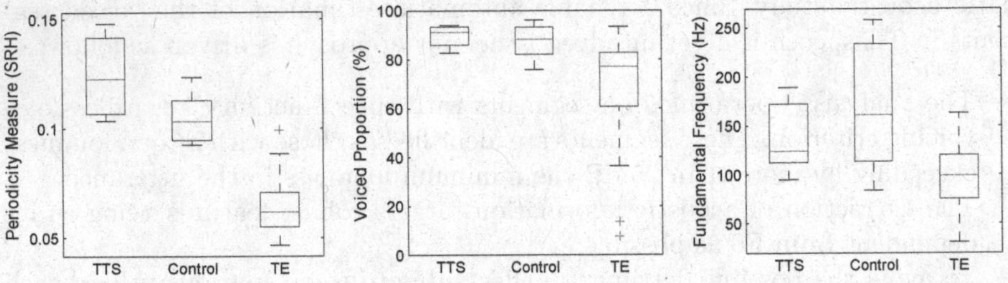

Fig. 1. *Distributions of the periodicity measures across the three datasets.* Left panel*: the SRH values indicating the level of perdiodicity,* Middle panel*: the proportion of voiced segments,* Right panel*: the fundamental frequency F0.*

3.2 Regularity of Phonation

In addition to the reduced periodicity, we observed the TE phonation to be less regular. This can be physiologically explained by the fact that turbulences are more important at the PE segment for TE patients, than at the glottis for normal subjects. The amount of irregularities is here assessed via three acoustic measures. The first one is the variation of the Chirp Group Delay (CGD) which is a phase-based feature shown in [12] (in the frame of voice pathology detection) to be particularly suited for capturing the signal irregularities. The second is the spectral variation [13] computed as the normalized cross-correlation between two successive amplitude spectra. Finally, the third measure is the normalized Linear Prediction (LP) error, i.e. the error made when considering an autoregressive model (whose order is standardly fixed to $F_s/1000 + 2$) to explain the speech signal. If the speech production statisfied ideally this modeling, voiced speech would be characterized by a LP residual signal being an ideal pulse train, and the LP error would be minimum. The more the turbulences during the phonation, the more the excitation signal contains noise and irregularities, and the more it deviates from the ideal pulse train. This will thus be reflected in the LP error.

The distributions of these 3 acoustic measures are displayed in Figure 2. These plots reflect coherently the same phenomenon: while the regularity in *TTS* and *Control* datasets is comparable, it is observed to be significatnly lower in TE speech. This turns out to hold for all TE patients. It is worth noting at this stage that periodicity and regularity are two complementary aspects of speech. For example, the Pearson correlation coefficient between SRH and CGD values only barely reaches -0.49. In this way, we noticed that some patients can produce TE speech with an acceptable periodicity and low regularity, and vice versa.

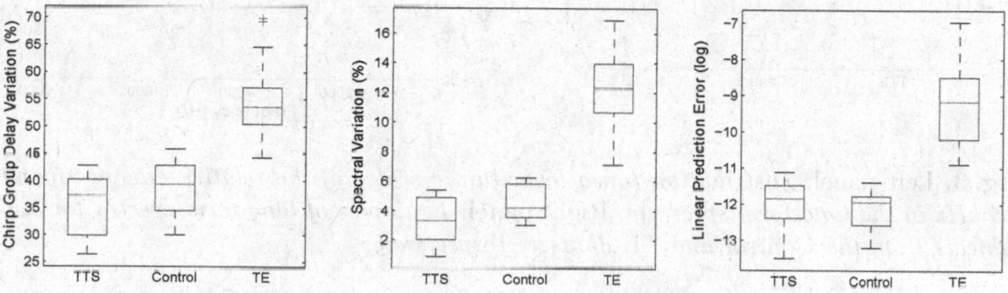

Fig. 2. *Distributions of the regularity measures across the three datasets.* Left panel: *the Chirp Group Delay variations,* Middle panel: *the spectral variations,* Right panel: *the normalized prediction error (on a logarithmic scale).*

3.3 High-Frequency Noise

For some patients, the presence of high-frequency (HF) noise can be particularly annoying. To quantify the amount of high frequencies, the long-term average spectrum is estimated for each speaker. For this, the spectrum of each frame (where speech activity has been detected) is computed and normalized in energy. Obtained spectra are then averaged over all sentences uttered by the speaker. In this way, since the text to be read is phonetically balanced, the effects of formants can be assumed to cancel each others, and the long-term spectrum contains averaged contributions of the vocal tract and of the source (either laryngeal or alaryngeal). A way to measure the average quantity of HF noise is to calculate the relative energy beyond a given frequency (fixed to 1.5 kHz in this work) in the long-term spectrum.

The left panel of Figure 3 exhibits the distributions of this measure for the 3 datasets. It can be seen that, on average, most of the TE patients have a greater amount of high-frequencies in their speech. Nonetheless, about 1 patient with a TE prosthesis over 4 produces speech with a proportion of HF similar to normal speech. On the opposite, for a few others, the amount of HF noise can be relatively high. This is illustrated in the right panel of Figure 3 where the long-term spectrum of such a TE patient is exhibited (with the one of a standard control speaker for comparison purpose). These differences can be explained by the noisy airflow evicted at the tracheostoma by some TE patients when speaking, and by the fact that the production at the PE segment differs strongly from the vibration at the glottis in normal laryngeal speech, and consequently that the spectral shaping imposed at source is different.

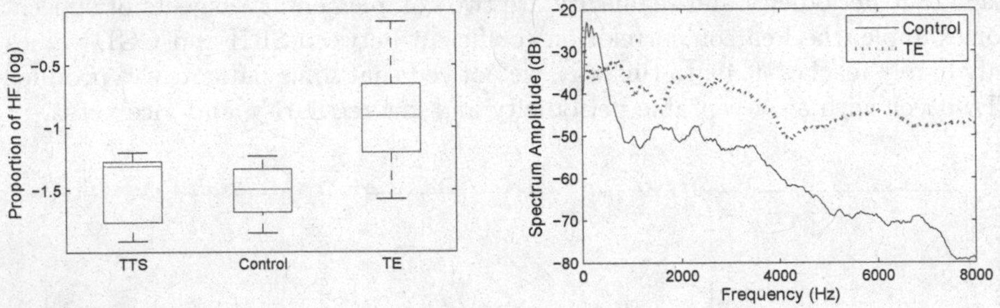

Fig. 3. Left panel: *Distribution (on a logarithmic scale) of the relative energy beyond 1.5 kHz in the long-term spectrum.* Right panel: *Examples of long-term spectra for two subjects from the* Control *and* TE *datasets respectively.*

3.4 Gargling Noise

Finally, a last artefact was observed in a minority (3 out of the 23) of patients with a TE puncture: the gargling noise. For such patients, speech is perceived as if they were talking with water in their throat. This is due to deglutition problems, which lead to the fact that saliva and/or nasal mucus may flow down in the throat. Because of these secretions, the resulting speech signal may sporadically exhibit artefacts, as illustrated in Figure 4 for a vowel /a/. The smoothed Hilbert envelope is indicated for information purpose. It can be seen that the gargling noise is reflected by uncontrolled energy bursts in the signal (generally spaced by more than 50 ms). Note that the reliable detection and quantification of this artefact would require further investigation.

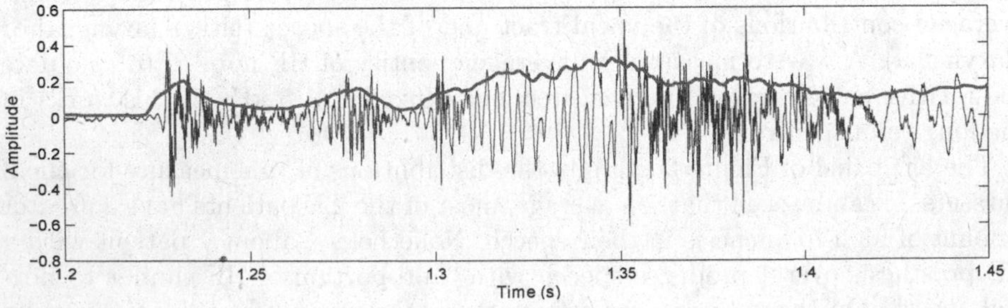

Fig. 4. Illustration of a gargling noise for a vowel /a/

4 Conclusion

This paper proposed an automatic quantification of the artefacts in tracheoesophageal speech. Four categories of acoustic artefacts were identified: a lower periodicity and regularity of the phonation, and the presence of high-frequency and gargling noises. Each artefact and its physiological origin were analyzed. Besides, robust acoustic features were proposed to characterize the first three artefacts. This allows a multidimensional assessment of the patient's voice which can be used by speech therapists during voice rehabilitation sessions. These findings are also of paramount interest for synthesis techniques targeting the enhancement of TE speech as these methods should compensated the artificats highlighted in this paper.

Acknowledgments. Thomas Drugman is supported by a FNRS Research Fellow grant.

References

1. Most, T., Tobin, Y., Mimran, R.: Acoustic and perceptual characteristics of esophageal and tracheoesophageal speech production. Journal Commun. Disord. 33(2), 165–180 (2000)
2. Singer, S., Wollbruck, D., Dietz, A., et al.: Speech rehabilitation during the first year after total laryngectomy. Head and Neck Journ. (2012) doi: 10.1002/hed.23183
3. Robbins, J., Fisher, H., Blom, E., Singer, M.: A comparative acoustic study of normal, esophageal, and tracheoesophageal speech production. Journal of Speech and Hearing Disorders 49(2), 202–210 (1984)
4. van As-Brooks, C., Koopmans-van Beinum, F., Pols, L., Hilgers, F.: Acoustic signal typing for evaluation of voice quality in tracheoesophageal speech. Journal of Voice 20(3), 355–368 (2006)
5. Siric, L., Sos, D., Rosso, M., Stevanovic, S.: Objective assessment of tracheoesophageal and esophageal speech using acoustic analysis of voice. Coll Antropol. 36(suppl. 2), 111–114 (2012)
6. Qi, Y., Weinberg, B., Bi, N.: Enhancement of female esophageal and tracheoesophageal speech. Journal of the Acoustical Society of America 98, 2461–2465 (1995)
7. del Pozo, A., Young, S.: Continuous tracheoesophageal speech repair. In: Proc. European Signal Processing Conference, EUSIPCO (2006)
8. Reza Sharifzadeh, H., McLoughlin, I., Ahmadi, F.: Recontruction of Normal Sounding Speech for Laryngectomy Patients Through a Modified CELP Codec. IEEE Trans. on Biomedical Engineering 57(10) (2010)
9. CMU ARCTIC speech synthesis databases, `http://festvox.org/cmuarctic/`
10. Drugman, T., Alwan, A.: Joint Robust Voicing Detection and Pitch Estimation Based on Residual Harmonics. In: Proc. Interspeech (2011)
11. Dehgan, A., Scherer, R., et al.: The Effects of Aging on Acoustic Parameters of Voice. Folia Phoniatr Logop. 64(6), 265–270 (2013)
12. Drugman, T., Dubuisson, T., Dutoit, T.: Phase-based information for voice pathology detection. In: Proc. IEEE ICASSP, pp. 4612–4615 (2011)
13. Peeters, G.: A large set of audio features for sound description (similarity and classification) in the CUIDADO project (2003)

Analysis of Speech from People with Parkinson's Disease through Nonlinear Dynamics

Juan Rafael Orozco-Arroyave[1,2], Julián David Arias-Londoño[1], Jesús Francisco Vargas-Bonilla[1], and Elmar Nöth[2]

[1] Universidad de Antioquia, Medellín, Colombia
[2] Friedrich-Alexander Universität, Erlangen - Nürnberg, Germany

Abstract. Different characterization approaches, including nonlinear dynamics (NLD), have been addressed for the automatic detection of PD; however, the obtained discrimination capability when only NLD features are considered has not been evaluated yet.

This paper evaluates the discrimination capability of a set with ten different NLD features in the task of automatic classification of speech signals from people with Parkinson's disease (PPD) and a control set (CS). The experiments presented in this paper are performed considering the five Spanish vowels uttered by 20 PPD and 20 people from the CS.

According the results, it is possible to achieve accuracy rates of up to 76,81% considering only utterances from the vowel /i/. When features calculated from the five Spanish vowels are combined, the performance of the system is not improved, indicating that the inclusion of more NLD features to the system does not guarantee better performance.

Keywords: Nonlinear dynamics, complexity measures, Parkinson's disease, speech signals.

1 Introduction

PD is a neurodegenerative disorder that results from the progressive death of dopaminergic cells in the substantia nigra, a region of the mid-brain. About 89% of PPD commonly develop speech impairments affecting different aspects such as respiration, phonation, articulation and prosody [1]. Speech impairments in PPD are related to the vocal fold bowing and incomplete vocal fold closure [2], besides the vocal production is a highly nonlinear dynamical system, thus the changes caused by impairments in the movement of different muscles, tissues and organs which are involved in the voice production process, such as those suffered by PPD, can be modeled using NLD analysis [3], [4].

NLD techniques have been applied for both the automatic assessment of pathological speech signals and the automatic evaluation of speech from PPD. In [5] the authors include four NLD features along with other 13 acoustic measures for the automatic detection of PD. The set of NLD features includes correlation dimension (D_2), Period Density Entropy (RPDE), Detrended Fluctuation Analysis (DFA) and Pitch Period Entropy (PPE). According to their results, it is possible to achieve classification rates of up to 91.4%. Additionally, in [6] the

T. Drugman and T. Dutoit (Eds.): NOLISP 2013, LNAI 7911, pp. 112–119, 2013.

evolution of the PD through the time is studied using a set of features composed by different dysphonia measures (including some from NLD) and analyze their correlation with the evolution of the patients according to the Unified Parkinson Disease Rating Scale (UPDRS) [7] in a period of six months. The authors stated that UPDRS scale can be mapped with a precision of up to 6 points.

Despite the interest of the scientific community to apply NLD for the automatic assessment of speech from PPD, the discrimination capability of NLD features is not clear yet because they have been combined with other features such as acoustics and noise measures. In this paper, different state of the art NLD features are implemented and their discrimination capability is objectively evaluated on the automatic classification of speech signals from PPD and CS. The set of features considered in this study includes a total of 10 measures which have been used for the automatic detection of different speech disorders such as hypernasality [8] and dysphonia [5], [9]. The features are: correlation dimension, largest Lyapunov exponent, Lempel-Ziv complexity, Hurst exponent, RPDE, DFA, approximate entropy, approximate entropy with Gaussian kernel, sample entropy, sample entropy with Gaussian kernel.

The paper is organized as follows: section 2 presents a brief description of the methods that are applied in this work, in the section 3 the details of the performed experiments is given, section 4 shows the obtained results and finally, the section 5 provides the conclusions that are derived from the presented work.

2 Methodology

The general methodology that is applied in this work is depicted in figure 1. The signal is first preprocessed by means of its division into frames. After, the characterization is performed. In this case, only NLD features have been considered for this stage. With the aim of eliminate possible redundancy in the information provided by all NLD a features selection stage is required. Finally, the decision about whether a speech signal comes from a person with PD or a CS is taken through an automatic classification strategy. In this work, this step is performed using support vector machines (SVM). In the following subsections, more details of each part of the methodology will be provided.

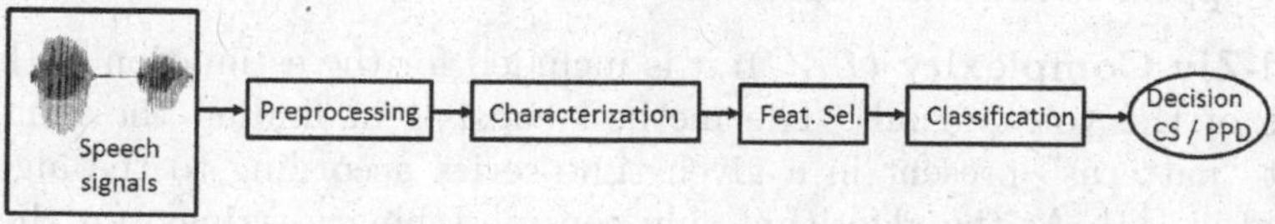

Fig. 1. General methodology

2.1 Nonlinear Dynamics Characterization

A set of ten NLD features is calculated to perform the automatic classification of speech signals from PPD and CS. The first step in the characterization process is to embed the signal into the state space following the the time-delay embedding theorem originally proposed by Takens [10]. This theorem establishes that where there is a single sampled quantity of a dynamical system, it is possible to reconstruct a state space that is equivalent or diffeomorphic to the original state space that is unknown. Points in the state space form trajectories, and a set of trajectories from a time series is known as attractor [3]. After the embedding process, the NLD features are estimated as it is briefly described below.

Correlation Dimension (D_2): it is a measure of the space dimensionality occupied by the points in the reconstructed attractor. In this work, (D_2) is implemented according to the Takens estimator method [3]. The estimation requires the use of the correlation sum ($C(r)$), which is defined as: $C(r) = \sum_{i=1}^{N} C_i^m(r)$. Where,

$$C_i^m(r) = \frac{2}{N(N-1)} \sum_{j=i+1}^{N} \Theta\left(r - \|\boldsymbol{x}_i - \boldsymbol{x}_j\|\right) \tag{1}$$

N is the number of points in the state space, Θ the Heaviside function and ($\|\cdot\|$) is a norm defined in any consistent metric space. D_2 is theoretically defined for an infinity amount of data ($N \to \infty$) and for small r, thus its general expression is written as:

$$D_2 = \lim_{r \to 0} \lim_{N \to \infty} \frac{\partial \ln C\,(r, N)}{\partial \ln\,(r)} \tag{2}$$

Larges Lyapunov Exponent (LLE): this feature is estimated as the average divergence rate of neighbor trajectories in the attractor, according to the Ronsenstein method [3]. For this algorithm, once again the nearest neighbors to every point in the trajectories must be estimated. In this case, a neighbor must fulfill a temporal separation greater than the "period" of the time series, to be considered as a nearest neighbor. It is possible to state that the separation of points in a trajectory is according to the expression $d(t) = Ce^{\lambda_1 t}$, where λ_1 is the maximum Lyapunov exponent, $d(t)$ is the average divergence taken at the time t, and C is a normalization constant. Assuming that the $j-th$ pair of nearest neighbors approximately diverge at a rate of λ_1, it is possible to obtain the expression $ln(d_j(i)) = ln(C_j) + \lambda_1(i\Delta t)$, where λ_1 is the slope of the average line that appears when such expression is drawn on a logarithmic plane [3].

Lempel-Ziv Complexity (LZC): it is included for the estimation of the randomness of the voice signals. The method consists in finding the number of different "patterns" present in a given time series according to the algorithm presented in [11]. As the algorithm only considers binary strings; for the practical case, a value of 0 is assigned when the difference between two successive samples is negative, and 1 when such a difference is positive or null (see [11] for additional details).

Hurst Exponent (H): the possible long term dependencies in a time series can be estimated trough H. It is calculated following the rank scaling method [3]. Where the relation between the variation rank (R) of the signal, evaluated in a segment, and its standard deviation S is given by $\frac{R}{S} = cT^H$, where c is a scaling constant, T is the duration of the segment and H is the Hurst exponent.

Entropy Measurements: in general, entropy is a measure of the uncertainty of a random variable. When there is a stochastic process with a set of independent but not identically distributed variables, the rate at which the joint entropy grows with the number of variables n is given by $H(X) = -\lim_{n\to\infty} \frac{1}{n} \sum_{i=1}^{n} H(X_i)$.

For the case of a state space, it can be partitioned into hypercubes of content ϵ^m and observed at time intervals δ, defining the Kolmogorov-Sinai entropy as:

$$H_{KS} = -\lim_{\substack{\delta\to\infty \\ \varepsilon\to 0 \\ n\to\infty}} \frac{1}{n\delta} \sum_{k_1,\ldots,k_n} p(k_1, ..., k_n) \log p(k_1, ..., k_n) \quad (3)$$

where $p(k_1, ..., k_n)$ is the joint probability that the state of the system is in the hypercube k_1 at the time $t = \delta$, k_2 at $t = 2\delta$, etc. For stationary processes, it can be shown that $H_{KS} = \lim_{\delta\to 0} \lim_{\varepsilon\to 0} \lim_{n\to\infty} (H_{n+1} - H_n)$.

In practical terms it is not possible to compute the equation 3 for $n \to \infty$, thus different estimation methods have been proposed in the literature. One of them is the *Approximate entropy* (A_E), which is designed for measuring the average conditional information generated by diverging points on a trajectory in the state space [12]. For fixed m and r, A_E is estimated as:

$$A_E(m, r) = \lim_{N\to\infty} \left[\Phi^{m+1}(r) - \Phi^m(r)\right] \quad (4)$$

where $\Phi^m(r) = \frac{1}{N-m+1} \sum_{i=1}^{N-m+1} \ln C_i^m(r)$, and $C_i^m(r)$ was defined in equation 1.

The main drawback of A_E is its dependence to the signal length due to the self comparison of points in the attractor. In order to overcome this problem, the *sample entropy* (S_E) is proposed as:

$$S_E(m, r) = \lim_{N\to\infty} \left(-\ln \frac{\Gamma^{m+1}(r)}{\Gamma^m(r)}\right) \quad (5)$$

The only difference between Γ in the equation 5 and Φ in the equation 4 is that the first does not evaluate the comparison of embedding vectors with themselves.

Another modification of A_E is the *approximate entropy with Gaussian kernel* $A_E GK$. It exploits the fact that Gaussian kernel function can be used to give greater weight to nearby points by replacing the Heaviside function by [13].

$$d_G(\boldsymbol{x}_i, \boldsymbol{x}_j) = \exp\left(-\frac{(\|\boldsymbol{x}_i - \boldsymbol{x}_j\|_1)}{10r^2},\right) \quad (6)$$

The same procedure of changing the distance measure can be applied to define the *sample entropy with Gaussian kernel* $S_E GK$.

On the other hand, considering that the voice signal has two components, deterministic and stochastic, in [14] was proposed to analyzed the deterministic component by means of the *recurrence period density entropy* ($RPDE$), considering a hypersphere of radius $r > 0$, containing a embedded data point $\boldsymbol{x}(t_i)$. The time $t_r = t_j - t_i$ is the recurrence time, where t_j is the instant at which the trajectory first returned to the same hypersphere. If $R(t)$ is the normalized histogram of the recurrence times estimated for all embedded points into a reconstructed attractor, the $RPDE$ can be defined as in the equation 7.

$$RPDE = \frac{-\sum_{i=1}^{t_{\max}} R(i) \ln R(i)}{\ln t_{\max}} \tag{7}$$

where t_{max} is the maximum recurrence time in the attractor. Besides, the stochastic component of the voice signals can be analyzed by means of the *detrended fluctuation analysis* (DFA) to estimate the scaling exponent α in non-stationary time series as is indicated in [14].

2.2 Feature Selection and Classification

In characterization stages large amounts of information are produced. Such information is represented in high dimensionality spaces which most of the times have redundant information. The reduction of the dimensionality of such spaces and the elimination of redundant information is performed applying the Sequential Floating Features Selection (SFFS) algorithm. It is such that finds the best subset of features of the original set through the inclusion and exclusion of features. In this procedure after each forward step, a number of backward steps are applied as long as the resulting subsets are better, in the sense of the accuracy, than the previous one [15]. The decision about whether a voice recording is from PPD or CS is taken by a SVM with Gaussian kernel which parameters are optimized in the training process [16]

3 Experimental Setup

3.1 Corpus of Speakers

Speech recordings from 20 PPD and 20 people from the CS are considered (10 women and 10 men). The ages of the men patients ranged from 56 to 70 (mean 62.9 ± 6.39) and the ages of the women patients ranged from 57 to 75 (mean 64.6 ± 5.62). For the case of the healthy people, the ages of men ranged from 51 to 68 (mean 62.6 ± 5.48) and the ages of the women ranged from 57 to 75 (mean 64.8 ± 5.65). All of the PPD have been diagnosed by neurologist experts and none of the people in the CS has history of symptoms related to Parkinson's disease or any other kind of movement disorder syndrome. The recordings consist of sustained utterances of the five Spanish vowels, every person repeated three times the five vowels, thus in total the database is composed of 60 recordings per vowel on each class. This database is built by *Universidad de Antioquia* in Medellín, Colombia.

3.2 Experiments

First, each Spanish vowel is considered separately. The recordings are preprocessed by means of its division into frames with $55ms$ of length with an overlap of 50%, according to [9]. After, NLD features are calculated for each frame and four statistics are calculated for each feature. The considered statistics are *mean value*, *standard deviation*, *skewness* and *kurtosis*, thus each recording will be represented by a total of 40 features (four statistics on ten features).

The validation of the system's performance is made by the division of the data into 70% for training and 30% for testing, following the methodology exposed in [17]. The 70% of the data are used for the feature selection and for training the classifier and the remaining 30% of the data are used for testing; the different subsets for training and testing are randomly formed ten times. For each pair of subsets (train and test), the classification process is repeated ten times, forming a total of 100 independent realizations of the experiment obtaining results with confidence intervals of the system's performance.

In order to look for better accuracies, the selected features per vowel are combined, collecting information from the five Spanish vowels. This combination is performed considering the same process that was described above. The features selection process is applied again and the decision about whether a speech recording is from PPD or CS is taken with a SVM. The results are presented according to [17], indicating accuracy rates, specificity and sensitivity. Specificity indicates the probability of a healthy register to be correctly detected and sensitivity is the probability of a pathological signal to be correctly classified.

4 Results

Table 1 shows the results obtained when each Spanish vowel is considered, and the last row of the table indicates the results obtained when all Spanish vowels are combined into the same space. According to the results, the best performance is obtained when the vowel /i/ is considered separately. This is an interesting result specially if it is considered that the production of the vowel utterances involved several muscles but among them the risorius muscles only participate in the phonation of vowels /e/ and /i/ [18]. Further experiments should be addressed to get a deeper understanding about the impact of PD in the movement of the muscles involved in speech production.

Although the combination of the five vowels can provide more information about the phenomena, the obtained results in such case are not as well as expected. It could happen because the combination of features from all vowels rises the dimensionality of the system and it can result in an increment of redundant information that does not contribute to the correct classification of the speech recordings. To present the results compactly, a detection error tradeoff (DET) curve is shown in figure 2. The line corresponding to the performance for vowel /i/ is separated from the others, indicating that such performance is the best among the Spanish vowels and even better than those obtained with the combination of features from the five vowels.

Table 1. Accuracy results obtained per vowel and with the combination of all vowels

Vowel	accuracy	sensitivity	specificity
/a/	72,49 ± 2,68	68,30 ± 7,08	76,67 ± 5,86
/e/	71,58 ± 5,29	69,50 ± 6,07	73,67 ± 8,72
/i/	**76,81 ± 3,77**	**76,61 ± 9,96**	**77,00 ± 7,62**
/o/	70,23 ± 3,71	69,99 ± 7,86	70,45 ± 7,83
/u/	73,36 ± 3,92	75,45 ± 3,85	71,28 ± 7,29
All vowels	74,03 ± 3,96	71,50 ± 8,92	76,06 ± 5,19

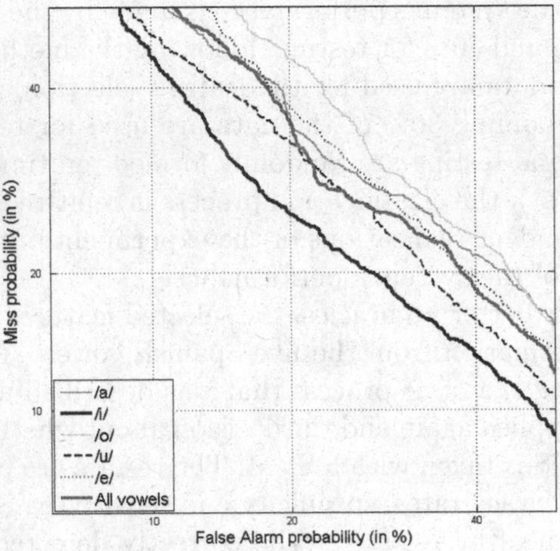

Fig. 2. DET curves for each vowel

5 Conclusions

Different state of the art NLD features have been evaluated in the automatic classification of speech recordings from PPD and CS. This work has considered experiments with the five Spanish vowels in order to state which of them provide better performance. According to our results, speech recordings from PPD and CS can be better classified considering NLD features by means of the evaluation of the vowel /i/. Additionally, with the voice samples evaluated, it is possible to state that the combination of features from the five vowels does not provides increases in the performance of the system.

Other works in the state of the art report higher accuracy rates; however, such works consider NLD features combined with other acoustic measures such as Harmonics to Noise Ratio, jitter and shimmer. The results reported in this work allow to state which is the real contribution of each NLD feature for the automatic classification of speech signals from PPD and CS.

Acknowledgments. Juan Rafael Orozco Arroyave is under grants of "Convocatoria 528 para estudios de doctorado en Colombia 2011" financed by COLCIENCIAS. The authors give a special thanks to all of the patients and collaborators in the "Fundalianza Parkinson-Colombia" foundation, without their valuable support it would be impossible to address this research.

References

1. Ramig, L.O., Fox, C., Shimon, S.: Speech treatment for parkinson's disease. Expert Review Neurotherapeutics 8(2), 297–309 (2008)
2. Perez, K.S., Ramig, L.O., Smith, M.E., Dromery, C.: The parkinson larynx: tremor and videostroboscopic findings. Journal of Voice 10(4), 353–361 (1996)
3. Kantz, H., Schreiber, T.: Nonlinear time series analysis, 2nd edn. Cambridge University Press, Cambridge (2006)
4. Giovanni, A., Ouaknine, M., Guelfucci, R., Yu, T., Zanaret, M., Triglia, J.M.: Nonlinear behavior of vocal fold vibration: the role of coupling between the vocal folds. Journal of Voice 13(4), 456–476 (1999)
5. Little, M.A., McSharry, P.E., Hunter, E.J., Spielman, J., Ramig, L.O.: Suitability of dysphonia measurements for telemonitoring of parkinson's disease. IEEE Transactions on Bio-Medical Engineering 56(4), 1015–1022 (2009)
6. Tsanas, A., Little, M., McSharry, P., Ramig, L.: Accurate telemonitoring of parkinson's disease progression by noninvasive speech tests. IEEE Transactions on Biomedical Engineering 57(4), 884–893 (2010)
7. Kostek, B., Kaszuba, K., Zwan, P., Robowski, P., Slawek, J.: Automatic assessment of the motor state of the parkinson's disease patient-a case study. Diagnostic Pathology 7(1), 1–8 (2012)
8. Orozco-Arroyave, J., Arias-Londoño, J.D., Bonilla, J.V., Nöth, E.: Automatic detection of hypernasal speech signals using nonlinear and entropy measurements. In: Proceedings of the INTERSPEECH (2012)
9. Arias-Londoño, J., Godino-Llorente, J., Sáenz-Lechón, N., Osma-Ruiz, V., Castellanos-Domínguez, G.: Automatic detection of pathological voices using complexity measures, noise parameters, and mel-cepstral coefficients. IEEE Transactions on Bio-medical Engineering 58(2), 370–379 (2011)
10. Takens, F.: Detecting strange attractors in turbulence. Dynamical Systems and Turbulence: Lecture Notes in Mathematics, vol. 898, pp. 366–381 (1981)
11. Kaspar, F., Shuster, H.G.: Easily calculable measure for complexity of spatiotemporal patterns. Physical Review A 36(2), 842–848 (1987)
12. Costa, M., Goldberger, A., Peng, C.: Multiscale entropy analysis of biological signals. Physical Review E 71, 1–18 (2005)
13. Xu, L.S., Wang, K.Q., Wang, L.: Gaussian kernel approximate entropy algorithm for analyzing irregularity of time series. In: Proceedings of the International Conference on Machine Learning and Cybernetics, pp. 5605–5608 (2005)
14. Little, M.A., McSharry, P.E., Roberts, S.J., Costello, D.E., Moroz, I.M.: Exploiting nonlinear recurrence and fractal scaling properties for voice disorder detection. Biomedical Engineering Online 6(23), 1–19 (2007)
15. Novovicova, J., Pudil, J.K.P.: Floating search methods in feature selection. Pattern Recognition Letters 15(11), 1119–1125 (1994)
16. Scholköpf, B., Smola, A.: Learning with Kernel. The MIT press (2002)
17. Sáenz-Lechón, N., Godino-Llorente, J., Osma-Ruiz, V., Gómez-Vilda, P.: Methodological issues in the development of automatic systems for voice pathology detection. Biomedical Signal Processing and Control 1, 120–128 (2006)
18. Phonetics, D.: Dissection of the speech production mechanism. Working Papers in Phonetics, UCLA (102), 1–89 (2002)

Synthesis by Rule of Disordered Voices

Jean Schoentgen[1] and Jorge C. Lucero[2]

[1] Department of Image and Signal Processing, Université Libre de Bruxelles, Faculty of Applied Sciences, 50, Av. F.-D. Roosevelt, B-1050, Brussels, Belgium
jschoent@ulb.ac.be

[2] Department of Computer Science, University of Brasilia, Brasilia DF, 70910-900 Brazil
lucero@unb.br

Abstract. The synthesis of disordered voices designates the use of numerical methods to simulate the vocal timbre of speakers suffering from laryngeal pathologies or dysfunctions to investigate the link between perceived timbre and speech signal properties. The simulation is based on a mapping of the amplitude of a narrow-band input signal onto the amplitude of a desired output signal, while the cycle lengths of the input and output are identical. The proposed amplitude-to-amplitude mapping, also known as waveshaping, makes possible simulating a wide range of timbres by fixing the control parameters of a cascade of elementary waveshapers. These enable evolving sample by sample the open quotient, pulse onset and offset rounding, speed quotient and formant ripple of the glottal airflow rate. Preliminary perceptual tests show that the perceived naturalness of the synthetic timbres is comparable to or better than the perceived naturalness of timbres generated via template-based waveshaping.

Keywords: speech synthesis, glottal source modeling, voice quality, voice disorders.

1 Introduction

Disordered voices refer to voices that are perceived as abnormal with regard to pitch, loudness or timbre. They are often the consequence of laryngeal pathologies or laryngeal, pulmonary or, occasionally, digestive dysfunctions (e.g. reflux). Synthesis here designates the use of models to numerically simulate speech sounds the timbre of which mimics the quality of disordered voices.

Perceptual evaluation plays a central role in the clinical assessment of speech and voice. The relevance of auditory assessment follows from the communicative function of oral speech that by default relies on the auditory channel. In running speech, voice, that is, the sound produced at the glottis via a pulsatile airflow, has a central place because approximately half the speech sounds are voiced. In addition, voice plays a major role in prosody (e.g. intonation) as well as paralinguistic communication (e.g. speaker attitude) and extralinguistic information (e.g. speaker identity). Speakers deprived of voice may therefore be

T. Drugman and T. Dutoit (Eds.): NOLISP 2013, LNAI 7911, pp. 120–127, 2013.

considered to be unable to communicate orally. One major unresolved issue in the assessment of speech and voice is the ill-understood link between perceived timbre and data that may be obtained instrumentally.

Synthetic speech stimuli have in the past played a major role in the study of the perception of the phonetic identity of speech sounds. Synthetic stimuli have played, however, a minor role only in the investigation of voice timbre. One reason is that the glottal source is usually modeled via the piecewise concatenations of curves that may request observed voice source signals to which they are fitted. Sample-to-sample updating of the source parameters is therefore not possible and continuity and smoothness constraints at the curve junctures are difficult to implement. Also, curve models do not enable source-tract interaction to be taken into account easily.

One approach that circumvents several of these problems is waveshaping, which maps the amplitude of an input signal onto the amplitude of an output signal. The input signal usually is a narrow-band signal the instantaneous frequency of which can be meaningfully interpreted in terms of its Fourier frequency. The cycle lengths of the input signal are identical to the cycle lengths of the output signal, which is the desired glottal area or flow rate or the derivative of the latter with regard to phase [2][6].

Existing applications of waveshaping to the modeling of the glottal area or airflow rate rest on a template cycle, which is turned via its Fourier series into a polynomial waveshaper [3]. The cycle lengths of the output are fixed via the instantaneous frequency of a driving harmonic. When the amplitude of the driving harmonic is changed from 0 to +1, polynomial waveshapers output cycle shapes that continuously evolve from a constant over a quasi-harmonic to the default template shape.

In this article, we discuss template-free waveshaping of different voice qualities, which is based on a cascade of waveshapers the input-to-output maps of which are so simple that they can be directly formulated mathematically on the base of the desired input-output relations.

2 Methods

2.1 Morphological Features of Glottal Area and Volume Velocity

Morphological features of the glottal area and flow rate waveforms that are relevant to timbre have been investigated by Fant and Titze [1][8]. Auditorily-relevant cues of the glottal area are the open quotient, onset and offset rounding as well as formant bandwidth modulation.

- The open quotient reports the percentage of the glottal cycle length over which the glottis is open. When the ligamental glottis does not close, the open quotient is equal to 100%. But, sound may be produced as long as the folds vibrate and modulate the flow rate.
- The glottis does not open or close abruptly. The area pulse shape has therefore a smooth onset and offset, which has a considerable impact on timbre.

- The bandwidths of the resonances of the vocal tract are modulated by the opening and closing of the glottis that connects or disconnects additional acoustic losses that occur in the trachea and lungs.

The opening and closing of the glottis turns the airflow from the lungs into a pulsatile flow rate that creates sound. Glottal area and flow rate share the open quotient as well as onset/offset rounding, but not cycle shape. Cycle shape skewing and formant ripples as well as the previously mentioned resonance bandwidth modulation are consequences of source-tract interaction.

- The flow rate cycle summit is delayed with regard to the area cycle summit. The delay is a consequence of the inertia of the air in the glottis and pharynx, which does not move instantaneously at glottal opening and which therefore skews the flow rate waveform to the right.
- Ripples at the frequency of the first formant are superimposed on the increasing flow rate at glottal opening. Rippling is a consequence of the vocal source emitting into the vocal tract in which sound waves propagate that disturb the pressure drop experienced by the airflow through the glottis.

2.2 Elementary Waveshapers

A waveshaper comprises one or several memory-less, continuous and smooth maps $y = f(x)$ the input x and output y of which share the same interval so that several waveshapers can be cascaded. The interval $(-1 \leq x, y \leq +1)$ is used the most often, assuming $x(t)$ to be sinusoidal or quasi-sinusoidal.

In waveshapers that comprise two maps, the switch occurs according to whether $\frac{dx}{dt} > 0$ or < 0 to enable increasing or decreasing input signal fragments to be shaped differently. Bi-maps $y = f_{\pm}(x)$ intersect at the interval boundaries, i.e. $f_{+}(x = \pm 1) = f_{-}(x = \pm 1)$, and share a common left-hand derivative at $x = +1$ and right-hand derivative at $x = -1$ to guarantee continuity and smoothness of output y.

Hereafter, four elementary waveshapers are discussed that fix (a) the open quotient, (b) pulse onset and offset rounding, (c) the speed quotient, as well as (d) formant ripples. The speed or skewing quotient is the ratio of the time intervals during which the flow rate decreases and increases.

Vertical Offsetting. Offsetting consists in shifting sinusoidal input x along the vertical axis to change its duty cycle to fix the open quotient of the glottal area or flow rate waveform.

$$y = (1 - \mathit{shift})x + \mathit{shift}, -1 < \mathit{shift} < +1. \tag{1}$$

Truncating and Rounding. Assuming zero leakage, truncating combined with rounding consists in the following.

$$y = 0 \text{ if } x \leq x_0,$$
$$y = x \text{ if } x \geq x_1,$$
$$y = interpol(x_0 = x_1 - d_r, y_0 = 0, [\tfrac{dy}{dx}]_{x=x_0} = 0, x_1 = y_1, y_1 = \tfrac{d_r}{\gamma},$$
$$[\tfrac{dy}{dx}]_{x=x_1} = 1, x) \text{ if } x_0 < x < x_1. \tag{2}$$

The interpolator is a cubic Hermite spline, $d_r > 0$ is fixed by the experimenter and $2 < \gamma < 3$ is a parameter that guarantees convex rounding.

Skewing. Formally $y = f_{\pm}(x)$ is written as follows, with $0 < s_k < 1$ fixed by the experimenter.

$$y = \frac{x}{\sqrt{1 + s_k^2 \pm 2s_k\sqrt{1 - x^2}}} \tag{3}$$

Waveshaper (3) is a bi-map inspired by [5]. It is easily interpreted and applied only when input $x(t)$ is a sinusoid because then $\pm\sqrt{1 - x^2}$ is the time derivative.

Selecting + or − in front of $\sqrt{1 - x^2}$ defines a map that is a slanted smooth hemi-"8" with $\frac{dy}{dx} \rightarrow \pm\infty$ when $x \rightarrow \pm 1$. The sign of the limit of $\frac{dy}{dx}$ depends on the sign of $\frac{dx}{dt}$. A thin "8" ($s_k \approx 0$) outputs a quasi-harmonic $y(t)$ the increase and decrease of which are similar in length. A fat "8" ($s_k \approx 1$) outputs an $y(t)$ the extrema of which are delayed with regard to the extrema of $x(t)$ and the cycle shape decrease of which occurs faster than the increase.

Rippling. The waveshaper simulates formant ripple during flowrate cycle increase by adding an exponentially decaying cosine to x when $\frac{dx}{dt} > 0$. No ripple is added when $\frac{dx}{dt} < 0$ because the formants are assumed to be dampened when the glottis is open. Ripple and first formant have opposite phases because positive acoustic pressure in the vocal tract decreases the pressure drop across the glottis and vice versa. Ripple size a_{ripple} is fixed by the user.

The decaying cosine is multiplied by sigmoidal Gompertz curves $gptz$ that assign to (4) an envelope with a slope $\frac{dy}{dx}$ equal to +1 when $x = \pm 1$ to guarantee smoothness when the waveshaper switches maps.

Formant frequency F_1 and bandwidth B_1 are normalized with regard to vocal frequency f_0 because $t = 1$ corresponds to one glottal cycle, irrespective of f_0.

$$t = 0.5x + 0.5$$
$$y = x + gptz(t, a, b, c)(-a_{ripple})e^{-\pi\frac{B_1}{f_0}t}\cos(2\pi\tfrac{F_1}{f_0}t) \text{ if } \tfrac{dx}{dt} > 0 \text{ and } t < 0.5$$
$$y = x + gptz(1 - t, a, b, c)(-a_{ripple})e^{-\pi\frac{B_1}{f_0}t}\cos(2\pi\tfrac{F_1}{f_0}t) \text{ if } \tfrac{dx}{dt} > 0 \text{ and } t \geq 0.5$$
$$y = x \text{ if } \tfrac{dx}{dt} \leq 0, \text{ with } a = 1,\ b = -6,\ c = -50. \tag{4}$$

2.3 Modulation Noise and Additive Noise

Other features involved in the genesis of vocal timbre that have been implemented are frequency modulation noise (vocal frequency jitter and vocal frequency tremor) as well as aspiration noise and pulsatile noise owing to turbulent airflow in the glottis. The size of pulsatile noise evolves with the clean flow rate, whereas aspiration noise is stationary. The added noise is Gaussian white noise low-pass filtered with the cut-off frequency in the interval $600Hz - 800Hz$, depending on perceived strain.

Jitter in natural voices is reported as a single quantity in % [7]. Expression (5) is therefore a quasi-definitional model of vocal frequency jitter depending on a single control parameter a_{jit} and white noise dW that perturbs intonation frequency f_0. Together they determine instantaneous frequency $\frac{d\theta}{dt}$ of the driving sinusoid of the waveshapers that output the glottal area or airflow rate.

$$d\theta = 2\pi f_0 dt + a_{jit} dW \tag{5}$$

However, voices simulated with (5) are perceived as hoarser than expected given the measured cycle perturbations at the glottis. The degree of perceived hoarseness can be brought into line with cycle length perturbations observed in natural voices by linear second-order low-pass filtering perturbations dW in the vicinity of $600Hz - 800Hz$ so that glottal cycle length jitter of 1% causes voices to be perceived as borderline hoarse. A second beneficial consequence of filtering is that the constraint $2\pi f_0 dt > a_{jit} dW_{lowpass}$ is satisfied for modal voices as well as feebly and moderately hoarse voices, which agrees with the usual view that dW in (5) is perturbative. Voices that are perceived as severely hoarse can be simulated by means of (5) only when the previous constraint is not satisfied by all samples of $dW_{lowpass}$.

Vocal frequency tremor is simulated by adding to model (5) Gaussian white noise that is filtered by a linear second-order filter [3]. The gain, center frequency and bandwidth of the filter respectively fix tremor size, tremor frequency and tremor irregularity. Experimenting with tremor and jitter confirms that perceived hoarseness depends not only on perturbation size but also on perturbation bandwidth. Data with regard to the latter are however not reported in the literature, neither for jitter nor tremor.

2.4 Asthenic versus Pressed Voice

During speech, open quotient, pulse onset and offset rounding as well as skewing are not expected to evolve independently for a given phonatory setting. One may expect larger open quotients and onset and offset rounding to co-occur with smaller skewing. The latter gives rise to voices that are perceived as asthenic, whereas the reverse causes voices to be perceived as pressed. Upper and lower limit values have therefore been fixed for parameters *shift*, d_r and s_k in (1), (2) and (3). They are evolved linearly between their extreme values by means of one control parameter comprised between -1 (asthenic) and $+1$ (pressed).

2.5 Modeling of the Glottal Area, Airflow Rate and Speech Signal

The glottal area is modeled by inserting a harmonic driving function into waveshaper (1), followed by truncating and rounding (2). If the user wishes to skew the glottal area waveform, the harmonic is first inserted into skewing waveshaper (3), followed by (1) and (2) in that order.

The output, which is comprised between 0 and +1, is then multiplied by the maximal glottal area $a_{g,max}$ and inserted into Fant's model that simulates the glottal flow rate taking into account lung pressure and tracheal and vocal tract loads [1]. Fant's model involves solving numerically a differential equation the solution of which may become unstable if rapidly evolving equation parameters are included, such as time-variable formant frequencies and bandwidths.

As an alternative, the glottal flow rate may be simulated exclusively by means of waveshapers by inserting the harmonic driving function into the skewing waveshaper, followed by rippling, offsetting, truncating and rounding. Output $0 \leq y \leq +1$ is then turned into the glottal airflow rate u_g by means of the following expression, with $\rho =$ density of air at human body temperature, $K =$ recovery coefficient ≈ 1 and $p_L =$ lung (excess) pressure [1].

$$u_g = a_{g,max} y \sqrt{\frac{2}{\rho K} p_L (1 - \mathit{shift})} \tag{6}$$

Parameter *shift* that is identical to the control parameter of waveshaper (1) enables simulating soft vowel onsets and offsets when the parameter evolves from +1 to its target value $\mathit{shift}_{target} \geq 0$ and back. In speech, shift_{target} is not expected to be smaller than 0, which corresponds to an open quotient of 50%.

When the glottis is wide open (i.e. $\mathit{shift} = 1$) then flow rate $u_g = 0$ because $p_L(1 - \mathit{shift})$ is zero. When the open quotient is at a minimum (i.e. $\mathit{shift} = \mathit{shift}_{target}$) pulmonary (excess) pressure evolves to its maximum $p_L(1 - \mathit{shift}_{target})$.

Finally, flow rate u_g is inserted into a formant synthesizer. The implementation of the vocal tract resonances closely follows the proposal by Klatt [4]. The sampling frequency of the synthetic speech signal equals $50kHz$. The first three formants are controllable by the user, the following two are fixed at default values that are $3500Hz$ and $4500Hz$ and the final 20 formants up to $25kHz$ are fixed to equally spaced default frequencies and large default bandwidths. The purpose of the latter is to keep the transfer function trend flat up to $25kHz$. Sound radiation is simulated by a numerical derivative of the formant synthesizer output and the synthetic stimuli are saved in .wav format.

3 Results and Discussion

Figures 1 to 4 demonstrate the sample by sample evolution of four morphological features of the glottal flow rate. They respectively show the glottal airflow rate with rounding, skewing, open quotient and formant ripple increasing with time.

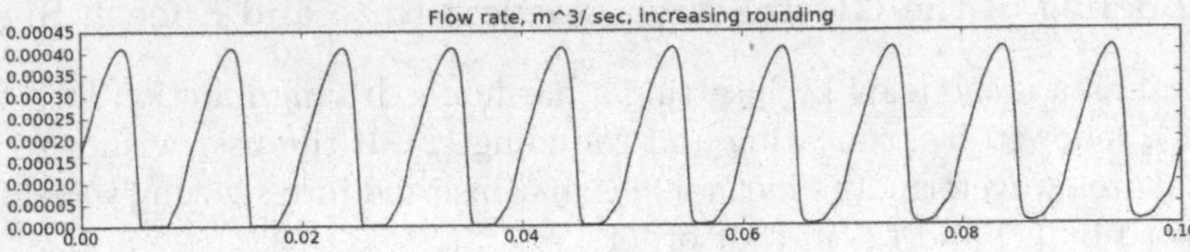

Fig. 1. Glottal airflow rate with increasing pulse onset and offset rounding r_d. The horizontal axis is in s, the vertical axis in $\frac{m^3}{s}$.

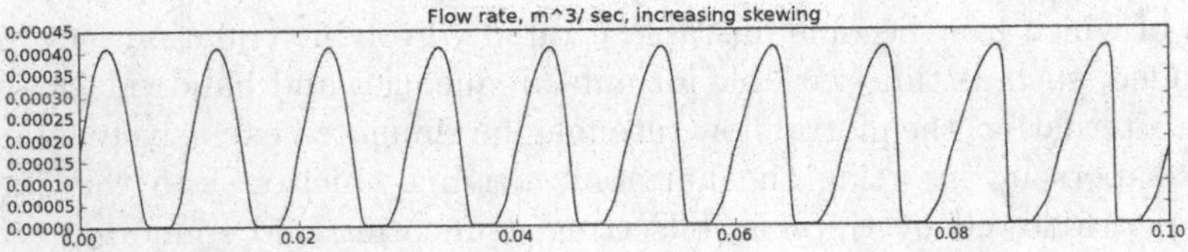

Fig. 2. Glottal airflow rate with skewing s_k evolving from 0 to 0.9. The horizontal axis is in s, the vertical axis in $\frac{m^3}{s}$.

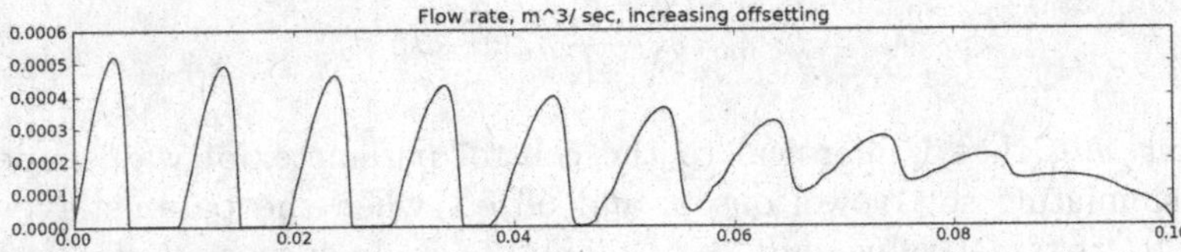

Fig. 3. Glottal airflow rate with offsetting *shift* evolving from 0 to 1. The horizontal axis is in s, the vertical axis in $\frac{m^3}{s}$.

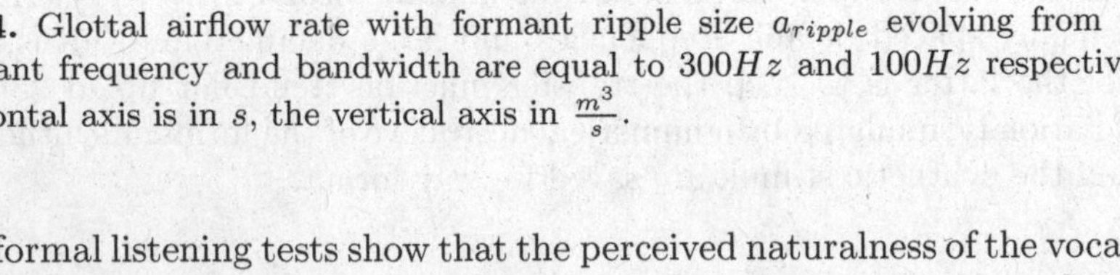

Fig. 4. Glottal airflow rate with formant ripple size a_{ripple} evolving from 0 to 0.4 Formant frequency and bandwidth are equal to $300Hz$ and $100Hz$ respectively. The horizontal axis is in s, the vertical axis in $\frac{m^3}{s}$.

Informal listening tests show that the perceived naturalness of the vocal timbre of the sounds synthesized via waveshaping by rule is equivalent to or better than the naturalness of the timbre of speech sounds simulated by means of a template-based waveshaper [3].

The difference between waveshaping by rule and by template is that for the former the user has a finer control over the morphological and timing features of the glottal area and flow rate, with a concomitant increased risk of selecting combinations of features that are unlikely. Also, waveshaping by rule does not contain an in-built protection against accidental aliasing.

In waveshaping by template, open quotient, rounding and skewing co-evolve plausibly with the amplitude of the driving harmonic. Also, waveshaping by template enables fixing the number of harmonics, making accidental aliasing unlikely when vocal frequency f_0 evolves slowly. Finally, waveshaping by template enables synthesis to be based on observed glottal areas or flow rates. Polynomial waveshapers are indeed linked to the Fourier series coefficients of an observed template cycle via a linear constant transform [6].

Acknowledgments. Part of the research reported here has been supported by CNPq (Brazil) and F.R.S-F.N.R.S. (French-speaking Community of Belgium).

References

1. Ananthapadmanaba, T.V., Fant, G.: Calculation of true glottal flow and its components, Speech Comm. Speech Comm. 1, 167–184 (1982)
2. Fant, G., Liljencrants, J., Lin, Q.G.: A four-parameter model of glottal flow. In: STL-QPSR 4, KTH, Stockholm (1985)
3. Fraj, S., Schoentgen, J., Grenez, F.: Development and perceptual assessment of a synthesizer of disordered voices. J. Acoust. Soc. Am. 132, 2603–2615 (2012)
4. Klatt, D.: Software for a cascade/parallel formant synthesizer. J. Acoust. Soc. Am. 67, 971–995 (1980)
5. Peters, B.T., Haddada, J.M., Heiderscheit, B.C., Van Emmerik, R.E.A., Hamill, J.: Limitations in the use and interpretation of continuous relative phase. J. Biomechanics 36, 271–274 (2003)
6. Schoentgen, J.: Shaping function models of the phonatory excitation signal. J. Acoust. Soc. Am. 114, 2906–2912 (2003)
7. Schoentgen, J.: Vocal cues of disordered voices. Acta Acustica 92, 667–682 (2006)
8. Titze, I.: The myoelastic aerodynamic theory of phonation. National Center for Voice and Speech, Denver CO (2006)

Towards a Low-Complex Breathing Monitoring System Based on Acoustic Signals

Pere Martí-Puig, Jordi Solé-Casals, Gerard Masferrer, and Esteve Gallego-Jutglà

Digital Technologies Group, University of Vic,
Sagrada Família 7, 08500 - Vic, Catalonia, Spain
{pere.marti,jordi.sole,gerard.masferrer,
esteve.gallego}@uvic.cat

Abstract. Monitoring the breathing is required in many applications of medical and health fields, but it can be used also in new game applications, for example. In this work, an automatic system for monitoring the breathing is presented. The system uses the acoustic signal recorded by a standard microphone placed in the area of the nostrils. The system is based on a low-complex signal parameterization performed on non-overlapped frames. From this parameterization, a reduced set of real parameters is obtained frame-to-frame. These parameters feed a classifier that performs a classification in three stages: inspiration, transition or retention and expiration providing a fine monitoring of the respiration process. As all of those algorithms are of low complexity and the auxiliary equipment required could only be a standard microphone from a conventional Bluetooth Headset, the system could be able to run in a smartphone device.

Keywords: Breathing monitoring, low-complex system, linear discriminant analysis, smartphone app.

1 Introduction

The breathing is one of the body's few autonomic functions that can be controlled and can affect functioning of the autonomic nervous system [5]. This paper specifically considers the fine real-time breathing monitoring using an acoustic signal recorded by a standard microphone placed in the area of the nostrils. By analyzing this acoustic signal, the breathing is continuously classified in terms of its cycles of inspiration-expiration and an intermediate stage that we call retention. A real-time breathing monitoring system can be used in some biofeedback applications and in this preliminary design it is thought to work in low noise environments.

The human breathing has been deeply studied in the context of respiratory illnesses and has received great attention from the biofeedback framework. Following the biofeedback breathing approach, some relevant works have been done in relation with stress and health [21-23],[25],[26], [30] especially in the area of respiratory illnesses [22], [32]. Respiratory sinus arrhythmia (RSA) is the phenomenon by which respiration modulates the heart rate in normal humans. As a result, the respiration affects the arterial blood pressure and the volume pulse, so, nowadays, an important part of those

T. Drugman and T. Dutoit (Eds.): NOLISP 2013, LNAI 7911, pp. 128–135, 2013.

biofeedback clinical studies relate the breath control with the heart rate coherence [28] and with the idea of developing a non-pharmacological treatment for hypertension. Many clinical studies are being done under this assumption [21], [31], [20], [10], [24].

Another interesting area in which the breathing monitoring can be of interest is the area of emotion detection. As it was early reported in [27], emotions are associated with distinct patterns of cardiorespiratory activity. According to [6][13], fast and deep breathing can indicate excitement such as anger or fear, but sometimes also joy. Rapid shallow breathing can indicate tense anticipation including panic, fear or concentration. Slow and deep breathing indicates a relaxed resting state, while slow and shallow breathing can indicate states of withdrawal, passive like depression or calm happiness. In the literature several non-intrusive methods have been proposed to detect the breathing. Some other classical methods are based on movement, volume and tissue composition detection. Methods included in this category are the transthoratic impedance monitoring, the measurement of chest and/or the abdominal circumference, the electromyography, various motion detectors and the photoplethysmography. A good compilation of these methods can be found in [11]. Recently, in [19], [12], [14] the breathing is detected using far-infrared (FIR) cameras by monitoring the air flow temperature in the nasal hole due of the inspiration and expiration. Those approaches involve some image processing techniques and have to deal with practical questions as head rotation, distance between camera and human and camera angle. Our approach follows the acoustic signal approximation like those appeared in [7], [8], where the respiratory sound is measured using a microphone placed either close to the respiratory airways or over the throat to detect the variation of sound. The acoustic breathing signal have been studied and modelled in different works [16-17], [29], [33].

On the other hand, today the smartphones have become more ubiquitous and provide high computing and connectivity capabilities, incorporating high-resolution touchscreens, portable media players, 3-axis accelerometers, 3-axis gyroscopes, cameras and microphones, among other accessories. So it is reasonable to consider trying advantage of those devices by developing biofeedback apps specifically for them, in order to allow a patient to perform training at home. A potential advantage of using smartphone's apps is the opportunity to collect large amount of data -with user permission if the apps are distributed for free- enabling large scale clinical studies.

Nowadays there are several applications available for Smartphone, mainly for iOS and Android operating systems, which work on different breathing aspects. Most of these apps come from fields like health [2], [5] relaxation [3] or meditation [1] techniques, and have a careful presentation but have a little control on monitoring the quality of the exercise as most of those apps are limited to provide breathing rhythms that should guide the exercise. Our system can overcome these limitations and provide an accurate control on breathing monitoring.

1.1 Acoustic Data Registration

A microphone detects the airflow due to the sound created by turbulence that occurs in the human respiratory system because, even for shallow breathing, turbulence occurs in parts of this system creating a noise which is transferred through tissue to the surface of the skin [15]. Some works have analyzed the acoustic breathing signal from the physical production and some models are proposed [16, 17, 29, 33]. In some of these the same studies the problematic of finding the best place to allocate the microphone is addressed, finding different appropriate locations on the human body where acoustic breathing signals may be detected.

In our case an inexpensive standard microphone from a conventional Bluetooth Headset is placed very close to the nostrils area with the amplifier gain near of its maximum. The signal is sampled at 8000 Hz and it is processed in a personal computer (PC). The recoding environment in which the user performs the breathing exercises is recommended to be noiseless. By means of an envelope detector the cycles of breathing are easy characterized as it is shown in figure 1. In order to detect the envelope, the input signal is digitally rectified and filtered by an infinite impulse response filter of one single pole at z = 0.995 that has been prepared to work frame-to-frame. The breathing signal can be automatically segmented in its three stages using a threshold on the envelope.

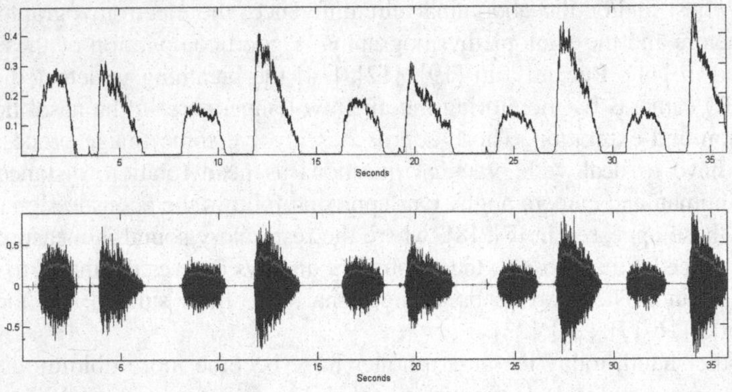

Fig. 1. On the top, 36 seconds of an acoustic breathing signal envelope. On the bottom, the same detected envelope represented together with the breathing signal.

1.2 Low-Complex Parameterization Method

The proposed simple parameterization is as follows: The signal is segmented into non-overlapped frames. The band of interest is divided into a given number of sub-bands and the frame is parameterized with the energy that has in each of this sub-bands. In order to simplify the process, a fast Fourier Transform (FFT) is performed with a square window. Only the moduli of the discrete Fourier coefficients are considered and the values belonging to the same sub-band are added in order to obtain a real parameter per sub-band. It means that if we consider, for example, a band partition in 4 sub-bands then only 4 real parameters are required to parameterize a frame. Those parameters are normalized. The normalization value is a reference value obtained from the highest parameter of a test signal.

To perform the experiments we have selected a group of 5 users and we have recorded their breathing for 5 minutes. In order to verify that the proposed parameterization is suitable for detecting the three stages considered in the respiration process, a manual segmentation is performed considering different frame lengths and different sub-band partitions. Figure 2 shows the process of the manual segmentation and the parameterization process.

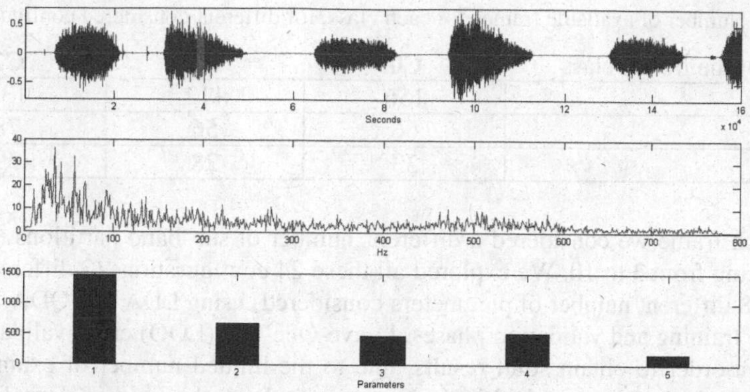

Fig. 2. On the top, a frame of 200 ms is represented (in red) that corresponds to an expiration breathing sound. In the middle, the modulus of the Fast Fourier Transform applied to this frame. On the bottom, the frame parameterization obtained from the integration of all coefficients of each equal-spaced sub-band, considering a five sub-band partition.

2 Experiments

2.1 Classification Techniques

Many possible techniques for data classification are available. Among them, Principal Component Analysis (PCA), Linear Discriminant Analysis (LDA) or Neural Networks (NN) are techniques commonly used for data classification and/or dimensionality reduction [9]. In our experiments we will use LDA due to his properties: the system works by projecting the data onto a lower-dimensional vector space such that the ratio of the between-class distances to the within-class distance is maximized, thus achieving maximum discrimination. The optimal projection (transformation) can be readily computed by applying the eigendecomposition on the scatter matrices. See [9] and [18] for details on the algorithm.

In our experiments we will hence use LDA and a variation of it, called Quadratic discriminant Analysis (QDA). The difference of both systems relies on the assumptions made for the distributions of each class. While for LDA a normal distribution is assumed with a pooled estimate of covariance, in QDA there is no assumption that the covariance of each of the classes is identical, and for each class this covariance matrix is estimated from training data.

2.2 Results and Discussion

In the following experiment we mixed all the users in order to have a more general system, not focussed in one solely user. After applying the pre-processing step explained in Section 2.2, we obtained the total number of frames per class depicted in Table 1, where C0 is inspiration, C1 is expiration and C2 is retention.

Table 1. Number of available frames for each class, for different considered configurations

Length of the frame\ class	C0	C1	C2
50 ms	156	112	132
100 ms	66	56	78
200 ms	33	28	39

For each frame we considered a different number of sub-band partitions (parameters), ranging from 3 to 10. We explored all these 24 configurations (3 different frame lengths x 8 different number of parameters considered) using LDA and QDA.

For the training and validation phases, Leave-One-Out (LOO) cross-validation was used [9] in order to obtain solid results, due to the limited number of examples per class (156 in the best case and 33 in the worst case). With this methodology for a data set with N samples, a single sample is retained as a validation, and all the N-1 samples are used as a training data. Then cross-validation process is repeated N times, using each time a different sample as a validation data. The obtained results once all the samples have been used as a validation data are averaged in order to compute a single measure of classification rate. The advantage of this method is that all observations are used for both training and validation, and each observation is used for validation exactly once. LOO could be computationally expensive because it requires many repetitions of training, but it is successful in dealing with very small data sets as it is our case.

In figure 1 we shown the evolution of the classification rate (in %), obtained with the LOO cross-validation strategy when LDA is used as classification system. We can observe that higher frame length obtains always better performance independently of the number of parameters considered. The best case is a 93% of classification rate, obtained with 4, 8, 9 or 10 sub-bands and frame length of 200 ms. For all the 3 cases, 8 parameters seems to be the best option, as the maximum classification rate is achieved in all configurations (93% for 200 ms frame length, and 90.5% for 100 ms and 50 ms frame length), but also 4 parameters is a good choice for 200 ms frame length.

On the other hand, using QDA results are improved as shown in figure 2. The best frame length is still 200 ms and the number of parameters is again 4 for this case, where the maximum classification rate of 96% is achieved, representing an improvement of 3 points compared to LDA case.

For the other frame lengths results also improve when QDA is used. For 100 ms frame length we achieve 95% of classification rate, with again 4 parameters, representing an improvement of 4.5 points compared to LDA case, while for 50 ms frame length we obtain a maximum of 94.75% of classification rate, for 8 parameters, that represents an improvement of 4.25 points compared to LDA case.

It seems that high frame lengths tend to be more adapted to our parameterisation system, and small number of parameters can be used. This result is interesting in the sense that audio signal will be faster processed if we have an small number of frames and also the classification system will be faster with less number of parameters.

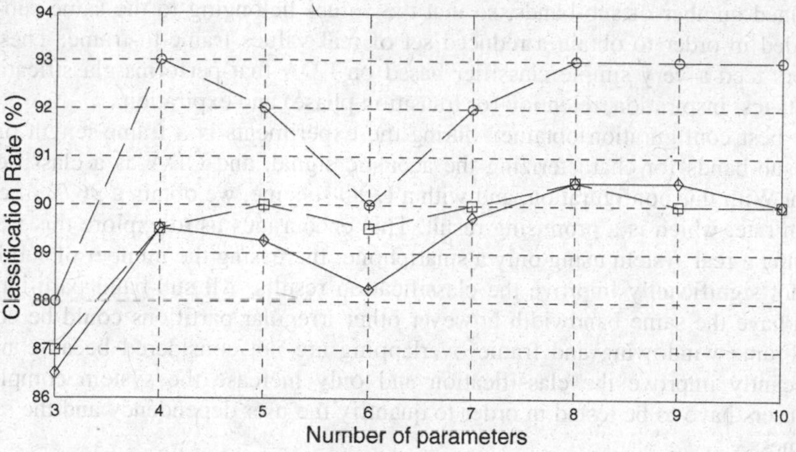

Fig. 3. Classification Rate (%) obtained for LDA, different number of sub-bands considered (different number of parameters for the classification system), from 3 to 10, and different frame lengths (50 ms, diamond marker; 100 ms, square marker; and 200 ms circle marker)

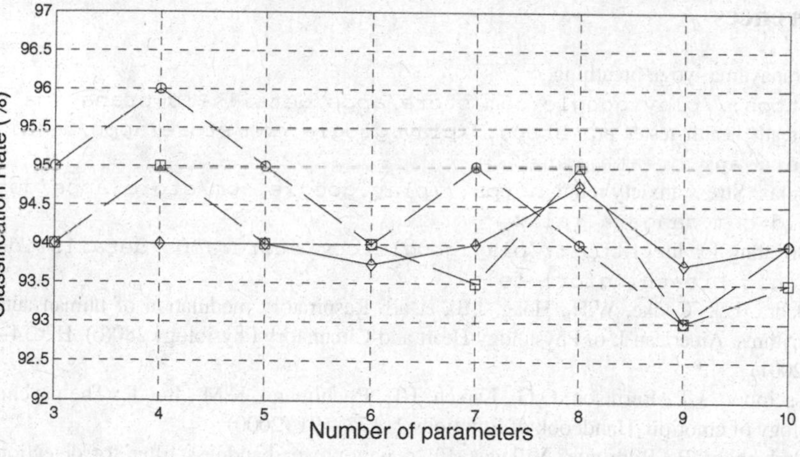

Fig. 4. Classification Rate (%) obtained for QDA, different number of sub-bands considered (different number of parameters for the classification system), from 3 to 10, and different frame lengths (50 ms, diamond marker; 100 ms, square marker; and 200 ms circle marker)

3 Conclusions

In this work, a preliminary study for developing a system for monitoring the breathing is presented. The system is designed in order to use the acoustic signal recorded by a standard microphone placed in the area of the nostrils, and based on a low-complex signal parameterization performed on non-overlapped frames. Parameters are obtained from the moduli of the discrete Fourier Transform coefficients considering a predefined number of sub-bands, so that the values belonging to the same sub-band are added in order to obtain a reduced set of real values frame-to-frame. These parameters feed a very simple classifier based on LDA that performs classification in three stages: inspiration, retention (or transition phase) and expiration.

The best configuration obtained during the experiments is a frame length on 200 ms, 4 sub-bands for characterizing the acoustic signal, and QDA as a classification system. With this configuration, and with a LOO scheme, we obtain a 96 % of classification rate, which is a promising result. This encourages us to explore this way for designing a real system using only a smartphone. Increasing the number of sub-bands does not significantly improve the classification results. All sub-band partitions explored have the same bandwidth however other irregular partitions could be considered. Frame windowing and frame overlapping are not considered because neither significantly improve the classification and only increase the system complexity. More users have to be tested in order to quantify the user dependency and the system robustness.

Acknowledgments. This work has been partially supported by the University of Vic (grant R904) and under a predoctoral grant to Mr. Esteve Gallego-Jutglà ("Amb el suport de l'ajut predoctoral de la Universitat de Vic").

References

1. Pranayama -yoga breathing, `https://play.google.com/store/apps/details?id=pranayama.home`
2. Breath health tester pro, `https://play.google.com/store/apps/details?id=org.app.breath_rate`
3. Relax: Stress anxiety relief, `https://play.google.com/store/apps/details?id=com.saagara.relax`
4. Breathng for life, `https://play.google.com/store/apps/details?id=com.soniq.breathingforlife1`
5. Badra, L.J., Cooke, W.H., Hoag, J.B., et al.: Respiratory modulation of human autonomic rhythms. American J. of Physiology-Heart and Circulatory Physiology 280(6), H2674–H2688 (2001)
6. Cacioppo, J.T., Berntson, G.G., Larsen, J.T., Poehlmann, K.M., Ito, T.: The psychophysiology of emotion. Handbook of Emotions 2, 173–191 (2000)
7. Corbishley, P., Rodriguez-Villegas, E.: A nanopower bandpass filter for detection of an acoustic signal in a wearable breathing detector. IEEE Transactions on Biomedical Circuits and Systems 1(3), 163–171 (2007)
8. Corbishley, P., Rodríguez-Villegas, E.: Breathing detection: Towards a miniaturized, wearable, battery-operated monitoring system. IEEE Transactions on Biomedical Engineering 55(1), 196–204 (2008)
9. Duda, R.O., Hart, P.E., Stork, D.G.: Pattern classification and scene analysis, 2nd edn. (1995)
10. Ferreira, J.B., Plentz, R.D.M., Stein, C., Casali, K.R., Arena, R., Lago, P.D.: Inspiratory muscle training reduces blood pressure and sympathetic activity in hypertensive patients: A randomized controlled trial. Int. J. Cardiol. (2011)
11. Folke, M., Cernerud, L., Ekström, M., Hök, B.: Critical review of non-invasive respiratory monitoring in medical care. Medical and Biological Engineering and Computing 41(4), 377–383 (2003)

12. Goldman, L.J.: Nasal airflow and thoracoabdominal motion in children using infrared thermographic video processing. Pediatr. Pulmonol. (2012)
13. Haag, A., Goronzy, S., Schaich, P., Williams, J.: Emotion recognition using bio-sensors: First steps towards an automatic system. Affective Dialogue Systems, 36–48 (2004)
14. Hanawa, D., Morimoto, T., Tearda, S., et al.: Nasal cavity detection in facial thermal image for non-contact measurement of breathing, 586–590 (2012)
15. Harper, V.P., Pasterkamp, H., Kiyokawa, H., Wodicka, G.R.: Modeling and measurement of flow effects on tracheal sounds. IEEE Trans. on Biomedical Engineering 50(1), 1–10 (2003)
16. Hossain, I., Moussavi, Z.: Relationship between airflow and normal lung sounds 2, 1120–1122 (2002)
17. Hossain, I., Moussavi, Z.: Respiratory airflow estimation by acoustical means 2, 1476–1477 (2002)
18. Fukunaga, K.: Introduction to statistical pattern recognition. Academic Pr. (1990)
19. Koide, T., Yamakawa, S., Hanawa, D., Oguchi, K.: Breathing detection by far infrared (FIR) imaging in a home health care system, 206 (2009)
20. Linden, W., Moseley, J.: The efficacy of behavioral treatments for hypertension. Appl. Psychophysiol Biofeedback 31(1), 51–63 (2006)
21. McGrady, A.: The effects of biofeedback in diabetes and essential hypertension. Cleve Clin. J. Med. 77(suppl. 3), S68–S71 (2010)
22. Mikosch, P., Hadrawa, T., Laubreiter, K., et al.: Effectiveness of respiratory-sinus-arrhythmia biofeedback on state-anxiety in patients undergoing coronary angiography. J. Adv. Nurs. 66(5), 1101–1110 (2010)
23. Moore, S.: Tools & toys: Calm in your palm. IEEE Spectrum 43(3), 60 (2006)
24. Mourya, M., Mahajan, A.S., Singh, N.P., Jain, A.K.: Effect of slow-and fast-breathing exercises on autonomic functions in patients with essential hypertension. The Journal of Alternative and Complementary Medicine 15(7), 711–717 (2009)
25. Pokrovskii, V.M., Polischuk, L.: On the conscious control of the human heart. Journal of Integrative Neuroscience 11(2), 213–223 (2012)
26. Rafferty, G.F., Gardner, W.: Control of the respiratory cycle in conscious humans. J. Appl. Physiol. 81(4), 1744–1753 (1996)
27. Rainville, P., Bechara, A., Naqvi, N., Damasio, A.: Basic emotions are associated with distinct patterns of cardiorespiratory activity. International Journal of Psychophysiology 61(1), 5–18 (2006)
28. Sharma, M.: RESPeRATE: Nonpharmacological treatment of hypertension. Cardiol. Rev. 19(2), 47–51 (2011)
29. Shykoff, B.E., Ploysongsang, Y., Chang, H.: Airflow and normal lung sounds. American Journal of Respiratory and Critical Care Medicine 137(4), 872–876 (1988)
30. Stock, M., Kontrisova, K., Dieckmann, K., Bogner, J., Poetter, R., Georg, D.: Development and application of a real-time monitoring and feedback system for deep inspiration breath hold based on external marker tracking. Med. Phys. 33(8), 2868–2877 (2006)
31. Tsai, P., Chang, N., Chang, W., Lee, P., Wang, M.: Blood pressure biofeedback exerts intermediate-term effects on blood pressure and pressure reactivity in individuals with mild hypertension: A randomized controlled study. The J. of Alternative and Complementary Medicine 13(5), 547–554 (2007)
32. Van Gestel, A.J.R., Kohler, M., Steier, J., Teschler, S., Russi, E.W., Teschler, H.: The effects of controlled breathing during pulmonary rehabilitation in patients with COPD. Respiration 83(2), 115–124 (2012)
33. Yap, Y.L., Moussavi, Z.: Acoustic airflow estimation from tracheal sound power 2, 1073–1076 (2002)

Automatic Detection of Laryngeal Pathologies in Running Speech Based on the HMM Transformation of the Nonlinear Dynamics

Carlos M. Travieso[1], Jesús B. Alonso[1], Juan Rafael Orozco-Arroyave[2], Jordi Solé-Casals[3], and Esteve Gallego-Jutglà[3]

[1] Signals and Communications Department, Institute for Technological Development and Innovation in Communications, University of Las Palmas de Gran Canaria, Campus University of Tafira, 35017, Las Palmas de Gran Canaria, Las Palmas, Spain
{ctravieso,jalonso}@dsc.ulpgc.es
[2] DIEyT, Universidad de Antioquia, Medellín, Colombia
rafael.orozco@udea.edu.co
[3] Digital Technologies Group, University of Vic, Sagrada Família 7,08500 Vic, Spain
{jordi.sole,esteve.gallego}@uvic.cat

Abstract. This work describes a novel system for characterizing Laryngeal Pathologies using nonlinear dynamics, considering different complexity measures that are mainly based on the analysis of the time delay embedded space. The model is done by a kernel applied on Hidden Markov Model and decision of the Laryngeal pathology/control detection is performed by Support Vector Machine. Our system reaches accuracy up to 98.21%, improving the current reported results in the state of the art in the automatic classification of pathological speech signals (running speech) and showing the robustness of this proposal.

Keywords: Nonlinear Dynamic parameterization, Pathological voice detection, Hidden Markov Models, Laryngeal Pathologies, Speech signal.

1 Introduction

For several years, voice pathology detection has been addressed by means of acoustic, Cepstral and perturbation analysis of voice. Good results have been obtained in sustained voices [1] and also in continuous speech [2]. However, these features present stability and accuracy problems in cases where the estimation of the pitch period is not possible, such as those where the level of the pathology is severe [3].

The nonlinear behavior of the vocal fold vibration was demonstrated in previous works [4, 5]; the research community is now working in nonlinear dynamics (NLD) for the development of methods to perform the automatic and accurate detection of voice pathologies. This problem can be addressed mainly from two different points: the evaluation of sustained phonations and the evaluation of continuous speech.

In the evaluation of sustained phonations using NLD features, the state of the art reports accuracy levels of 99.69% considering a set of six NLD features such as first

T. Drugman and T. Dutoit (Eds.): NOLISP 2013, LNAI 7911, pp. 136–143, 2013.

minimum of the mutual information (FMMI), correlation dimension (D_c), first-order Renyi block entropy, second-order Renyi block entropy and Shannon entropy [6]. More recently, Vaziri et al. [7] report a success rate of 94.44% considering only the correlation dimension.

Additionally, there are recent works that consider the evaluation of sustained voices by mixing acoustic, Cepstral, perturbation and NLD features, reporting accuracy levels of 98.23% [8].

For continuous speech, it is already demonstrated that it contains more information about different variations of pitch period, rhythm, intonation and other suprasegmental features [9]. In [2] the authors report accuracy levels of 96.3% considering fourteen Mel Frequency Cepstral Coefficients (MFCC), energy content, harmonics to noise ratio (HNR), normalized noise energy (NNE), glottal to noise excitation ratio (GNE) and the first derivates of each feature, building a representation space with 36 dimensions estimated over a sub set of the *Massachusetts Eye & Ear Infirmary (MEEI)* database that includes 117 pathological and 23 healthy speech signals. In [10] the authors consider all of the speech recordings in the MEEI database and perform the automatic detection of the laryngeal pathologies in running speech signals by means of different implementations of the jitter, reporting accuracy rates of up to 94.82%.

Recently, in [11] different statistics from NLD features are considered for characterizing continuous speech signals obtained from a sub set of the MEEI database. The experiments reported in that work are performed over 396 speech recordings, 360 from people with different laryngeal pathologies and 36 with healthy voices. The results reported by the authors indicate accuracy rates of up to 95%.

With the aim of performing the automatic classification of pathological speech signals and healthy recordings, the application of different NLD features is introduced in this paper considering speech recordings from a sub set of the MEEI database. Four complexity measures are implemented for the characterization of the speech signals: correlation dimension (D_c), Lyapunov exponent (λ_{max}), Hurst exponent (H) and Lempel-Ziv complexity (LZC).

The features are modeled by a Hidden Markov Model (HMM) [12] and a kernel applied to HMM. Finally, a Support Vector Machine (SVM) [13] is used as classifier for identifying the pathology.

The paper is organized as follows: Section 2 includes the description of NLD features. Section 3 provides the details about our classification system. In Section 4, the database, the experimental methodology, results and comments are shown. Finally, in Section 5, general conclusions of this work are presented.

2 Nonlinear Dynamics (NLD) Characterization

Some works in the state of the art demonstrate the existence of nonlinear dynamics in the voice production process and analyze its capability for the automatic detection of pathologies [6, 13]. The different complexity measures which were implemented for the automatic detection of laryngeal pathologies in Spanish vowels and words will be described in the following sections. This measures have not studied from medical point of view, but it will be demonstrated its good behavior for Laryngeal Pathologies. The goal of this parameterization doesn't depend on pitch [15], and it has invariance of the age and gender.

2.1 Correlation Dimension D_c

In an Euclidean space with dimensionality d, a volume measure V can be described by "longitude" L measurements, such that $V\alpha L^d$, or equivalently $d\alpha\frac{\log V}{\log L}$. To describe D_c, it is necessary to introduce the concept of "correlation sum" in the state space $C_\vartheta(\varepsilon)$, which can quantify the number of points x_i that are correlated with the others inside an sphere with radius ε. Intuitively, this sum can be interpreted as the probability of having pairs of points in a trajectory in the attractor inside the same sphere of radius ε. This event can be described by a uniform distribution, so it is possible to define the expression for the correlation sum using the Heaviside function, as in Equation 1:

$$C_\vartheta(\varepsilon) = \lim_{N\to\infty}\frac{1}{N^2}\sum_{i=1}^{N}\sum_{j=1}^{N}\Theta(\varepsilon - \|x_i - x_j\|) \quad (1)$$

where $\Theta(z) = \begin{Bmatrix} 0, & z \le 0 \\ 1, & z > 0 \end{Bmatrix}$ and $\|x_i - x_j\|$ is the Euclidean distance between every pair of points inside the sphere of radius ε.

In [16], Grassberger and Procaccia demonstrated that $C_\vartheta(\varepsilon)$ represents a volume measure, thus the correlation dimension is defined by Equation 2.

$$D_c = \lim_{\varepsilon\to 0}\left(\frac{\log(C_\vartheta(\varepsilon))}{\log(\varepsilon)}\right) \quad (2)$$

In the process of the estimation of D_c it is necessary to draw the figure $log(C_\vartheta(\varepsilon))$ *vs* $log(\varepsilon)$. The slope of the obtained straight line after a linear regression for the small values of ε is the correlation dimension D_c. A proper estimation of D_c must guarantee that the embedding dimension complies withthe expression $\vartheta = 2D_c + 1$ [17].

2.2 Maximum Lyapunov Exponent λ_{max}

This feature represents the average divergence rate of neighbor trajectories in the state space. Due to its robustness to noisy and short term signals, its estimation in this work has been developed according to the algorithm proposed by Rosenstein, et al. [18].

In this algorithm, once again the nearest neighbors to every point in the trajectories must be estimated. In this case, a neighbor must fulfill a temporal separation greater than the period of the time series, to be considered as a nearest neighbor. Considering every pair of neighbors on each trajectory as the representation of the initial conditions of the phenomena, the maximum Lyapunov exponent is estimated as the average separation rate of the nearest neighbors in the embedding space.

Applying the Oseledec's theorem [19], it is possible to state that two points in the attractor are separated at a rate of $d(t) = C{\cdot}e^{\lambda max t}$, where λ_{max} is the maximum Lyapunov exponent, $d(t)$ is the average divergence taken at the time t, and C is a normalization constant. Considering that the distance between the jth pair of nearest neighbors approximately diverge at a rate of λ_{max}, it is possible to obtain the expression $ln(d_j(i)) = ln(C_j)+\lambda_{max}(i\Delta t)$,where λ_{max} is the slope of the average line that appears when such expression is drawn on a logarithmic plane.

2.3 Hurst Exponent *H*

This parameter allows to analyze the long term dynamics of a system, stating the possible long term dependencies of the different elements in a given time series.

The estimation of H for a time series $x(n)$ with $n = 1, 2, ...,N$, is based on the rank scaling method, proposed by Hurst, et al. in [20]. Hurst demonstrated that the relation between the variation rank of the signal R, evaluated in a segment, and the standard deviation of the signal S is given by $\frac{R}{S}=cT^H$, where c is a scaling constant, T is the duration of the segment and H is the Hurst exponent. A value of H=0.5 indicate a completely uncorrelated series (Brownian time series), meaning that there is no correlation between any element and a future element and there is a 50% probability that future return values will go either up or down. A value of H in the range $0 < H < 0.5$ exists for time series with "anti-persistent behaviour", meaning that a single high value will probably be followed by a low value. Finally, a value of H in the range $0.5 < H < 1$ indicates positive autocorrelation, that is the time series is trending. If there is an increase from t_{n-1} to t_n there will probably be an increase from t_n to t_{n+1}. Of course, the same rule applies for decreases, where a decrease will tend to follow a decrease.

2.4 Lempel-Ziv Complexity *LZC*

As LZC is used for estimating the complexity of computer algorithms, it can also be used for the estimation of complexity in time series. Its implementation consists in finding the number of different "patterns" present in a given sequence. The algorithm only considers binary strings; for the practical case, it is necessary to assign 0 when the difference between two successive samples is negative; and 1 for the case when the difference is positive or null. The estimation of the LZC is based on the reconstruction of a sequence X by means of the copying and insertion of symbols in a new sequence. Considering the sequence $X = x_1, x_2,... x_n$, it is analyzed from left to right, the first bit of the string is taken by default as initial point. The variable S is defined to store the bits that have been inserted, i.e. at the beginning S only has x_1. The variable Q is defined for the accumulation of the bits that have been analyzed from left to right in the bit stream. On each iteration, the union of S and Q, denoted by SQ is generated. When the sequence Q does not belong to the string $SQ\pi$, which is the result of eliminating the last bit in the stream SQ, the insertion of the bits in the subset of symbols finishes. The value of LZC will be the number of subsets used for the representation of the original signal [21].

3 Classification System

This part has been divided on two subparts: (i) the use direct of NLD characterization on Hidden Markov Models (HMM) [12]; (ii) the transformation of HMM as parameterization (HMMK), and its classification by means of SVM [12].

The proposed classification system is based on the HMMs [12]. An HMM is a string of states $\boldsymbol{q}$, jointed with a stochastic process which takes values in an alphabet $\boldsymbol{S}$ which depends on $\boldsymbol{q}$. These systems evolve in time passing randomly from one state to another and issuing in each moment a random symbol of the $\boldsymbol{S}$ alphabet. When the system is in the state $\boldsymbol{q_{t-1} = i}$, it has a probability $\boldsymbol{a_{ij}}$ of moving to the state $\boldsymbol{q_t = j}$ in the next instant of time and the probability $\boldsymbol{b_j(k)}$ of issuing the symbol $\boldsymbol{o_t = vk}$ in time $\boldsymbol{t}$. Only the symbols issued by the state $\boldsymbol{q}$ are observable, nor the route or the sequence of states $\boldsymbol{q}$. That is why the HMM obtain the appellative "hidden", since the Markov process is not observable.

In this investigation, we have worked with a Bakis HMM, also called left to right, which is particularly appropriate for sequences. The Bakis HMM is especially appropriate for sequential sound data because the transitions between states are produced in a single direction. Therefore, it always advances during the transitions of its states, providing the ability to keep a certain order in this type of models with respect to the observations produced where the temporary distance among the most representative changes [22]. Finally, the HMM model used has been configured with a range from 5 to 20 states and 32 symbols per state, following the recommendations from [22].

The next step is the transformation of HMM probabilities, relating to the approach of the Kernel building [13]. With this goal, the aim is to merge the probability given by the HMM to the given discrimination by the classifier based on SVM. This score calculates the gradient with respect to HMM parameters, in particular, on the probabilities of emission of a vector of data x, while it is found in a certain state $q \in \{1,..,N\}$, given by the matrix of symbol probability in state q ($b_q(x)$), as it is indicated in equation 3;

$$P(x/q,\lambda) = b_q(x) \tag{3}$$

If the derivative of the logarithm of the previous probability is calculated (gradient calculation), the HMM kernel is obtained, whose expression is given by [22];

$$\frac{\partial}{\partial P(x,q)} \log P(x/q,\lambda) = \frac{\xi(x,q)}{b_q(x)} - \xi(q) \tag{4}$$

Details for the previous equation can be found in [21].

In our case, and using Discrete HMM (DHMM), $\xi(x,q)$ represents the number of times that it is localized in a state q, during the generation of a sequence, emitting a certain symbol x [22]. And $\xi(q)$ represents the number of times which it has been in q during the process of sequence generation [22]. These values are directly obtained from the forward backward algorithm, applied to DHMM by [10].

The application of this score (U_X) to the SVM is given by the expression of equation 5, using the technique of the natural gradient;

$$U_X = \nabla_{P(x,q)} \log P(x / q, \lambda) \quad (5)$$

where U_X defines the direction of maximum slope of the logarithm of the probability of having a certain symbol in a state.

Finally, the final decision will be done by Support Vector Machine (SVM) [13]. SVM is based on a bi-class system, in other words only two classes are considered. In particular for this present work, we have worked with 2 classes, pathological and control classes [13].A linear kernel has been used in our SVM.

4 Experimental Methodology

In this section, the used database, the experiments and the results will be shown.

4.1 Sound Collections

With the aim of eliminating balance problems between the classes, a total of 72 recordings of the "rainbow passage" which are included in the MEEI database are randomly chosen: 36 of the voice recordings are from patients with a variety of voice impairments such as organic, neurological, and traumatic disorders, and the remaining 36 are from healthy people. The speech samples are captured using a condenser microphone in a sound-proof booth and the distance between the microphone and the speakers is 15 cm. The original frequency sampling is 44100 Hz with a resolution of 16 bits, and they are down sampled at 25kHz using the CSL system model 4300.

4.2 Experiments and Results

NLD features described in Section 2 are calculated for each time window of 30 ms, forming four feature vectors (one per feature) per voice recording. A 20% hold-out cross validation were implemented, and it was repeated 10 times in order show the accuracy by mean and standard deviation in the Table 1. We used 20% of samples for training and the rest of samples for testing. Two classification approaches were evaluated, HMM with NLD features and SVM with the HMM transformation of NLD features (see Table 1).

Table 1. Accuracy for NLD features for our classification systems

Number of states	HMM accuracy	Linear SVM accuracy
5	79.24% ± 14.41	96.82% ± 6.36
10	88.69% ± 4.09	97.42% ± 6.44
15	84.73% ± 9.42	98.21% ± 2.36
20	86.50% ± 6.19	96.23% ± 4.59

Looking at the experiments, it can be observed that the transformation of the NLD features reaches better accuracy than the use of HMM with NLD characterization directly. It is also interesting to note the decrease of the standard deviation when using transformation of the NLD features, obtaining the smallest value of 2.36 for the better classification accuracy of 98.21%. Therefore, jointing HMM transformation and non-linear features is a good solution to the automatic detection of laryngeal pathologies in voice. If we compare our results with the state of the art ones we observe that our proposal works better. Hence it can be an option to be considered for the detection of laryngeal pathologies.

5 Conclusions and Future Work

In this work we propose a novel strategy for an automatic detection of laryngeal pathologies based on a fusion of HMM transformation of the nonlinear parameters and the use of a SVM classification system. After experiments, the accuracy reached up to 98.21%, applying a hold-out cross validation. Laryngeal voices have been detected using NLD, achieving better accuracy rates than other systems that are based on acoustic features and only NLD features. According to the results presented in this work, NLD features and its HMM transformation can be used for automatic detection of laryngeal pathologies.

The comparison versus the state of the art, for references, which have used the same database, show the improvement of our approach based on the parameterization and its classifier. In [2, 9, 10-11], authors have used temporal information (pitch, etc…), MFCC, jitter and statistics from NLD, but their accuracy rates don't reach the success of our proposal.

The next step will be to increase the number of experiments and different databases and different pathologies for verification approach and to use another SVM kernel.

Acknowledgments. This work has been supported by funds with reference "e-Voice" from "Cátedra Telefónica - ULPGC 2013". Besides, this work has been partially supported by the University of Vic under the grant R904, and under a predoctoral grant from the University of Vic to Mr. Esteve Gallego-Jutglà, ("Amb el suport de l'ajut predoctoral de la Universitat de Vic"). Juan Rafael Orozco Arroyave is under grants of "Convocatoria 528 para estudios de doctorado en Colombia, generación del bicentenario, 2011"financed by COLCIENCIAS.

References

[1] Hadjitodorov, S., Mitev, P.: A computer system for acoustic analysis of pathological voices and laryngeal diseases screening. Medical Engineering & Physics 24(6), 419–429 (2002)

[2] Godino, J.I., Fraile, R., Sáenz, N., Osma, V., Gómez, P.: Automatic detection of voice impairments from text-dependent continuous speech. Biomedical Signal Processing and Control 4(3), 176–182 (2009)

[3] Zhang, Y., Jiang, J.J.: Acoustic analyses of sustained and continuous voices from patients with laryngeal pathologies. Journal of Voice 22(1), 1–9 (2008)

[4] Titze, L.R.: Principles of Voice Production. Prentice Hall, Englewood Cliffs (1994)

[5] Giovanni, A., Ouaknine, M., Guelfucci, R., Yu, T., Zanaret, M., Triglia, J.M.: Nonlinear behavior of vocal fold vibration: the role of coupling between the vocal folds. Journal of Voice 13(4), 456–476 (1999)

[6] Henríquez, P., Alonso, J.B., Ferrer, M.A., Travieso, C.M., Godino, J.I., Díaz, F.: Characterization of Healthy and Pathological Voice Through Measures Based on Nonlinear Dynamics. IEEE Transactions on Audio, Speech, and Language Processing 17(6), 1186–1195 (2009)

[7] Ghazaleh, V., Farshad, A., Roozbeh, B.: Pathological assessment of patients' speech signals using nonlinear dynamical analysis. Journal of Computers in Biology and Medicine 40(1), 54–63 (2010)

[8] Arias, J.D., Godino, J.I., Sáenz, N., Osma, V., Castellanos, G.: Automatic detection of pathological voices using complexity measures, noise parameters, and mel-Cepstral coefficients. IEEE Transactions on Bio-medical Engineering 58(2), 370–379 (2011)

[9] Fourcin, A., Abberton, E.: Hearing and phonetic criteria in voice measurement: clinical applications. Logopedics Phoniatrics Vocology 33(1), 35–48 (2007)

[10] Vasilakis, M., Stylianou, Y.: Voice pathology detection based con short-term jitter estimations in running speech. Folia Phoniatrica et Logopaedica 61(3), 153–170 (2009)

[11] Orozco-Arroyave, J.R., Vargas-Bonilla, J.F., Alonso-Hernández, J.B., Ferrer-Ballester, M.A., Travieso, C.M., Henríquez, P.: Voice pathology detection in continuous speech using nonlinear dynamics. In: Proceedings of the 11th IEEE International Conference on Information Science, Signal Processing and their Applications (ISSPA), pp. 1030–1033 (2012)

[12] Rabiner, L.R.: A tutorial on Hidden Markov models and Selected Applications in Speech Recognition. Proceedings of the IEEE 77(2), 257–286 (1989)

[13] Taylor, J.S., Cristianini, N.: Support Vector Machines and other kernel-based learning methods. Cambridge University Press, Cambridge (2000)

[14] Shaheen, A., Roy, N., Jiang, J.J.: Nonlinear dynamic analysis of disordered voice:the relationship between the correlation dimension (D2) and pre-/post-treatment changein perceived dysphonia severity. Journal of Voice 24(3), 285–293 (2010)

[15] Jiang, J.J., Zhang, Y., McGilligan, C.: Chaos in Voice, From Modeling to Measurement. Journal in Voice 20(1), 2–17 (2006)

[16] Grassberger, P., Procaccia, I.: Measuring the strangeness of strange attractors. Physica D 9, 189–208 (1983)

[17] Abarbanel, H.D.I.: Analysis of observed chaotic data. Institute of Nonlinear Science (1999)

[18] Rosenstein, M.T., Collins, J.J., De Luca, C.J.: A practical method for calculatinglargest Lyapunov exponents from small data sets. Physica D 65, 117–134 (1993)

[19] Oseledec, V.A.: A multiplicative ergodic theorem. Lyapunov characteristic numbers fordynamical systems. Transactions of Moscow Mathematic Society 19, 197–231 (1968)

[20] Hurst, H.E., Black, R.P., Simaika, Y.M.: Long-term storage: an experimental study, 1st edn., Constable, London (1965)

[21] Kaspar, F., Shuster, H.G.: Easily calculable measure for complexity of spatiotemporalpatterns. Physical Review A 36(2), 842–848 (1987)

[22] Briceño, J.C.: Metodología para la Identificación de Formas mediante las Transformación Markoviana de su Contorno. Ph.D. Thesis. University of Las Palmas de Gran Canaria (2013)

Feature Extraction Approach Based on Fractal Dimension for Spontaneous Speech Modelling Oriented to Alzheimer Disease Diagnosis

Karmele López-de-Ipiña[1], Harkaitz Egiraun[1], Jordi Sole-Casals[2], Miriam Ecay[3], Aitzol Ezeiza[1], Nora Barroso[1], Pablo Martinez-Lage[3], and Unai Martinez-de-Lizardui[1]

[1] Department of System Engineering and Automation, University of the Basque Country, Spain
karmele.ipina@ehu.es
[2] Digital Technologies Group, Universitat de Vic
[3] Neurology Department CITA-Alzheimer Foundation

Abstract. Alzheimer's disease (AD) is the most prevalent form of progressive degenerative dementia; it has a high socio-economic impact in Western countries. The purpose of our project is to contribute to earlier diagnosis of AD and better estimates of its severity by using automatic analysis performed through new biomarkers extracted from non-invasive intelligent methods. The methods selected in this case are speech biomarkers oriented to Spontaneous Speech. Thus the main goal of the present work is feature search in Spontaneous Speech oriented to pre-clinical evaluation for the definition of test for AD diagnosis. Nowadays our feature set offers some hopeful conclusions but fails to capture the nonlinear dynamics of speech that are present in the speech waveforms. The extra information provided by the nonlinear features could be especially useful when training data is scarce. In this work, the Fractal Dimension (FD) of the observed time series is combined with lineal parameters in the feature vector in order to enhance the performance of the original system.

Keywords: Nonlinear Speech Processing, Alzheimer disease diagnosis, Spontaneous Speech, Fractal Dimensions.

1 Introduction

Alzheimer's Disease (AD) is the most common type of dementia among the elderly. It is characterized by progressive and irreversible cognitive deterioration with memory loss and impairments in judgment and language, together with other cognitive deficits and behavioral symptoms. The cognitive deficits and behavioral symptoms are severe enough to limit the ability of an individual to perform everyday professional, social or family activities. As the disease progresses, patients develop severe disability and full dependence. An early and accurate diagnosis of AD helps patients and their families to plan for the future and offers the best opportunity to treat the symptoms of the disease. According to current criteria, the diagnosis is expressed with different degrees

T. Drugman and T. Dutoit (Eds.): NOLISP 2013, LNAI 7911, pp. 144–151, 2013.

of certainty as possible or probable AD when dementia is present and other possible causes have been ruled out. The diagnosis of definite AD requires the demonstration of the typical AD pathological changes at autopsy [1,2,3]. The clinical hallmark and earliest manifestation of AD is episodic memory impairment. At the time of clinical presentation, other cognitive deficits are present in areas like language, executive functions, orientation, perceptual abilities and constructional skills [4,5]. All these symptoms lead to impaired performance in everyday activities. Approaches to the early diagnosis of AD have in the past few years made significant advances in the development of reliable clinical biomarkers [6]. However, the cost and technology requirements make it impossible to apply such biomarkers to all patients with memory complaints. Given these problems, non-invasive Intelligent Techniques of diagnosis may become valuable tools for early detection of dementia. Non-technical staff in the habitual environments of the patient could use these methodologies, which include e.g. Automatic Spontaneous Speech Analysis (ASSA) without altering or blocking the patients' abilities, as the spontaneous speech involved in these techniques is not perceived as a stressful test by the patient. Moreover, these techniques are very low-cost and do not require extensive infrastructure or the availability of medical equipment. They are thus capable of yielding information easily, quickly, and inexpensively [7,8].In addition to the loss of memory, one of the major problems caused by AD is the loss of language skills. We can meet different communication deficits in the area of language, including aphasia (difficulty in speaking and understanding) and anomia (difficulty in recognizing and naming things). The specific communication problems the patient encounters depend on the stage of the disease [3,4,5]:

1. First Stage or Early Stage (ES): difficulty in finding the right word in spontaneous speech. Often remains undetected.
2. Second Stage or Intermediate Stage (IS): impoverishment of language and vocabulary in everyday use.
3. Third Stage or Advanced Stage (AS): answers sometimes very limited and restricted to very few words.

The main goal of the present work is feature search in Spontaneous Speech oriented to pre-clinical evaluation for the definition of test for AD diagnosis. These features will define control group (CR) and the three AD levels. One of the most relevant nonlinear techniques for Automatic Speech Recognition (ASR) is the consideration of the Fractal Dimension (FD) of the speech signal as a feature to be used in the training process. The interest on fractals in speech date back to the mid-80's [9], and they have been used for a variety of applications, including consonant/vowel characterization [10-11], speaker identification [12], and end-point detection [13], even for whispered speech [14].The approach of this work is to improve the system developed in our previous work [8] augmenting the features with FD. The FD is one of the most significant features which describe the complexity of a system and could help in the detection of subtle changes for early diagnosis. Moreover this feature has in the ability to capture the dynamics of the system and thus relevant variations in speech utterances. More precisely, an implementation of Higuchi's algorithm [18] in order to add this new feature to the set that feeds the training process of the model.

The rest of this paper is organized this way: In Section 2, the materials are presented. Section 3 explains the methodology of the experiments, Section 4 shows the experimental results, and finally, conclusions are presented in Section 5.

2 Materials

This study is focuses on early AD detection and its objective is the identification of AD in the pre-clinical (before first symptoms) and prodromic (some very early symptoms but no dementia) stages. The research presented here is a complementary preliminary experiment to define thresholds for a number of biomarkers related to spontaneous speech. Feature search in this work is oriented to pre-clinical evaluation for the definition of test for AD diagnosis Obtained data will complement the biomarkers of each person.

Trying to develop a new methodology applicable to a wide range of individuals of different sex, age, language and cultural and social background, we have built up a multicultural and multilingual (English, French, Spanish, Catalan, Basque, Chinese, Arabian and Portuguese) database with video recordings of 50 healthy and 20 AD patients (with a prior diagnosis of Alzheimer) recorded for 12 hours and 8 hours respectively. The age span of the individuals in the database was 20-98 years and there were 20 males and 20 females. This database is called AZTIAHO. All the work was performed in strict accordance with the ethical guidelines of the organizations involved in the project. The recordings consisted of videos of Spontaneous Speech – people telling pleasant stories or recounting pleasant feelings as well as interacting with each other in friendly conversation. The recording atmosphere was relaxed and non-invasive. The shorter recording times for the AD group are due to the fact that AD patients find speech more of an effort than healthy individuals: they speak more slowly, with longer pauses, and with more time spent on efforts to find the correct word and uttering speech disfluencies or break messages. In the advanced stage of the disease, they find this effort tiring and often want to stop the recording. We complied with their requests. The video was processed and the audio extracted in wav format (16 bits and 16 Khz). The first step was removing non-analyzable events: laughter, coughing, short hard noises and segments where speakers overlapped. Next, background noise was removed using denoiser adaptive filtering. After the pre-processing, about 80% of the material from the control group and 50% of the material from the AD group remained suitable for further analysis. The complete speech database consists of about 60 minutes of material for the AD group and about 9 hours for the control. The speech was next divided into consecutive segments of 60 seconds in order to obtain appropriate segments for all speakers, resulting finally in a database of about 600 segments of Spontaneous Speech. Finally for experimentation from the original database, a subset of 20 AD patients was selected (68-96 years of age, 12 women, 8 men, with a distribution in the three stages of AD as follows: First Stage [ES=4], Secondary Stage [IS=10] and Tertiary stage [AS=6]). The control group (CR) was made up of 20 individuals (10 male and 10 female, aged 20-98 years) representing a wide range of speech responses. This subset of the database is called AZTIAHORE.

3 Methods

3.1 Feature Extraction

3.1.1 Features Oriented to Automatic Spontaneous Speech Analysis (ASSA)

Spoken language is one of the most important elements defining an individual's intellect, social life, and personality; it allows us to communicate with each other, share knowledge, and express our cultural and personal identity. Spoken language is the most spontaneous, natural, intuitive, and efficient method of communication among people. Therefore, the analysis by automated methods of Spontaneous Speech (SS – free and natural spoken communication), possibly combined with other methodologies, could be a useful non-invasive method for early AD diagnosis. The analysis of Spontaneous Speech fluency is based on three families of features (SSF set), obtained by the Praat software package [15] and software that we ourselves developed in MATLAB. For that purpose, an automatic Voice Activity Detector (VAD) [16,17] has extracted voiced/unvoiced segments as parts of an acoustic signal.

These three families of features include: 1) *Duration:* the histogram calculated over the most relevant voiced and unvoiced segments, the average of the most relevant voiced/unvoiced, voiced/unvoiced percentage and spontaneous speech evolution along the time dimension, and the voiced and unvoiced segments' mean, max and min; 2) *Time domain:* short time energy; 3) *Frequency domain, quality*: spectral centroid.

The energy of a signal is typically calculated on a short-time basis, by windowing the signal at a particular time, squaring the samples and taking the average. The spectral centroid is commonly associated with the measure of the brightness of a sound. This measure is obtained by evaluating the "center of gravity" using the Fourier transform's frequency and magnitude information.

3.1.2 Fractal Dimension

Most of the fractal systems have a characteristic called self-similarity. An object is self-similar if a close-up examination of the object reveals that it is composed of smaller versions of itself. Self-similarity can be quantified as a relative measure of the number of basic building blocks that form a pattern, and this measure is defined as the Fractal Dimension. There are several algorithms to measure the Fractal Dimension, but this current work focus on the alternatives which are specially suited to time series analysis and which don't need previous modelling of the system. Two of these algorithms are Higuchi [18] and Katz [19], named after their authors. Higuchi was choice because it has been reported to be more accurate in previous works with under-resourced conditions [20]. Higuchi [18] proposed an algorithm for measuring the Fractal Dimension of discrete time sequences directly from the time series $x(1),x(2),\ldots,x(n)$. Without going into detail, the algorithm calculates the length $L_m(k)$ (see Equation 1) for each value of m and k covering all the series.

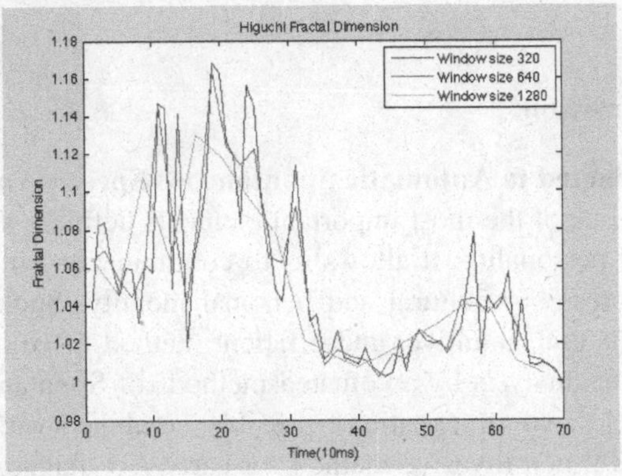

Fig. 1. Higuchi Fractal Dimension (HFD) for an AD signal for different window sizes

$$L_m(k) = \frac{\sum_{i=1}^{\left\lfloor \frac{N-m}{k} \right\rfloor} \left| x(m+ik) - x(m+(i-1)k) \right| (n-1)}{\left\lfloor \frac{N-m}{k} \right\rfloor k} \tag{1}$$

After that, a sum of all the lengths $L_m(k)$ for each k is determined with Equation 2.

$$L(k) = \sum_{m=1}^{k} L_m(k) \tag{2}$$

And finally, the slope of the curve ln(L(k))/ln(1/k) is estimated using least squares linear best fit, and the result is the Higuchi Fractal Dimension (HFD).

3.1.3 Feature Sets

In the experimentation four feature set will be used: 1) SSF: Spontaneous Speech features; 2) SSF+HFD1: SSF set and Higuchi Fractal Dimension (HFD). 3) SSF+HFD2: SSF set, HFD, maximum HFD, minimum HFD, variance HFD and standard deviation HFD.

3.2 Automatic Classification Method

The automatic classification of speech is based on the Multi Layer Percetron (MLP). WEKA software [21] has been used in carrying out the experiments. The results were evaluated using Accuracy (Acc) and Classification Error Rate (CER) measurements. For the training and validation steps, we used *k*-fold cross-validation with *k*=10. Cross validation is a robust validation for variable selection [22]. These features will define the CR group and the three AD levels. The main goal of the present work is feature search in Spontaneous Speech oriented to pre-clinical evaluation for the definition of test for AD diagnosis. These features will define CR group and the three AD levels.

Table 1. Global Accuracy (%) with MLP for Automatic Spontaneous Speech Analysis and different Neuron Number in Hidden Layer (NNHL) and Training Step (TS)

NNHL	TS	SSF	SSF+HFD1	SSF+HFD2
50	500	75.96	76.74	85.27
	1000	75.96	76.44	83.72
	1500	74.41	76,44	82.94
100	500	76.74	79.06	85.27
	1000	75.96	77,51	86.04
	1500	75.96	77,51	**86.82**
150	500	75.96	79,84	84.49
	1000	75.96	79.06	83.72
	1500	74.41	79.06	82.84

4 Experimental Results

The task was Automatic Classification, with the classification targets being: healthy speakers without neurological pathologies and speakers diagnosed with AD. The experimentation is carried out with AZTIAHORE. The results have been analyzed with regard to: global results and also to AD level results.

1. Global System Results: The results are satisfactory for this study. The new fractal features improve the system, being SSF+HFD2 the best option. This feature set includes both HFD and its detailed variations, which are able to model non-linear signal features (Table 1).
2. MLP Selection: Table 1 shows detailed results with regard to the selection of MLP characteristics. The best results are obtained with one hidden layer of 100 neurons with 1500 training steps.
3. Window Size: For HFD algorithm three different window size have been used: 1280, 640 and 320 samples. The best results have been obtained for a window size of 320 samples mainly for SSF+HFD2 set.

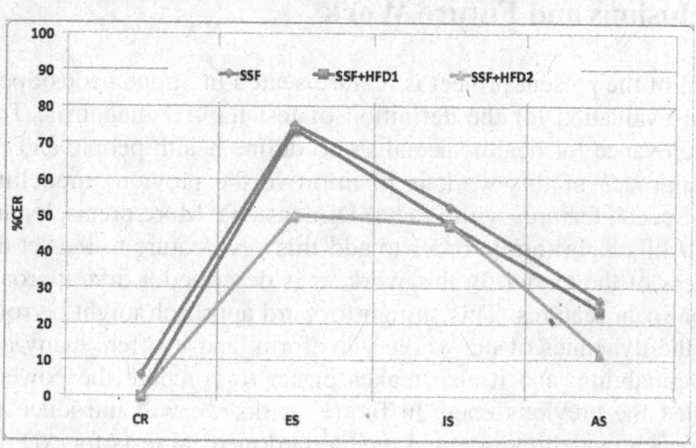

Fig. 2. Classification Error Rate (%) with MLP for different classes: CR, ES, IS and AS

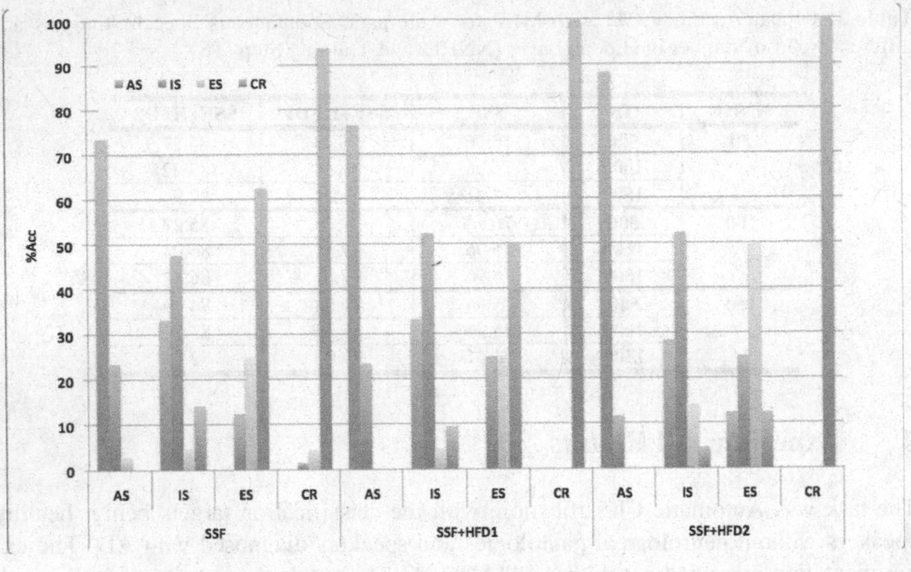

Fig. 3. Accuracy (%) with MLP for different classes: CR, ES, IS and AS

4. <u>Classes' Results:</u> SSF+HFD2 set obtains the best results for all classes (Figure 2). This set improves also the classification with regard to early detection (ES class, (Figure 3). IS has also better rate to discriminate middle AD level. The model is able also to discriminate pathological and non-pathological segments in each patient.

Health specialists note the relevance of the system's ability to carry out both the analysis of independent biomarkers as spontaneous speech and/or the integral analysis of several biomarkers.

5 Conclusions and Future Work

The main goal of the present project is feature search in Spontaneous Speech oriented to pre-clinical evaluation for the definition of test for AD diagnosis. These features are of great relevance for health specialists to define health people and the three AD levels. The approach of this work is to improve the previous modelling based on Spontaneous Speech features with Fractal Dimensions. More precisely, an implementation of Higuchi's algorithm in order to add this new feature to the set that feeds the training process of the model. In this work, it is described a first approach to the inclusion of nonlinear features. This straightforward approach might be robust in terms of capturing the dynamics of the whole waveform, and it offers many advantages in terms of computability, and it also makes easier to compare the power of the new features against the previous ones. In future works we will introduce new features relatives to speech modelling oriented to standard medical tests for AD diagnosis and to emotion response analysis. We will also model Fractal Dimension by other algorithms based on previous works in Automatic Speech Recognition [20].

References

1. Mc Kahn, G., Drachman, D., Folstein, M., Katzman, R., Price, D., Stadlan, E.M.: Clinical diagnosis of Alzheimer's disease: report of the NINCDS-ADRDA Workgroup on Alzheimer's disease 24, 939–944 (1984)
2. McKhann, G.M., et al.: The diagnosis of dementia due to Alzheimer's disease: Recommendations from the National Institute on Aging-Alzheimer's Association workgroups on diagnostic guidelines for Alzheimer's disease. Alzheimers Dement 7(3), 263–269 (2011)
3. Van de Pole, L.A., et al.: The effects of age and Alzheimer's disease on hippocampal volumes, a MRI study. Alzheimer's and Dementia, 1(1, suppl. 1), 51 (2005)
4. Morris, J.C.: The Clinical Dementia Rating (CDR): current version and scoring rules. Neurology 43, 2412b–2414b (1993)
5. American Psychiatric Association, Diagnostic and Statistical Manual of Mental disorders, 4th Edition Text Revision, Washington DC (2000)
6. Alzheimer's Association, `http://www.alz.org/`
7. Faundez-Zanuy, M., et al.: Biometric Applications Related to Human Beings: There Is Life beyond Security. Cognitive Computation (2012), doi:10.1007/s12559-012-9169-9
8. López de Ipiña, K., Alonso, J.B., Solé-Casals, J., Barroso, N., Faundez, M., Ecay, M., Travieso, C., Ezeiza, A., Estanga, A.: Alzheimer Disease Diagnosis based on Automatic Spontaneous Speech Analysis. In: Proceedings of NCTA 2012, Barcelona (2012)
9. Pickover, C.A., Khorasani, A.: Fractal characterization of speech waveform graphs. Comput. Graph. 10(1), 51–61 (1986)
10. Martinez, F., Guillamon, A., Martinez, J.: Vowel and consonant characterization using fractal dimension in natural speech. In: Proceedings of NOLISP 2003 (2003)
11. Langi, A., Kinsner, W.: Consonant Characterization Using Correlation Fractal Dimension for Speech Recognition. In: Proceedings of Communications, Power, and Computing. Conference Proceedings. IEEE (1995)
12. Nelwamondo, F.V., Mahola, U., Marwola, T.: Multi-Scale Fractal Dimension for Speaker Identification Systems. WSEAS Trans. Syst. 5(5), 1152–1157 (2006)
13. Li, Y., Fan, Y., Tong, Q.: Endpoint Detection In Noisy Environment Using Complexity Measure. In: Proceedings of the 2007 International Conference on Wavelet Analysis and Pattern Recognition, Beijing, China (2007)
14. Chen, X., Zhao, H.: Fractal Characteristic-Based Endpoint Detection for Whispered Speech. In: Proceedings of the 6th WSEAS International Conference on Signal, Speech and Image Processing, Lisbon, Portugal (2006)
15. Praat: doing Phonetics by Computer, `http://www.fon.hum.uva.nl/praat`
16. Voice Activity Detector algorithm (VAD), `http://www.mathwork.com`
17. Solé, J., Zaiats, V.: A Non-Linear VAD for Noisy Environment. Cognitive Computation 2(3), 191–198 (2010)
18. Higuchi, T.: Approach to an irregular time series on the basis of the fractal theory. Physica D 31277, 283 (1988)
19. Katz, M.: Fractals and the analysis of waveforms. Comput. Biol. Med. 18(3), 145–156 (1988)
20. Ezeiza, A., de Ipiña, K.L., Hernández, C., Barroso, N.: Enhancing the feature extraction process for automatic speech recognition with fractal dimensions. Cognitive Computation (2012)
21. WEKA, `http://www.cs.waikato.ac.nz/ml/weka/`
22. Picard, R., Cook, D.: Cross-Validation of Regression Models. Journal of the American Statistical Association 79(387), 575–583 (1984), doi:10.2307/2288403. JSTOR 2288403

Robust Hierarchical and Sparse Representation of Natural Sounds in High-Dimensional Space

Simon Brodeur and Jean Rouat

Groupe de recherche en Neuroscience Computationelle
et Traitement Intelligent des Signaux (NECOTIS),
Département génie électrique et génie informatique, Université de Sherbrooke,
Sherbrooke QC Canada J1K 2R1
{Simon.Brodeur,Jean.Rouat}@usherbrooke.ca

Abstract. Based on general findings from the field of neuroscience and their algorithmic implementations using signal processing, information theory and machine learning techniques, this paper highlights the advantages of modelling a signal in a sparse and high-dimensional feature space. The emphasis is put on the hierarchical organisation, very high dimensionality and sparseness aspects of auditory information, that allow unsupervised learning of meaningful auditory objects from simple linear projections. When the dictionaries are learned using independent component analysis (ICA), it is shown that specific spectro-temporal modulation patterns are learned to optimally represent speech, noise and tonal components. In a noisy isolated-word speech recognition task, sparse and high-dimensional features have shown greater robustness to noise compared to a standard system based on a dense low-dimensional feature space. This brings new ways of thinking in the field of recognition and classification of acoustic signals.

1 Introduction

It is typically assumed that complex sounds such as speech are composed of fundamental and intermediate sub-units (e.g. phones, syllables), where composition allows to generate higher-level auditory objects such as words. It is still unclear how to define such auditory objects exactly, as well as their temporal and spectral spans (i.e. scales) in the acoustic signals. In realistic environments, multiple sources of useful and noisy signals are mixed together and this situation brings a large ambiguity in the estimation of the underlying components. It is known from the field of neuroscience that neuronal population sparseness and high-dimensional representation are basic properties of the brain [1], as well as the hierarchical processing of speech in the central auditory system [2] and language-related areas of the cerebral cortex [3]. Closer to human-engineered systems, the use of a greater acoustic context integration in a hierarchical framework was recently a major success in the recognition of spontaneous speech [4]. Sparse and high-dimensional spaces can also exhibit a large discriminative power if the dictionary learning algorithm is chosen properly [5]. Unsupervised learning algorithms should be preferred so that the estimated components are intrinsically

T. Drugman and T. Dutoit (Eds.): NOLISP 2013, LNAI 7911, pp. 152–159, 2013.

adapted to the statistics of the signals. Commonly used signal processing and information theory algorithms allow to derive a sparse and high-dimensional representation of any acoustic signal, which are expected to lead to better model quality and increased robustness [6]. Recently, hierarchical spectro-temporal feature extraction methods integrating all those aspects have shown the ability to outperform standard approaches in a continuous digit recognition task [7]. However, dimensionality reduction is often used prior to the classifier [8], removing many advantages of having a model parameter space of similar properties (i.e. sparse and high-dimensional).

In this paper, the aim is to transform the acoustic signal into a meaningful and robust object-based representation, adapted to the recognition or classification task at hand. Leveraging the sparse and high-dimensional space within the classifier, and not just during feature extraction, is also thought to be a solution to mitigate the interference and variability induced by undesirable acoustic components. The focus will only be on components defined by specific spectro-temporal modulation patterns. Such patterns can be easily learned in an unsupervised manner from natural sounds, and often exhibit the property of being localised in both time and frequency [9,10]. This means that specific and independent event-like components are extracted from the input signals, leading to a better modelling of speech in background additive noises.

2 Proposed Approach

The cochleagram is a spectro-temporal representation of sounds where parameters of the band-pass filters are derived from neurophysiological observations of the cochlea, favouring a better temporal resolution (as a trade-off to spectral resolution) compared to the commonly used narrow-band spectrogram. Amplitude modulations at the output of each filter then carry the information. In the experiments, the output of a 64-channel Gammatone filterbank [11] covering the frequency range [80, 8000 Hz] was post-processed with half-wave rectification, followed by a cubic-root compression and low-pass filtering [12] with frequency cut-off at 40 Hz. Sampled local patches (windows) were taken from the resulting image and used as input to a hierarchical dictionary-based projection stage. The cochleagram was used because its slow-modulation patterns emphasize stable structures, such as syllabic segmentation cues in speech [13].

The mathematical formulation of the hierarchical projection is as follows: Let $\mathbf{S}^{(h)}$ be a set of n signals of dimensionality N, input to the hierarchical level h, i.e. $\mathbf{S}^{(h)} = [\mathbf{s}_1 \dots \mathbf{s}_n] \in \Re^{N \times n}$. Let $\mathbf{D}^{(h)}$ a dictionary of K bases of dimensionality N, at hierarchical level h, i.e. $\mathbf{D}^{(h)} = [\mathbf{d}_1 \dots \mathbf{d}_K] \in \Re^{N \times K}$. The dimensionality N is allowed to vary across levels, to perform either a dimensionality reduction or expansion (with overcomplete representation). The projection of coefficients from the previous level on the dictionary produces a new set of coefficients $\mathbf{C}^{(h)} = [\mathbf{c}_1 \dots \mathbf{c}_n] \in \Re^{K \times n}$, as shown in equation (1) and valid for $h > 0$. The Moore-Penrose pseudo-inverse $\left(\mathbf{D}^{(h)}\right)^+$ estimates $\left(\mathbf{D}^{(h)}\right)^{-1}$, because $\mathbf{D}^{(h)}$ is a non-square matrix.

$$\mathbf{C}^{(h)} = \left(\mathbf{D}^{(h)}\right)^{+} \cdot \mathbf{S}^{(h-1)} = \left(\mathbf{D}^{(h)^T}\mathbf{D}^{(h)}\right)^{-1} \mathbf{D}^{(h)^T} \cdot \mathbf{S}^{(h-1)}$$
$$\text{for all abstract levels, i.e. where } h > 0 \qquad (1)$$

The hierarchical projection has here a spatial aspect, where adjacent patches are concatenated and the resulting vector projected on the next level. The reformulation following coordinates (i, j) in the local referential of each level is given by equation (2). At the first level $h = 0$, input signals correspond to patches $\mathbf{W}^{(i,j)} \in \Re^{L_C \times L_T}$ distributed spatially over the spectro-temporal representation, and converted to column vectors $\mathbf{X}^{(i,j)} \in \Re^{L_C \cdot L_T}$. The constants L_C et L_T are respectively the number of channels and temporal samples covered by each patch (e.g. $L_C = 16$ channels by $L_T = 40$ ms). For all level $h > 0$, the projection is applied on the concatenated coefficients of the lower level $h - 1$. The constants $M_{(h)}$ et $N_{(h)}$ define the number of adjacent projection patches considered respectively on the spectral (channel) and temporal dimensions. Figure 1 illustrates more intuitively the spatial aspect of the projection. Overlapping between patches is also possible and should be considered to avoid the discontinuities caused by the spectro-temporal framing process.

$$\mathbf{C}_{(h)}^{(i,j)} = \begin{cases} \mathbf{D}_{(0)}^{+} \cdot \mathbf{X}^{(i,j)} & \text{if } h = 0, \\ \mathbf{D}_{(h)}^{+} \cdot \Big\Vert_{i=0}^{M_{(h)}-1} \Big\Vert_{j=0}^{N_{(h)}-1} \mathbf{C}_{(h-1)}^{(i,j)} & \text{if } h > 0. \end{cases} \qquad (2)$$

The symbol $\Big\Vert$ defines the concatenation operator over P adjacent matrices of coefficients:

$$\Big\Vert_{i=0}^{P-1} \mathbf{C}^{(i)} = \left[\mathbf{C}^{(i)}\ \mathbf{C}^{(i+1)} \ldots \mathbf{C}^{(i+P-1)}\right] \qquad (3)$$

Independent component analysis (ICA) [14] is a linear decomposition algorithm commonly used for blind source separation [15] and denoising of speech signals [16]. The FastICA implementation [17] was used in the experiments to learn the dictionary $\mathbf{D}^{(h)}$ at each level h. The training was performed level-wise and went successively from the lowest-level dictionary to the higher-level dictionaries. This hierarchical integration scheme allows to derive bases that represent parts of auditory objects of increasing temporal and spectral contexts, without a priori knowledge of the characteristics of the sounds. Figure 2 shows that specific objects are extracted depending on the category of the sound (e.g. speech, music, nature), with only 1 hour of training data per category. For all categories, the dictionary size K for each of the 3 levels were respectively 128, 256 and 256. The dictionary learning was performed on at least 25,000 examples of coefficient vectors randomly sampled for each level. The initial window $\mathbf{W}^{(i,j)}$ of size $L_C = 16$ channels by $L_T = 40$ ms included no overlapping. There was the concatenation of $M_{(h)} = 2$ spectrally-distributed patches and $N_{(h)} = 3$ temporally-distributed

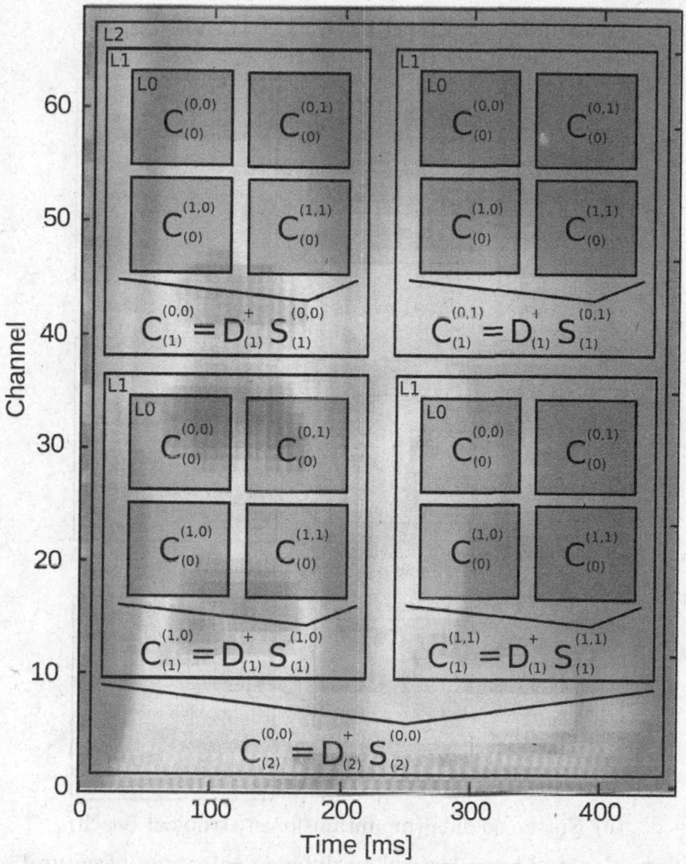

Fig. 1. Hierarchical projection by successive linear decompositions on dictionaries. The concatenation of adjacent projections at lower levels aim to extract from the cochleagram features covering increasing spectral and temporal contexts. In the given example, $M_{(h)} = N_{(h)} = 2$ for $h = \{1, 2\}$, the concatenation of 4 adjacent patches at each level. The figurative contours of patches are shown over the cochleagram corresponding to the pronunciation of "seven" by a male speaker. Note that in reality, levels L1 and L2 will never cover more area than what is defined by L0 (in shaded).

patches. With this configuration, the last projection level covered all 64 channels and 360 ms of temporal context. This object-based representation seems adequate for the recognition and classification of any acoustic signal, regardless of the particular dynamics.

3 Experiment: Isolated-Word Recognition in Noise

To assess the robustness and versatility of sparse and hierarchical features derived from a cochleagram, a speaker-independent isolated-word recognition system was validated on the TI46 database [18]. All 46 classes (i.e. digits, alphabet,

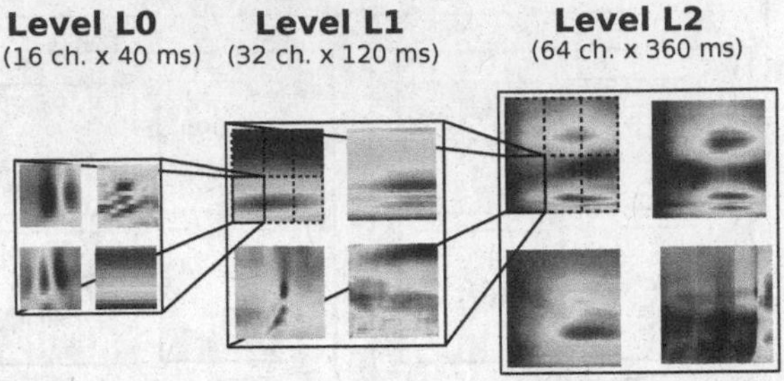

(a) Isolated words (TI46 corpus)

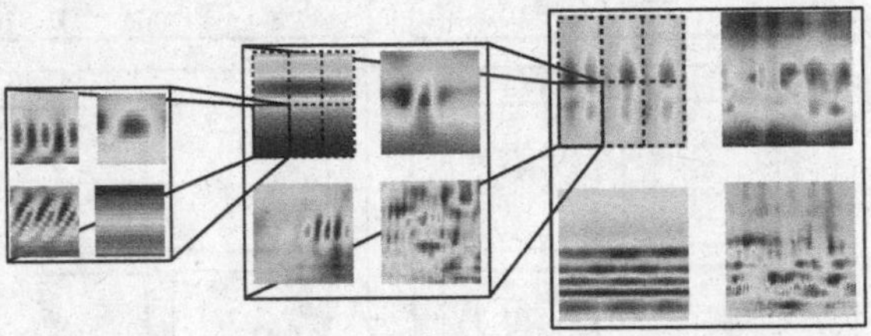

(b) Classical music (Vivaldi)

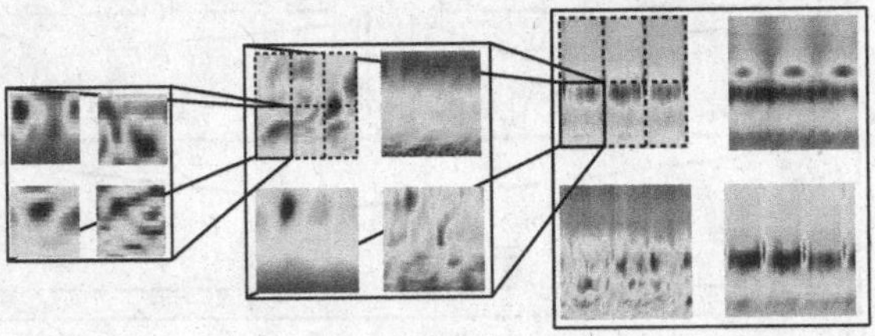

(c) Nature sounds (mountain forest, tropical beach)

Fig. 2. Configuration and bases learned on different categories of natural sounds for a classification task. Noticeable differences in the spectro-temporal interpretation of the bases appear between categories, regardless of the level in the hierarchical projection. Many high-level bases trained on speech extract configurations of formants, while bases trained on music extract constant harmonics and short tonal sequences. Very diversified bases are obtained for nature sounds.

commands) were considered in order to increase the difficulty of the task. The reference system was based on a commonly used Mel-frequency cepstral coefficients (MFCC) frontend, with standard parameters [19]. It consisted of a 39-dimensional dense representation of the amplitude spectrum profile and its local evolution. This greatly contrasted with the proposed system (SPARSE) who featured a 700-dimensional sparse representation, although both approaches accounted for the temporal context. The MFCC features included the first and second-order temporal derivatives of the cepstral coefficients, while the SPARSE features embedded the temporal context directly through the hierarchical projection. To create the observation vectors for the MFCC system, there was a 25 ms temporal framing with 10 ms overlap between frames. For the SPARSE system, the coefficients of the projections at all levels were taken every 10 ms in the acoustic signal, resulting in a greater overlapping. The dictionary size K for each of the 3 levels were respectively 64, 128 and 256. The dictionary learning was performed with independent component analysis (ICA) on at most 25,000 examples of coefficient vectors randomly sampled for each level. The initial window $\mathbf{W}^{(i,j)}$ of size $L_C = 32$ channels by $L_T = 40$ ms used 50% temporal and spectral overlapping. There was the concatenation of $M_{(h)} = 2$ spectrally-distributed and $N_{(h)} = 2$ temporally-distributed patches. With this configuration, the last projection level covered all 64 channels and 160 ms of temporal context, allowing the extraction of supra-segmental or syllabic features. Both systems used a whole-word modelling technique implemented with Hidden Markov models (HMMs) [20], having the same left-right topology and number of states. For a given utterance, the classification scheme selected the model with the highest likelihood of having generated the observation sequence. The influence of each feature extractor and classifier meta-parameter (e.g. number of mixtures) on the recognition rate of clean speech was validated for both systems, so as to obtain the optimal configurations[1].

The proposed system (SPARSE) and reference system (MFCC) were validated using a multi-condition training, with realistic additive noises from the NOISEX-92 database [21]. The training was thus performed under noisy speech (20 dB SNR) and included all noise types (i.e. the system is noise-independent). The recognition rates in table 1 show that the usage of a sparse high-dimensional representation improves the generalisation capacity compared to a dense representation. There is also a minimal degradation of performance when tested on clean speech, where the SPARSE and MFCC systems achieved respective recognition rates of 87.0% and 41.0%. This shows that noise during training didn't impair the ability to learn robust speech components for the SPARSE system, whereas the artificially-induced variability was problematic for the standard approach. The main explanation is that the MFCC system models the noise within the same dimensions as of the useful speech signal, because the representation is constrained to be dense and low-dimensional. The SPARSE system uses a sparse and high-dimensional representation derived from hierarchical projections, such that speech and noise components are distributed on different subspaces (i.e. subsets of dimensions), as shown by figure 3. In the parameter space of the acoustic model (for each state of the HMMs) where the statistical independence of the dimensions is assumed, the noise components then have their own probability density functions. The variability induced by noise is concentrated within a subspace, rather than being accounted by the probability density functions of speech components.

The results support similar findings where bases learned on a non-ideal noisy training dataset can significantly improve performances by modelling the noise components [7]. In this paper, the attention is however brought on the reason to avoid dimensionality reduction at the input of the classifier, such as principal component analysis (PCA) used in [7]. The reason is that this inhibits all advantages of working in high-dimensional space (e.g. linear separability).

[1] In this paper, the details of the configurations are omitted due to the lack of space.

Table 1. Recognition rates with training and testing in adverse conditions, for different types of additive noises and signal-to-noise ratios (SNRs). The results show that a system built on a sparse and high-dimensional representation (SPARSE) allows a better generalisation over a wide range of SNRs and noise types, compared to a reference system (MFCC) using a low-dimensional representation. This reflects the inherent ability to separate speech and noise components in high-dimensional spaces.

(a) Babble noise

SNR	0 dB	10 dB	20 dB	40 dB
MFCC	**10.3**	34.6	55.0	59.9
SPARSE	9.6	**63.3**	**88.8**	**88.1**

(b) Engine room noise

SNR	0 dB	10 dB	20 dB	40 dB
MFCC	**8.2**	**43.5**	62.9	61.5
SPARSE	3.5	37.5	**83.1**	**79.9**

(c) Car noise

SNR	0 dB	10 dB	20 dB	40 dB
MFCC	46.6	56.5	59.8	43.1
SPARSE	**67.2**	**87.6**	**88.6**	**87.8**

(d) White noise

SNR	0 dB	10 dB	20 dB	40 dB
MFCC	**7.6**	38.8	58.4	45.1
SPARSE	3.4	**43.0**	**84.6**	**87.0**

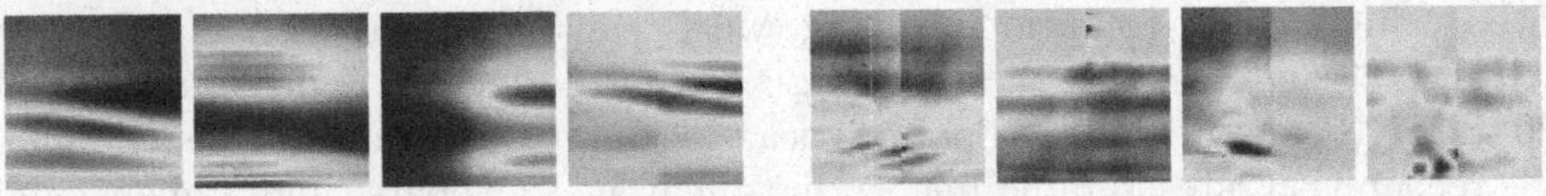

(a) Speech bases (64 ch. x 160 ms) (b) Noise bases (64 ch. x 160 ms)

Fig. 3. Example of bases learned from noisy speech (20 dB SNR) using the proposed approach. There is a clear separation between (a) the components of speech, and (b) the components of noise. This non-overlapping subspace property allows to model any useful signal in a parameter space with reduced dimension-wise variability, because of the minimal interference from non-useful components.

4 Conclusion

A sparse and high-dimensional representation of speech was proposed based on hierarchical linear projections that aim to extract localized spectro-temporal modulation patterns. Each level-specific dictionary is intrinsically adapted to the statistics of the input signal, because independent component analysis (ICA) was used for the unsupervised learning of the dictionary bases. It was observed that for a variety of sound categories (e.g. speech, music, nature), bases extracted relevant auditory objects from the signal, such as formant transitions (at low level) and formant configurations (at high level). When such bases were trained and used as input features to a noisy isolated-word speech recognition system, a separation of speech and noise components occurred in both feature and classifier parameter spaces. The proposed system has shown greater robustness to noise compared to a standard system based on a dense low-dimensional feature space. This highlights the fact that sparse and high-dimensional spaces have useful properties to exploit (e.g. overcompleteness, linear separability), and should be pushed forward for recognition and classification tasks on natural sounds and speech.

Acknowledgments. Authors would like to thank Compute Canada for the allocated high-performance computing resources. This work received funding from the Natural Sciences and Engineering Research Council (NSERC) of Canada and from the Fonds de Recherche Québec en Nature et Technologies (FRQ-NT).

References

1. Molotchnikoff, S., Rouat, J.: Brain at work: Time, Sparseness and Superposition Principles. Frontiers in Bioscience (Landmark Edition) 17(1), 583–606 (2012)
2. Winer, J., Schreiner, C.: The inferior colliculus. Springer (2005)
3. Hickok, G., Poeppel, D.: The cortical organization of speech processing. Nature Reviews Neuroscience 8(5), 393–402 (2007)
4. Dahl, G.E., Yu, D., Deng, L., Acero, A.: Context-Dependent Pre-Trained Deep Neural Networks for Large-Vocabulary Speech Recognition. IEEE Transactions on Audio, Speech, and Language Processing 20(1), 30–42 (2012)
5. Tosic, I., Frossard, P.: Dictionnary Learning: What is the right representation for my signal? IEEE Signal Processing Magazine 28(2), 27–38 (2011)
6. Klein, D.J., König, P., Körding, K.P.: Sparse Spectrotemporal Coding of Sounds. EURASIP Journal on Advances in Signal Processing 2003(7), 659–667 (2003)
7. Heckmann, M., Domont, X., Joublin, F., Goerick, C.: A Hierarchical Framework for Spectro-Temporal Feature Extraction. Speech Communication 53, 736–752 (2011)
8. Papageorgiou, C.P., Oren, M., Poggio, T.: A general framework for object detection. In: Proceedings of ICCV, pp. 555–562 (1998)
9. Lewicki, M.: Efficient coding of natural sounds. Nat. Neurosci. 5(4), 356–363 (2002)
10. Lee, J., Lee, T., Jung, H., Lee, S.: On the efficient speech feature extraction based on independent component analysis. Neural Process. Lett. 15(3), 235–245 (2002)
11. Hohmann, V.: Frequency analysis and synthesis using a Gammatone filterbank. Acta Acustica united with Acustica 88(3), 433–442 (2002)
12. Avendaño, C., Deng, L., Hermansky, H., Gold, B.: The analysis and representation of speech. Speech Processing in the Auditory System 18, 63–100 (2004)
13. Greenberg, S., Kingsbury, B.: The modulation spectrogram: In pursuit of an invariant representation of speech. In: Proceedings of ICASSP, pp. 1647–1650 (1997)
14. Hyvärinen, A., Oja, E.: Independent component analysis: algorithms and applications. Neural Networks 13(4-5), 411–430 (2000)
15. Obradovic, D., Deco, G.: Blind signal separation revisited. In: Proceedings of the 36th IEEE Conference on Decision and Control, pp. 1591–1596 (1997)
16. Lee, J., Jung, H., Lee, T., Lee, S.: Speech enhancement with MAP estimation and ICA-based speech features. Electronics Letters 36(17), 1506–1507 (2000)
17. Hyvärinen, A.: Fast and robust fixed-point algorithms for independent component analysis. IEEE Transactions on Neural Networks 10(3), 626–634 (1999)
18. Liberman, M., et al.: TI 46-Word Linguistic Data Consortium, Philadelphia (1993)
19. Young, S., Evermann, G., Kershaw, D., Moore, G., Odell, J., Ollason, D., Valtchev, V., Woodland, P.: The HTK Book Version 3.4. Cambridge University Press (2009)
20. Rabiner, L.: A tutorial on hidden Markov models and selected applications in speech recognition. Proceedings of the IEEE 77(2), 257–286 (1989)
21. Varga, A., Steeneken, H.: Assessment for automatic speech recognition: II. NOISEX-92: A database and an experiment to study the effect of additive noise on speech recognition systems. Speech Communication 12(3), 247–251 (1993)

On the Importance of Pre-emphasis and Window Shape in Phase-Based Speech Recognition

Erfan Loweimi[1], Seyed Mohammad Ahadi[1],
Thomas Drugman[2], and Samira Loveymi[3]

[1] Speech Processing Research Laboratory (SPRL),
Electrical Engineering Department, Amirkabir University of Technology,
424 Hafez Ave, Tehran, Iran
[2] TCTS Lab., University of Mons, 31, Boulevard Dolez, B7000 Mons, Belgium
[3] Computer Engineering Department, Buali Sina University, Hamedan, Iran
{eloveimi,sma}@aut.ac.ir, thomas.drugman@umons.ac.be,
s.loveymi@basu.ac.ir

Abstract. This paper aims at investigating the potentials of the phase spectrum in automatic speech recognition (ASR). We show that speech phase spectrum could potentially provide features with high discriminability and robustness. Out of such belief and to realize a higher portion of the phase spectrum potentials, we propose two simple amendments in two common blocks in feature extraction, namely pre-emphasis and windowing, without changing the workflow of the algorithms. Recognition tests over Aurora 2 indicate up to 11.2% and 14.7% performance improvement in average in the presence of both additive and convolutional noises for phase-based MODGDF and CGDF features, respectively. It proves the high potentials of the phase spectrum in robust ASR.

Keywords: Phase spectrum, speech recognition, feature extraction, discriminability, robustness, pre-emphasis, window shape.

1 Introduction

There is a general belief among the signal processing researchers that phase spectrum does not play a significant role in speech processing. Taking a glance on different areas of this field shows that only the magnitude spectrum is put under the center of attention. Phase spectrum is either directly transferred to the output without any processing (e.g. in speech enhancement) or discarded immediately after taking Fourier transform (e.g. in feature extraction for speech recognition).

Looking for the reasons behind the aversion toward speech phase spectrum, three issues could be found. In 19th century Ohm [1] and Helmholtz [2] stated that human ear performs Fourier analysis and only the magnitude spectrum is utilized in perception process. It implies that human ear is phase deaf. This misleading historical consideration, to some extent, biased the researchers against the sounds phase spectrum.

The second problem with phase spectrum, which seems to be the main one, is phase wrapping. It overwhelmingly complicates the interpreting and consequently

T. Drugman and T. Dutoit (Eds.): NOLISP 2013, LNAI 7911, pp. 160–167, 2013.

processing of the phase spectrum and creates a chaotic and noise-like shape lacking any meaningful trend or extrema points while the magnitude spectrum is much more understandable and matches well with our psychoacoustical knowledge.

The third problem is that it has been shown that speech phase spectrum is informative only in long frames while in short frames (20 to 40 ms) it does not carry notable deal of information [3]-[6]. Based on the current paradigms in signal processing, the non-stationary signals should be decomposed into short frames in which the stationarity assumption is held. As a result, working with long frame lengths does not make sense. Incidentally, this trend was remained unreasoned for about three decades.

Nonetheless, a number of phase (group delay)-based features such as modified group delay function (MODGDF) [7] and chirp group delay function (CGDF) [8] were proposed for automatic speech recognition (ASR). The recognition rates of these methods are comparable with MFCC in the presence of additive noise. However, channel noise distortion may highly degrade their performance. A missing point is that if this is really a fact that the phase spectrum is not informative in short frames, why are the recognition rates of the phase-based features comparable with those of the magnitude-based ones? This point also remained unaddressed and unreasoned.

In [9], we justified the two aforementioned questions and showed that, in contrast to the prevailing belief, speech phase spectrum is highly informative, even in short frames. This finding implies that much unexplored potential exists in the speech phase spectrum. In this paper, we aim at dealing with the possible capabilities of the phase spectrum in extracting strong features for ASR. We will show that this spectrum could potentially provide features with high discrimination abilities and robustness. After proving this point, we will propose two modifications in pre-emphasis and windowing stages, without changing the main workflow of the MODGDF and CGDF, aiming at realizing a higher portion of the phase spectrum potentials. Notable recognition rate improvements supports the idea that speech phase spectrum is worth more in ASR than what has been thought of it.

The rest of this paper is organized as follows. In Section 2 we will investigate the possible capabilities of the phase spectrum in speech recognition. In Section 3 two modifications which could provide more efficient usage of the phase spectrum information will be discussed. Section 4 includes the simulation results as well as their analysis and Section 5 concludes the paper.

2 Potentials of Speech Phase Spectrum in Feature Extraction

Usefulness of the phase spectrum in feature extraction, in the first degree, depends on both its information content and noise sensitivity in the short frame lengths. High information content and low noise sensitivity could potentially lead to features with high discriminability and robustness, respectively. The second concern is ambiguities in the behavior of this spectrum due to the phase wrapping because it complicates understanding and modeling of it. To some extent, this problem could be alleviated while working with GDF, since it can be computed without encountering the wrapping problem. It can also provide an estimate of the power spectrum which is an understandable and important function. However, GDF's spiky nature is an issue. MODGDF and CGDF are two possible solutions for dealing with this problem.

For checking potentials of the phase spectrum in providing features with high discriminability, we should determine its information content in short frame lengths. The information content of phase (or magnitude) spectrum could be evaluated by reconstructing the signal only from that spectrum. The quality and/or intelligibility of the reconstructed signal can be considered as an indicator of such information.

In [9], we have investigated this issue and shown that speech phase spectrum, even in short frame lengths, could be highly informative. In fact, we have shown that the quality and/or intelligibility of the phase-only reconstructed speech in all frame lengths, including short ones (16 and 32 ms), could be very high. It is an evidence for the capabilities of the speech phase spectrum in developing features with high discriminability. Moreover, the high recognition rates of the phase-based methods in the clean/matched condition could be justified considering this point.

The second issue, which is really challenging, is robustness. Although most of the features perform well in the clean/matched conditions, reduction of SNR leads to rapid degradation of their performance. In [10], we have investigated the sensitivity of the phase and magnitude spectra to (additive) noise and have shown that for speech signal decomposed into frame lengths of 32 ms, replacing the phase spectrum of noisy signal in 0 dB SNR, with its clean version could improve the quality up to 0.8 in PESQ scale. Similarly, substituting the magnitude spectrum with its clean version in the same situation could elevate the quality up to 2.1 in PESQ scale.

This observation may be interpreted in two ways. First, the quality of the signal primarily pertains to the magnitude spectrum and the phase spectrum's relation with the quality of the signal and consequently its importance is not as high as the magnitude spectrum. Second, the phase spectrum is less deviated from its clean version after contaminating the signal with noise whereas the magnitude spectrum is more sensitive to such disturbances. The first justification does not appear to be true since we have already shown that even in short frame lengths speech phase spectrum is highly informative. It seems that the second idea is the right case. This supports the high capabilities of the phase spectrum in providing more robust features in comparison with the magnitude spectrum due to its lower noise-sensitivity.

3 Possible Improvement for Phase-Based Features

Despite the aforementioned potentials of the speech phase spectrum, the features which are extracted from it such as MODGDF [7] and CGDF [8] do not show eye-capturing performance. Although their discrimination abilities seem to be high, their robustness is not remarkable. However, based on the arguments presented in the previous section, it appears logical to expect to reach better recognition rates for the phase-based features. In other words, phase spectrum seems to have something more than what is captured by these features.

The neglected and important point which should be noted is that due to the predominant role of the magnitude spectrum in speech processing, common stages of feature extraction algorithms such as pre-emphasis and windowing are based on the properties of the magnitude spectrum, not the phase spectrum. In this section, we will show that modification and adjustment of these two ostensibly simple blocks could lead to more efficient realization of the phase spectrum capabilities.

3.1 Pre-emphasis and Phase Spectrum

Generally, pre-emphasis is performed for flattening the magnitude spectrum and balancing the high and low frequency components. The point is that this task is defined based on the magnitude spectrum properties. However, the power spectrum which is estimated by the GDF, as depicted in Figure 1, is relatively flat. Therefore, pre-emphasis appears not to be a much needed block in phase-based speech processing. Nevertheless, since the magnitude-based paradigms are prevailed in speech processing, even in the case of phase-based features, pre-emphasis is used, without any modification. As illustrated in Figure 1, the group delay-based estimations of the power spectrum are relatively flat (far less negative slope) and pre-emphasis does not show any particular balancing influence. Hamming window is applied in this stage.

3.2 Window Shape and Phase Spectrum

Generally windowing is performed for getting a better smear-leakage trade-off. In [9], we have investigated the effect of 13 windows on the quality/intelligibility of the phase and magnitude-only reconstructed speech over different frames. In case of magnitude-only signal reconstruction, Hamming window results in the maximum quality. However, this window does not seem to be a good option for working with the phase spectrum since the quality of the phase-only reconstructed signal after applying it was quite poor. We observed that Chebyshev window with dynamic range of 25 to 35 dB results in the maximum quality for the phase-only reconstructed signal.

Changing the window from Hamming to Chebyshev (25 dB) in frame length of 32 ms, improved the quality of the phase-only reconstructed speech up to 1.4 in PESQ scale [9] which is quite significant and proves the impact of the windowing in working with phase spectrum. However, despite the notable influence of the window shape and unsuitability of the Hamming window, in all of the phase-based features extraction methods, such as MODGDF and CGDF, this window is applied. It appears that utilizing more suitable windows could be considered as a factor which may help in reaching more effective realization of the speech phase spectrum potentials.

Figures 2 and 3 depict the magnitude spectrum, MODGDF, and CGDF after applying rectangular and Chebyshev windows (30 dB), respectively, with and without pre-emphasis. As seen, in case of Chebyshev window, more distortion is introduced and only around the formant frequencies notable activities could be observed. It could have both positive and negative outcomes. In clean condition the introduced distortion may negatively affect the performance. On the other hand, it potentially could help in better retaining of the formants frequencies structure and also to some degrees alleviates the noise influence on the power spectrum. As a result, it could lead to more robust features. Our recognition test results interestingly verify these points.

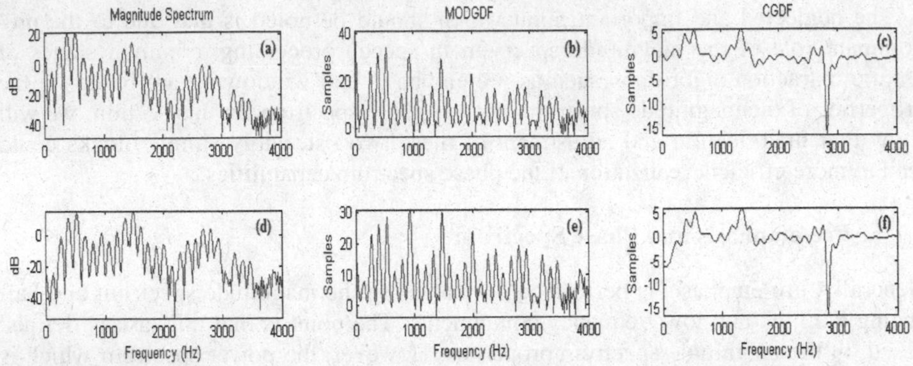

Fig. 1. Influence of application of pre-emphasis and Hamming window on the magnitude spectrum, MODGDF, and CGDF. (a), (b), (c) without pre-emphasis, (d), (e), and (f) with pre-emphasis (0.97).

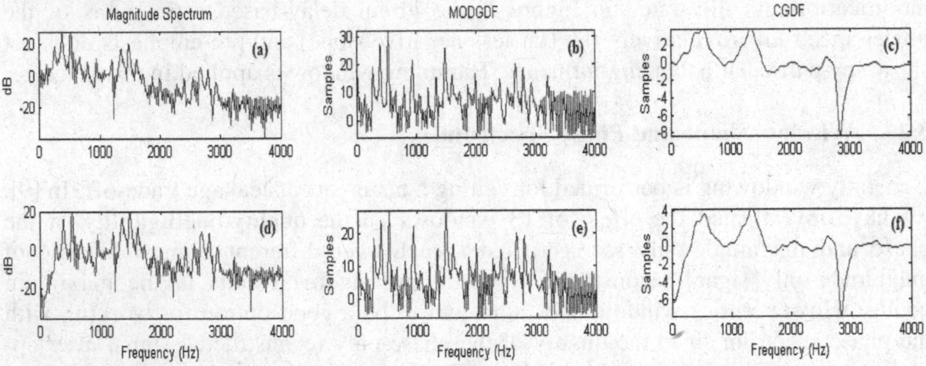

Fig. 2. Influence of application of pre-emphasis and Rectangular window on the magnitude spectrum, MODGDF, and CGDF. (a), (b), (c) without pre-emphasis, (d), (e), and (f) with pre-emphasis (0.97).

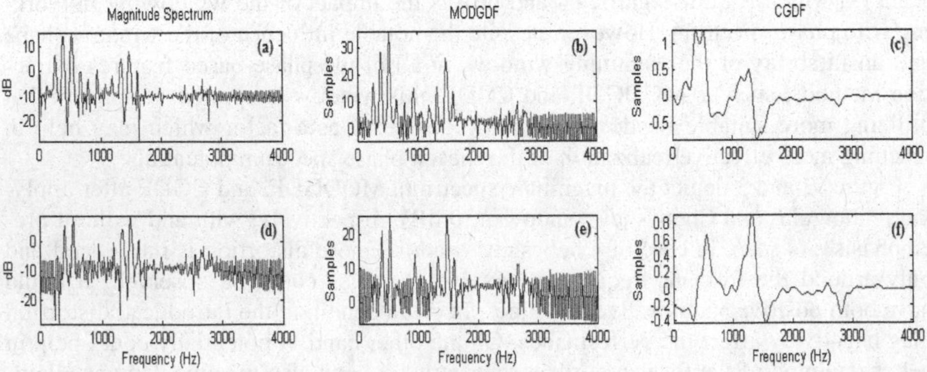

Fig. 3. Influence of application of pre-emphasis and Chebyshev window on the magnitude spectrum, MODGDF, and CGDF. (a), (b), (c) without pre-emphasis, (d), (e), and (f) with pre-emphasis (0.97).

4 Experimental Evaluation

4.1 Dataset and Feature Extraction Setting

Performance of the features is assessed on the Aurora 2 database [11]. It includes three test sets (A, B, and C) with SNRs varying from -5 dB to 20 dB by steps of 5 dB. A and B test sets include additive noises while speech signals in C test set are contaminated with both additive and channel distortions. We used the clean-data training in all our experiments and standard training of HMMs carried out with HTK [12].

For feature extraction techniques, we have used the default parameters reported in their respective publications. For investigating the effect of pre-emphasis, we have checked the effect of applying 0.97 ($a_{0.97}$), zero ($a_{0.0}$), and $r(1)/r(0)$ ($a_{r1/r0}$) [13] (where $r(n)$ is autocorrelation of the signal) as pre-emphasis coefficient. For examining the influence of window, Hamming, Rectangular, and Chebyshev (30 dB) windows are applied. Feature vector consists of 36 elements including 12 static coefficients as well as Δ and $\Delta\Delta$ components. CMN is also performed in all cases. Table 1 shows the average of the recognition rates of 20, 15, 10, 5, and 0 dB SNRs in percent.

4.2 Results and Discussion

As seen in Table 1 and Figure 4, modifying the pre-emphasis and window can notably affect the performance of both phase and magnitude-based features. Results should be compared with those of applying 0.97 as pre-emphasis coefficient and Hamming window which are displayed in italic and underlined form in Table 1.

For phase-based features (MODGDF and CGDF) both pre-emphasis and window shape seem to be influential. As previously mentioned, phase-based features return poor results in the presence of the convolutional noises. However, by applying adaptive pre-emphasis (r_1/r_0) as well as appropriate window this shortcoming is highly alleviated and their performance in the presence of both additive and channel noise notably improves. As seen, over the C test set, performance is elevated up to 11.2% and 14.7% for MODGDF and CGDF, respectively. This is quite remarkable and proves that there is much potential in the phase spectrum which has remained unused. For realizing it, we should rethink some prevalent facts and paradigms, however.

Contrary to MODGDF and CGDF, pre-emphasis is not very influential in case of MFCC and discarding this block even seems to be a better choice, especially in the presence of channel noise. For the C test set in which the high frequency components are strengthened to some extent by MIRS filter [11], further amplifying these components by pre-emphasis does not appear to be an appropriate action. That is why discarding this block in this case leads to better results. On the other hand, changing the window has a noticeable positive effect on the performance of MFCC. Chebyshev window (30 dB) clearly improves the performance of MFCC and results in interesting recognition rates. In addition, applying Rectangular window without performing pre-emphasis leads to good results and practically, it is a more economical choice.

Another interesting point is that based on our previous study [9] in which the Hamming window results in maximum quality in the magnitude-only speech reconstruction, we were expecting maximum recognition rates for magnitude-based features using this window. However, as seen in Table 1, this is not the case. It shows that the required smear-leakage trade-off which is expected to be provided by the window, not only depends on whether we are working with the magnitude or phase spectrum, but also depends on the task. In speech reconstruction all the information either related to vocal tract or excitation component are important whereas in recognition only a specific part of the speech data are significant. So, the window which more helps in capturing the required information leads to higher performance.

Table 1. Average (0-20 dB) word accuracy in percent

		Test Set A			Test Set B			Test Set C		
		$a_{0.0}$	$a_{0.97}$	$a_{r1/r0}$	$a_{0.0}$	$a_{0.97}$	$a_{r1/r0}$	$a_{0.0}$	$a_{0.97}$	$a_{r1/r0}$
MFCC	*Ham.*	62.8	62.3	62.7	67.3	67.2	66.9	64.8	63.4	60.0
	Rect.	68.9	65.2	65.4	71.7	68.4	69.6	71.9	69.6	67.3
	Ch(30dB)	69.6	70.3	**71.1**	68.2	73.0	**73.1**	**75.6**	68.3	73.4
Max Improvement (%)		**+ 8.8%**			**+ 5.9%**			**+12.2%**		
MODGDF	*Ham.*	59.2	63.1	64.0	60.4	67.0	67.7	52.3	57.6	62.6
	Rect.	64.6	66.0	66.4	65.4	69.6	69.8	64.5	62.6	67.4
	Ch(30dB)	64.0	68.1	**69.9**	62.6	70.1	**71.2**	67.1	62.3	**68.8**
Max Improvement (%)		**+ 6.8%**			**+ 4.2%**			**+ 11.2%**		
CGDF	*Ham.*	66.1	62.3	63.1	67.4	67.2	67.8	68.5	55.1	61.9
	Rect.	67.5	63.0	64.2	68.4	68.3	68.9	69.6	55.8	62.5
	Ch(30dB)	66.4	67.2	**69.0**	65.6	71.1	**72.1**	**69.8**	58.1	66.9
Max Improvement (%)		**+ 6.7**			**+ 4.9%**			**+ 14.7%**		

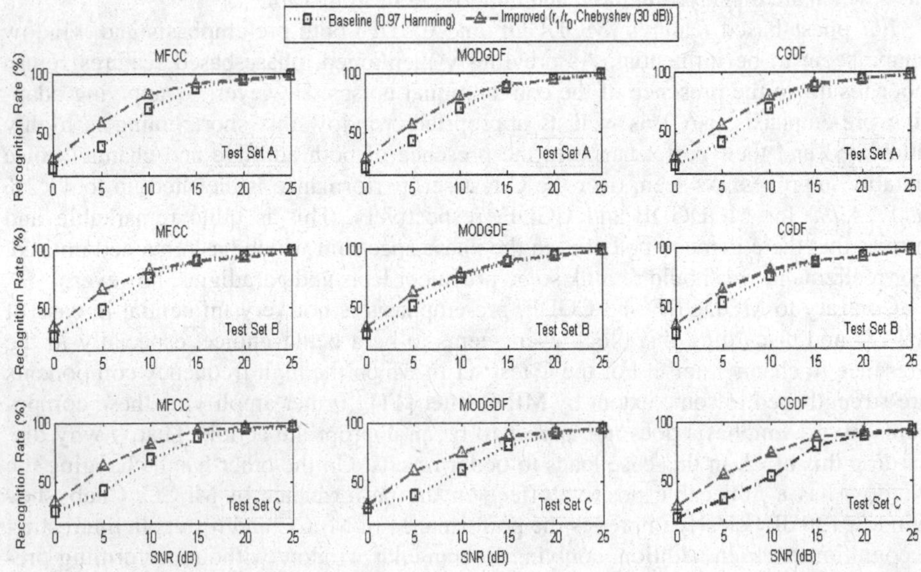

Fig. 4. Performance improvement after modifying pre-emphasis and window shape vs. SNR

Figure 4 depicts comparison between the recognition rates of the traditional scenario (0.97 + Hamming) with those of our proposed scenario ($\frac{r1}{r0}$ + Chebyshev (30 dB))

versus SNR for different test sets. As seen, pre-emphasis and window shape could notably affect the robustness of both phase-based and magnitude-based features. It should be noted that in clean condition traditional scenario slightly works better. However, by decreasing the SNR, the benefits of our modifications stand out. The last point is that these blocks do not provide any new information and only pave the way for employing the phase and magnitude spectra information in a more efficient way.

5 Conclusion

The main target of this paper was investigating the potentials of the phase spectrum in speech recognition. We showed that phase spectrum could result in features with high discriminability and robustness. Out of such idea, we proposed some modifications in two common blocks of feature extraction algorithms aiming at reaching more efficient realization of the phase spectrum potentials. The recognition tests results indicated that pre-emphasis and windowing could notably affect the performance of the phase-based (and also magnitude-based) features. Looking for novel models which explicate the phase spectrum behavior is a broad avenue for future researches.

References

1. Ohm, G.S.: Uber die Definition des Tones, nebst daran geknupfter Theorie der Sirene und ahnlicher tonbildender Vorrichtungen. Ann. Phys. Chem. 59, 513–565 (1843)
2. von Helmholtz, H.L.F.: On the Sensations of Tone (English translation by A.J. Ellis). Longmans, Green and Co., London (1912) (original work published 1875)
3. Oppenheim, A.V., Lim, J.S.: The importance of phase in signals. Proc. IEEE 69, 529–541 (1981)
4. Wang, D.L., Lim, J.S.: The unimportance of phase in speech enhancement. IEEE Trans. Acoust. Speech Signal Process, ASSP 30(4), 679–681 (1982)
5. Liu, L., He, J., Palm, G.: Effects of phase on the perception of intervocalic stop consonants. Speech Commun. 22(4), 403–417 (1997)
6. Paliwal, K.K., Alsteris, L.D.: Usefulness of phase spectrum in human speech perception. In: Proc. of Eurospeech, pp. 2117–2120 (September 2003)
7. Murthy, H.A., Gadde, V.: The modified group delay function and its application to phoneme recognition. In: Proc. ICASSP, pp. 68–71 (April 2003)
8. Bozkurt, B., Couvreur, L., Dutoit, T.: Chirp group delay analysis of speech signals. Speech Commun. 49(3), 159–176 (2007)
9. Loweimi, E., Ahadi, S.M., Sheikhzadeh, H.: Phase-only speech reconstruction using short frames. In: Proc. InterSpeech, Florence, Italy (2011)
10. Loweimi, E., Ahadi, S.M., Loveymi, S.: On the importance of phase and magnitude spectra in speech enhancement. In: Proc. ICEE, Tehran, Iran (May 2011)
11. Hirsch, H.G., Pearce, D.: The AURORA experimental framework for the performance evaluation of speech recognition Systems under noisy conditions. In: Proc. ASR 2000, Paris, France (September 2000)
12. Young, S.J., Kershaw, D., Odell, J., Ollason, D., Valtchev, V., Woodland, P.: The HTK Book Version 3.4. Cambridge University Press, Cambridge (2006)
13. Makhoul, J., Viswanathan, R.: Adaptive preprocessing for linear predictive speech compression systems. Journal of Acoustic Society of America 55, 475 (1974)

Smoothed Nonlinear Energy Operator-Based Amplitude Modulation Features for Robust Speech Recognition

Md. Jahangir Alam[1,2], Patrick Kenny[2], and Douglas O'Shaughnessy[1]

[1] INRS-EMT, University of Quebec, Montreal (QC) Canada
[2] CRIM, Montreal (QC) Canada
{jahangir.alam,patrick.kenny}@crim.ca, dougo@emt.inrs.ca

Abstract. In this paper we present a robust feature extractor that includes the use of a smoothed nonlinear energy operator (SNEO)-based amplitude modulation features for a large vocabulary continuous speech recognition (LVCSR) task. SNEO estimates the energy required to produce the AM-FM signal, and then the estimated energy is separated into its amplitude and frequency components using an energy separation algorithm (ESA). Similar to the PNCC (Power Normalized Cepstral Coefficients) front-end, a medium duration power bias subtraction (MDPBS) is used to enhance the AM power spectrum. The performance of the proposed feature extractor is evaluated, in the context of speech recognition, on the AURORA-4 corpus, which represents additive noise and channel mismatch conditions. The ETSI advanced front-end (ETSI-AFE), power normalized cepstral coefficients (PNCC), Cochlear filterbank cepstral coefficients (CFCC) and conventional MFCC and PLP features are used for comparison purposes. Experimental speech recognition results on the AURORA-4 task depict that the proposed method is robust against both additive and different microphone channel environments.

Keywords: Amplitude modulation, SNEO, Speech recognition, AURORA-4.

1 Introduction

Traditional Mel Frequency Cepstral Coefficients (MFCCs) [1] and Perceptual Linear Prediction (PLP) [2] features are frequently used as a low-dimensional set of features to represent short segments of speech. Since it was first conceived in 1974, MFCC has remained a powerful sound representation tool as it partly mimics human perception of sound color [3], and thus is popular in the signal processing community in almost its original form. MFCCs and PLP features along with the standard Hidden Markov Model (HMM)-based speech recognizer perform well if the training and test environments are the same. Different operating conditions during signal acquisition (e.g., channel response, handset type, additive background noise, reverberation, etc.) lead to feature mismatch across training and testing and thereby degrade the performance of the MFCCs and PLP-based speech recognition systems.

The methods to compensate for the effects of environmental mismatch can be implemented at the front-end (or feature extractor) or at the back-end or both. The main

T. Drugman and T. Dutoit (Eds.): NOLISP 2013, LNAI 7911, pp. 168–175, 2013.

goal of a robust feature extractor for a recognition task is to develop features that retain useful variability in speech while minimizing variability due to environmental mismatch. Various robust feature extractors are employed in speech recognition tasks such as the ETSI advanced front-end (ETSI-AFE) [4], power normalized cepstral coefficients (PNCC) [5], and the robust feature extractors proposed in [6, 7, 8].

Amplitude modulation-frequency modulation (AM-FM) of speech signal plays an important role in speech perception and recognition [8]. The AM-FM model has been successfully used in various areas of signal processing. Specifically in speech processing this model has been applied for speech analysis and modeling [9, 10, 11, 17, 19], speech synthesis [10], emotion, speech and speaker recognition [12-13, 14-15, 16-18]. A standard approach to the AM-FM demodulation problem is to use the Hilbert transform and the related Gabor's analytic signal [20]. An alternative approach is to use a nonlinear energy operator (NEO) to track the energy required to generate an AM-FM signal and separate it into amplitude and frequency components. The NEO approach to demodulation has many attractive features such as simplicity, efficiency, and adaptability to instantaneous signal variations [9]. In this paper we use smoothed nonlinear energy operator (SNEO) [20, 21]-based amplitude modulation features for a robust large vocabulary continuous speech recognition (LVCSR) task. The advantage of SNEO (or NEO) is that it uses only a few samples of the input signal to estimate the energy required to generate an AM-FM signal and separate it into amplitude and frequency components without imposing any stationarity assumption as done by linear prediction or Fourier transforms [8]. The SNEO approach has smaller computational complexity and faster adaptation due to its instantaneous nature [28]. Since SNEO (or NEO) uses only a few samples to estimate the energy, it is sensitive to noise. We use a medium duration power bias subtraction (MDPBS) technique, proposed in [5], to enhance estimated AM power. Power function nonlinearity with a coefficient of 0.07 is applied as it has been found in [5] that it is more robust than the logarithmic nonlinearity used in a conventional MFCC framework. The final features are obtained by taking the Discrete Cosine Transform (DCT) and normalizing the features using the full utterance-based cepstral mean normalization method.

The AURORA-4 LVCSR corpus [22] is used for performance evaluation of the proposed feature extractor. To compare the performances, the following front-ends are used: conventional MFCC, PLP, ETSI-AFE [4], power normalized cepstral coefficient (PNCC) [5], Cochlear filterbank cepstral coefficients (CFCC) [24], and the robust front-end (RFE) of [6]. Experimental results on the AURORA-4 LVCSR task show that the proposed feature extractor outperforms all the front-ends mentioned above.

2 Overview of the Proposed Feature Extractor

The various steps of the proposed feature extractor are shown in Fig. 1. In this method, processing of a speech signal begins with pre-processing (including DC removal and pre-emphasis, typically using a first-order high-pass filter with a transfer function of $(1-0.97z^{-1})$). The pre-processed speech signal is then framed (analysis frame length is 25 msec with a frame shift of 10 msec) and windowed using a Symmetric Hamming window. Each frame of the speech signal is then decomposed into a

C-channel (here, C = 40 is used) gammatone filterbank covering the frequency range of 100-3800 Hz (sampling frequency = 8000 Hz). The AM power spectrum for each gammatone channel is then estimated using the smoothed nonlinear energy operator (SNEO). Before applying the medium duration power bias subtraction (MDPBS) [5] to enhance the AM power spectrum, the AM power across each frame and channel is normalized using 95th percentile power [5]. The 13-dimensional static features, obtained after applying a power function nonlinearity, using a coefficient of 0.07 and discrete cosine transform (DCT), are normalized using the conventional cepstral mean normalization method.

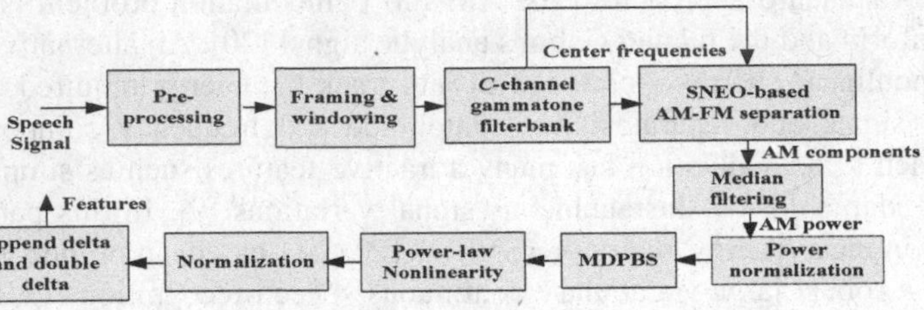

Fig. 1. Block diagram showing various steps of the proposed robust feature extractor

2.1 SNEO-Based AM-FM Separation

Extensive research by Teager resulted in a nonlinear approach for computing the energy of a signal denoted as the nonlinear energy operator (NEO) or Teager Kaiser Energy operator (TKEO) [23]. The NEO uses only a few samples of the input signal to track the energy required to generate an AM-FM signal and separate it into amplitude and frequency components in a nonlinear manner, which provides an advantage over the conventional Fourier transform (FT) or linear prediction (LP) methods in capturing the energy fluctuations. Let $x(c,n)$ represent the speech frame of the cth channel, where $c = 1,2,...,C$ is the channel (or filterbank) index of the C-channel gammatone filterbank, $n = 1,2,...,N$ is the discrete time index, N is the frame length in samples and C is the number of channels of the gammatone filterbank. Standard NEO (or TKEO) of $x(c,n)$ can be expressed as a special case of the following kth order (k=0,1,2,...) and lth lag (l=1,2,3,...) generalized discrete energy operator:

$$\Psi_{k,l}\left(x(c,n)\right) = x(c,n)\,x(c,n+k) - x(c,n-l)\,x(c,n+k+l). \tag{1}$$

For k=0 and l=1, eqn. (1) reduces to the standard NEO or TKEO. The NEO has the problem of cross terms and few negative values. To alleviate these problems we use the smoothed NEO (SNEO) [20, 21], which is expressed as:

$$\Psi^{s}_{0,1}\left(x(c,n)\right) = \Psi_{0,1}\left(x(c,n)\right) \otimes w(n), \tag{2}$$

where $w(n)$is the smoothing window and $\otimes$ represents the convolution operator. For smoothing, a Bartlett window was used in [21], whereas in [20] a 7-point binomial smoothing filter with impulse response (1, 6, 15, 20, 15, 6, 1) was applied. In this work we use the latter smoothing filter. Since SNEO (or NEO) is an energy operator and energy is a positive quantity, in order to avoid any negative values in eqn. (1) (if $x(c,n)x(c,n+k) < x(c,n-l)x(c,n+k+l)$ for k=0, l=1) we have taken the absolute values of eqn. (1) [25, 8]. Now, for the cth channel, the AM and FM components can be estimated using the discrete energy separation algorithm (DESA) when k=0, l=1as follows [20]:

$$\left|\hat{a}(c,n)\right| = \sqrt{\frac{\Psi^{s}_{0,1}\left(x(c,n)\right)}{1-\left(1-\dfrac{\Psi^{s}_{0,1}\left(y(c,n)\right)+\Psi^{s}_{0,1}\left(y(c,n+1)\right)}{4\Psi^{s}_{0,1}\left(x(c,n)\right)}\right)^{2}}}, \tag{3}$$

$$\left|\hat{\varphi}(c,n)\right| = \cos^{-1}\left(1-\left(\frac{\Psi^{s}_{0,1}\left(y(c,n)\right)+\Psi^{s}_{0,1}\left(y(c,n+1)\right)}{4\Psi^{s}_{0,1}\left(x(c,n)\right)}\right)\right), \tag{4}$$

where $y(c,n)) = x(c,n)) - x(c,n-1))$. In order to reduce the dynamic range, estimated AM and FM components are smoothed using a median filter with a window size of 5. For the mth speech frame the AM power for the cth channel is computed as:

$$P(m,c) = \sum_{n=1}^{N}\left(\left|\hat{a}(c,n)\right|^{2}\right). \tag{5}$$

2.2 Normalization and Enhancement of the AM Power Spectrum

Since SNEO (or NEO) uses only a few samples to estimate the energy, it is sensitive to noise. Therefore, the AM power estimated using (5) may be corrupted due to noise. In order to compensate for the noise, a medium duration power bias subtraction (MDPBS) [5] is applied on the AM power $P(m,c)$ after normalizing by the 95th percentile power across all frames and channels [5, 8].

2.3 Post-processing

13-dimensional static features, obtained after applying a power function nonlinearity using a coefficient of 0.07 and discrete cosine transform (DCT) on the bias subtracted AM power, are normalized using the conventional cepstral mean normalization method over the entire utterance. Delta and double-delta features are computed with a 5-frame window using regression formula [27].

3 Performance Evaluation

3.1 Speech Corpus and Experimental Setup

The AURORA-4 continuous speech recognition corpus is derived from the Wall Street Journal (WSJ0) corpus. 14 evaluation sets were defined in order to study the degradations in speech recognition performance due to microphone conditions, filtering and noisy environments [22]. The 14 test sets are grouped into the following 4 families [22, 26]: Test sets A, B, C and D. For the large-vocabulary continuous speech recognition task on the AURORA-4 corpus, all experiments employed state-tied crossword speaker-independent triphone acoustic models with 4 Gaussian mixtures per state. A single-pass Viterbi beam search-based decoder was used along with a standard 5K lexicon and bigram language model with a prune width of 250 [22, 26]. The HTK (Hidden Markov Model Toolkit) recognizer [27] is employed for the recognition task.

3.2 Results and Discussion

In order to verify the effectiveness of the proposed robust feature extractor, speech recognition experiments were conducted on the AURORA-4 large vocabulary continuous speech recognition (LVCSR) corpus. Percentage word accuracy was used as a performance evaluation measure for comparing the recognition performances of the proposed method to that of the following feature extractors: MFCC, PLP, ETSI-AFE [4], power normalized cepstral coefficient (PNCC) [5], Cochlear filterbank cepstral coefficients (CFCC) [24], and the robust front-end (RFE) of [6]. Features in the MFCC and PLP front-ends are normalized using the mean and variance normalization method. CFCC and the front-end proposed in [6] utilize a short-time mean and scale normalization technique [28] to normalize the features. PNCC and the proposed method use cepstral mean normalization whereas ETSI-AFE uses a blind equalization technique, which is based on the comparison to a flat spectrum and the application of the LMS algorithm, for improving robustness of ASR systems against additive noise distortions and channel effects. Speech recognition experiments were conducted on the four test sets (A, B, C, and D) of the AURORA-4 corpus. Test set A represents the matched training/test condition (same channel) where acoustic models were trained using clean training features and recognition were performed on the clean test features. Test set B represents the mismatched training/test condition (same channel) where mismatch was created randomly adding each of the 6 noise types (car, babble, restaurant, street traffic, airport, and train-station noises) at a randomly chosen SNR between 5 and 15 dB to the test data. Training data is the same as the training data of test set A. Test set C represents the mismatched training/test condition due to different channels where acoustic models were trained using clean training features extracted from the clean training data recorded with a Sennheiser microphone and recognition was performed on the clean test features extracted from the clean test data recorded with a secondary microphone. Test set D represents the mismatched training/test condition due to additive noise and different microphone channels where acoustic models were trained using clean training features extracted from the clean training data recorded with a Sennheiser microphone and recognition was performed on the noisy test features extracted from the noisy test data recorded with a secondary microphone.

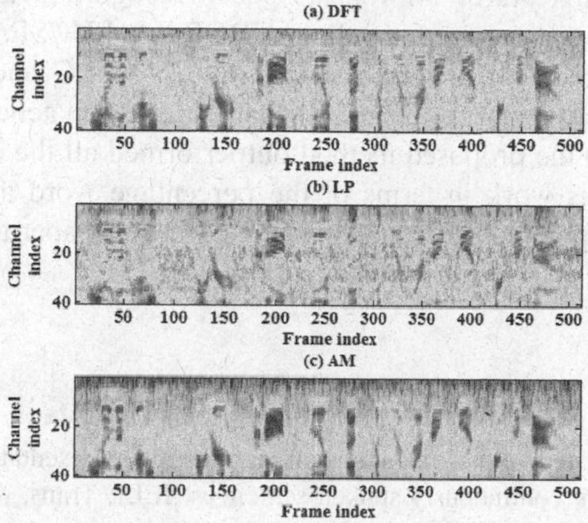

Fig. 2. Speech spectrograms after auditory filterbank integration, street noise, SNR = 5 dB, (a) DFT-based periodogram with Mel-filterbank, (b) LP spectrum with Mel-filterbank, and (c) AM power spectrum with gammatone filterbank

Table 1. Word accuracies (%) obtained by the various feature extractors on the AURORA-4 corpus. The higher the word accuracy the better is the performance of the feature extractor.

	Word Accuracy (%)				
	A	**B**	**C**	**D**	**Average**
MFCC	**90.02**	49.19	71.12	35.44	61.44
PLP(HTK)	89.72	50.41	74.44	39.64	63.55
CFCC	86.34	63.05	78.60	54.70	70.67
ETSI-AFE	88.59	69.58	79.52	61.51	74.80
PNCC [5]	88.64	69.85	81.07	60.00	74.89
RFE [6]	88.90	68.87	80.94	59.25	74.49
Proposed	87.41	**71.46**	**82.10**	**62.99**	**75.99**

Fig. 2 presents the speech auditory spectrograms of a noisy speech signal, corrupted with the street noise (SNR = 5 dB), obtained by the DFT-based periodogram, LP (linear prediction) spectrum, and AM power spectrum estimators. It is observed from this figure that compared to the other estimators, AM spectrum estimator results in a reduction of the noise while preserving the formant structure. Experimental results presented in Table 1 show that in matched environments the proposed method provides less word recognition accuracy compared to the other front-ends. It is observed from Table 1 that under mismatched environments (due to additive noise and different microphone channels) the proposed feature extractor outperformed the other feature extractors in terms of the recognition word accuracy. Therefore, the proposed method is found to be robust under environmental mismatch conditions.

4 Conclusion

A robust feature extractor that incorporates smoothed nonlinear energy operator-based amplitude modulation features for robust speech recognition is presented. Speech recognition results were reported on the AURORA-4 LVCSR corpus and performances were compared with the ETSI-AFE, PNCC, CFCC and the robust feature extractor of [6]. Experimental results depict that under mismatched condition (e.g., in test sets B, C, and D) the proposed method outperformed all the other feature extractors considered in this work in terms of the percentage word accuracy. Our future work will be to incorporate AM features presented in this paper to the feature extraction framework of [6].

References

1. Davis, S., Mermelstein, P.: Comparison of parametric representations for monosyllabic word recognition in continuously spoken sentences. IEEE Trans. Acoustics, Speech, and Signal Processing 28(4), 357–366 (1980)
2. Hermansky, H.: Perceptual linear prediction analysis of speech, J. Acoust. Soc. Am. 87(4), 1738–1752 (1990)
3. Terasawa, H.: A Hybrid Model for Timbre Perception: Quantitative Representations of Sound Color and Density. Ph.D. Thesis, Stanford University, Stanford, CA (2009)
4. ETSI ES 202 050, Speech Processing, Transmission and Quality aspects (STQ); Distributed speech recognition; advanced front-end feature extraction algorithm; Compression algorithms (2003)
5. Kim, C., Stern, R.M.: Feature extraction for robust speech recognition based on maximizing the sharpness of the power distribution and on power flooring. In: IEEE Int. Conf. on Acoustics, Speech, and Signal Processing, pp. 4574–4577 (March 2010)
6. Alam, M.J., Kenny, P., O'Shaughnessy, D.: Robust Feature Extraction for Speech Recognition by Enhancing Auditory Spectrum. In: Proc. INTERSPEECH, Portland Oregon (September 2012)
7. van Hout, J., Alwan, A.: A novel approach to soft-mask estimation and log-spectral enhancement for robust speech recognition. In: Proc. of ICASSP, pp. 4105–4108 (2012)
8. Vikramjit Mitra, H., Franco, M., Graciarena, A.: Mandal, Normalized Amplitude modulation features for large vocabulary noise-robust speech recognition. In: Proc. of ICASSP, pp. 4117–4120 (2012)
9. Maragos, Kaiser, J.F., Quatieri, T.F.: On amplitude and frequency demodulation using energy operators. IEEE Trans. Signal Processing 41(4), 1532–1550 (1993)
10. Potamianos, A., Maragos, P.: Speech analysis and synthesis using an AM–FM modulation model. Speech Communication 28, 195–209 (1999)
11. Dimitriadis, D., Maragos, P.: Continuous energy demodulation methods and application to speech analysis. Speech Communication 48(7), 819–837 (2006)
12. Zhou, G., Hansen, J.H.L., Kaiser, J.F.: Nonlinear feature based classification of speech under stress. IEEE Transactions on Speech and Audio Processing 9, 201–216 (2001)
13. Gao, H., Chen, S.G.: Emotion classification of mandarin speech based on TEO nonlinear features. Software Engineering, Artificial Intelligence, Networking and Parallel/Distributed Computing, 394–398 (2007)

14. Jabloun, F., Cetin, A.E., Erzin, E.: Teager energy based feature parameters for speech recognition in car noise. IEEE Signal Processing Letters 6(10), 259–261 (1999)
15. Dimitriadis, D., Maragos, P., Potamianos, A.: Robust AM–FM features for speech recognition. IEEE Signal Processing Letters 12(9), 621–624 (2005)
16. Jankowski Jr., C.R., Quatieri, T.F., Reynolds, D.A.: Measuring fine structure in speech: Application to speaker identification. In: ICASSP 1995, Detroit, USA (May 1995)
17. Plumpe, M.D., Quatieri, T.F., Reynolds, D.A.: Modeling of the glottal flow derivative waveform with application to speaker identification. IEEE Trans. Speech and Audio Processing 7(5), 569–586 (1999)
18. Grimaldi, M., Cummins, F.: Speaker identification using instantaneous frequencies. IEEE Trans. Audio, Speech and Language Processing 16(6), 1097–1111 (2008)
19. Tsiakoulis, P., Potamianos, A.: Statistical Analysis of Amplitude Modulation in Speech Signals using an AM-FM Model. In: Proc. Intl. Conf. on Acoustics, Speech and Signal Processing (ICASSP 2009), Taipei, Taiwan (April 2009)
20. Potamianos, A., Maragos, P.: A comparison of energy operator and Hilbert transform approach to signal and speech demodulation. Signal Process 37(1), 95–120 (1994)
21. Mukhopadhyay, S., Ray, G.C.: A new interpretation of nonlinear energy operator and its efficacy in spike detection. IEEE Tans. on Biomedical Engg. 45(2), 180–187 (1998)
22. Parihar, N., Picone, J., Pearce, D., Hirsch, H.G.: Performance analysis of the Aurora large vocabulary baseline system. In: Proceedings of the European Signal Processing Conference, Vienna, Austria (2004)
23. Kaiser, J.F.: On a Simple Algorithm to Calculate the 'Energy' of a Signal,". In: Proceedings of IEEE International Conference on Acoustics, Speech, and Signal Processing, Albuquerque, NM, pp. 381–384 (April 1990)
24. Li, Q(P.), Huang, Y.: Robust speaker identification using an auditory-based feature. In: Proc. ICASSP, pp. 4514–4517 (2010)
25. Kvedalen, E.: Signal processing using the Teager energy operator and other nonlinear operators, Cand. Scient Thesis, University of Oslo (May 2003)
26. Au Yeung, S.-K., Siu, M.-H.: Improved performance of Aurora-4 using HTK and unsupervised MLLR adaptation. In: Proceedings of the Int. Conference on Spoken Language Processing, Jeju, Korea (2004)
27. Young, S.J., et al.: HTK Book, Entropic Cambridge Research Laboratory Ltd., 3.4 edition (2006), `http://htk.eng.cam.ac.uk/`
28. Alam, M.J., Ouellet, P., Kenny, P., O'Shaughnessy, D.: Comparative Evaluation of Feature Normalization Techniques for Speaker Verification. In: Travieso-González, C.M., Alonso-Hernández, J.B. (eds.) NOLISP 2011. LNCS, vol. 7015, pp. 246–253. Springer, Heidelberg (2011)

Fuzzy Phonetic Decoding Method in a Phoneme Recognition Problem

Lyudmila V. Savchenko[1] and Andrey V. Savchenko[2]

[1] Nizhniy Novgorod State Linguistic University, Russia
LyudmilaSavchenko@yandex.ru
[2] National Research University Higher School of Economics, Nizhniy Novgorod, Russia
avsavchenko@hse.ru

Abstract. The definition of a phoneme as a fuzzy set of minimal speech units from the model database is proposed. On the basis of this definition and the Kullback-Leibler minimum information discrimination principle the novel phoneme recognition algorithm has been developed as an enhancement of the phonetic decoding method. The experimental results in the problems of isolated vowels recognition and word recognition in Russian are presented. It is shown that the proposed method is characterized by the increase of recognition accuracy and reliability in comparison with the phonetic decoding method.

Keywords: Automatic phoneme recognition, Kullback-Leibler minimum information discrimination principle, phonetic decoding method, fuzzy set theory.

1 Introduction

In recent years, automatic speech recognition (ASR) technology has reached a certain level of maturity [1]. Among the many ASR algorithms a particular interest is represented by an information-theoretic approach [2, 3] based on the Kullback-Leibler minimum information discrimination principle [4]. This principle has been successfully applied in the phonetic decoding method (PD) in isolated words recognition problem for Russian language [5]. According to this method, the input utterance is divided into the sequence of minimal speech units (phonemes). Each unit is recognized separately by using the speaker's phonetic database. Then the whole utterance is recognized as a sequence of phonetic codes. At last, the measure of similarity between this sequence and the phonetic code sequences of each word from the vocabulary is estimated. To get the final solution of the ASR, the nearest neighbor rule is applied.

The key part of this method is the assignment of the phonetic code to a minimal speech unit (allophone, phoneme, triphone, syllable, etc). This problem is usually referred to as phoneme recognition [6, 7]. Unfortunately, if each phoneme corresponds to the distinct code, the PD method's accuracy is usually low [5]. Hence, several phonemes closed to each other are united into one cluster and match to the same phonetic code. This approach leads to a significant reduction in the number of distinct phonemes and, as a consequence, to increase of the count of alternative solutions, especially for recognition of short words. The present article seeks a solution of this

T. Drugman and T. Dutoit (Eds.): NOLISP 2013, LNAI 7911, pp. 176–183, 2013.

issue with the fuzzy set theory [8]. It is proposed to define the phoneme as a fuzzy set of minimal speech units whose grades of membership are determined by the phonemes distance matrix.

The rest of the paper is organized as follows: Section 2 presents the phoneme recognition problem with the PD method. In Section 3, we propose the novel method of phoneme recognition on the basis of the PD and fuzzy set theory. In Section 4, we present experimental results in the tasks of isolated vowel phoneme and word recognition in Russian. Finally, concluding comments are given in Section 5.

2 Phonetic Decoding Method

Let a set of $R>1$ model phonemes (minimal speech units) $\{\mathbf{x}_r^*\}$ is given. Here r is the number of the model phoneme in the database. The phoneme recognition task is to assign a query utterance $\mathbf{x}$ to one of the model $\mathbf{x}_r^*$.

First, $\mathbf{x}$ is divided into non-overlapping segments $\{\mathbf{x}(t)\}$, $t=\overline{1,T}$ of the length $\tau \approx 0.01-0.03$ s. Each partial signal $\mathbf{x}(t)=[x_1(t)...x_M(t)]$ (here $M=\tau \cdot F$ and F is a sample rate (in Hz)) is identified with the model phoneme $\mathbf{x}_{\nu(t)}^*$, which complies the nearest neighbor rule with the Kullback-Leibler [4] information discrimination $\rho(\mathbf{x}(t)/\mathbf{x}_r^*)$ between the signal $\mathbf{x}(t)$ and the model $\mathbf{x}_r^*$: $\nu(t)=\arg\min_{r=\overline{1,R}} \rho(\mathbf{x}(t)/\mathbf{x}_r^*)$. This distance is calculated on the basis of the Itakura-Saito divergence [1] between the power spectral densities (PSD). The latter distance is widely used in the ASR task as it is strongly correlated with subjective estimates of speech signals closeness, namely, MOS (mean opinion score) [1]. The PSD is estimated on the basis of the LPC-coefficients (with order p), obtained by the Levinson-Durbin procedure and the Burg method [9].

Next, we use the PD method [5] to \assign the utterance $\mathbf{x}$ to a model class. According to this method, each phoneme $\mathbf{x}_r^*$ is put in correspondence with a numerical code $c(r)\in\{1,...,C\}$; in general case $C \le R$. Usually it is assumed [5] that the count of codes C is equal to the model database size $C=R$. The decision is made in favor of the most frequently occurring phoneme code

$$c^* = \arg\max_{c=\overline{1,C}} \sum_{t=1}^{T} \delta(c(\nu(t))-c), \tag{1}$$

where $\delta(x)$ is the discrete Dirac delta function. Unfortunately, if $C=R$, then the phoneme confusion error rate of the PD method is quite high [5]. To overcome this issue, it is necessary to unite similar phonemes into one cluster, so that $\mathbf{x}_i^*$ and $\mathbf{x}_j^*$ belong to the same cluster if $\rho(\mathbf{x}_i^*/\mathbf{x}_j^*)$ does not exceed a fixed threshold.

The phonetic code $c(r)$ for model $\mathbf{x}_r^*$ is defined as its cluster number. The disadvantage of this "PD with clustering" method is that the count R of phonemes usually exceeds the clusters count C. As the phonemes from the same cluster are not distinguished, it is the real problem in word recognition task, because it leads to a significant increase of the count of alternative words in a solution.

3 Fuzzy Phonetic Decoding Method

To resolve the mentioned issues of the PD method, we propose here to define the phoneme as a fuzzy set of model phonemes (minimal speech units). Namely, the j-th ($j=\overline{1,R}$) phoneme is represented not only by a model $\mathbf{x}_j^*$, but by a fuzzy set $\{(\mathbf{x}_r^*, \mu_j(\mathbf{x}_r^*))\}$, where $\mu_j(\mathbf{x}_r^*)$ is the grade of membership of $\mathbf{x}_r^*$ to the j-th phoneme. This definition is a generalization of the phoneme representation in the PD with clustering method. Really, $\mu_j(\mathbf{x}_r^*)=1$ if $\mathbf{x}_r^*$ and $\mathbf{x}_j^*$ belong to the same cluster, otherwise $\mu_j(\mathbf{x}_r^*)=0$.

In this article we propose the novel algorithm, in which the grade of membership $\mu_j(\mathbf{x}_r^*)$ is defined as the conditional probability of belonging $\mathbf{x}_r^*$ to j-th phoneme: $P(\mathbf{x}_j^* | \mathbf{x}_r^*)$. To estimate this probability, the matrix of model distances $\rho_{ij} = \rho(\mathbf{x}_i^* / \mathbf{x}_j^*)$ should be evaluated. It is known [4, 5] that the Kullback-Leibler information discrimination between objects from j-th and r-th classes is asymptotically distributed as noncentral χ^2 with $(M\text{-}p)$ degrees of freedom and noncentrality parameter ρ_{jr}. Thus, if M is high, we apply the central limit theorem and estimate conditional probability from a distribution of the minimum of independent *normal* random variables [10] as follows

$$P(\mathbf{x}_j^* | \mathbf{x}_r^*) = \frac{1}{\sqrt{2\pi}} \int_{-\infty}^{+\infty} \exp(-t^2/2) \cdot \prod_{\substack{i=1 \\ i\neq j}}^{R} \left(1 - \Phi\left(\frac{t\sqrt{8(M-p)\cdot\rho_{rj} + p - 1} + 2(M-p)(\rho_{rj} - \rho_{ri})}{\sqrt{8(M-p)\cdot\rho_{ri} + p - 1}}\right)\right) dt \qquad (2)$$

Here $\Phi(\cdot)$ is a cumulative distribution function of $N(0;1)$. The grades of membership defined by (2) constitute the elements of the decomposition matrix in the Fuzzy C-Means method [11]. The difference is only in the definition of kernel function.

By using the same procedure, the segment $\mathbf{x}(t)$ is assigned to the fuzzy set $\{(\mathbf{x}_r^*, \mu(x(t)/\mathbf{x}_r^*))\}$. The final decision $\{(\mathbf{x}_r^*, \mu(r,t))\}$ for $\mathbf{x}(t)$ is defined with the fuzzy intersection operation [8] of sets $\{(\mathbf{x}_r^*, \mu_j(\mathbf{x}_r^*))\}$ and $\{(\mathbf{x}_r^*, \mu(x(t)/\mathbf{x}_r^*))\}$:

$$\mu(r,t)=\min\left(\mu_{\nu(t)}\left(\mathbf{x}_r^*\right),\mu\left(\mathbf{x}(t)/\mathbf{x}_r^*\right)\right), \tag{3}$$

where $\mu_{\nu(t)}\left(\mathbf{x}_r^*\right)$ is determined by (2) after substitution $j=\nu(t)$. It is known [4] that, if $\mathbf{x}(t)$ belongs to the same class as the model $\mathbf{x}_\gamma^*$, then asymptotically $\forall r \in \{1...R\}$, $\rho\left(\mathbf{x}(t)/\mathbf{x}_r^*\right) \to \rho\left(\mathbf{x}_\gamma^*/\mathbf{x}_r^*\right)$. Therefore, if $\gamma=\nu(t)$, then, according to (3), $\mu(\nu(t),t)\approx 1$. Otherwise, $\mu(\nu(t),t)=\mu\left(\mathbf{x}(t)/\mathbf{x}_{\nu(t)}^*\right) << 1$. Thus, equation (3) leads to lower grades of membership in the case of recognition error ($\gamma \neq \nu(t)$).

Finally, decision for the whole utterance $\mathbf{x}$ is made in favor of fuzzy set $\left\{\left(\mathbf{x}_r^*,\mu(r)\right)\right\}$ on the basis of all $\mu(r,t)$ (3) by simple voting [12].

$$\mu(r)=\frac{1}{T}\sum_{t=1}^{T}\mu(r,t). \tag{4}$$

Thus, equations (2)-(4) determin the proposed fuzzy phoneme decoding (FPD) method in the phoneme recognition task.

4 Experimental Results

In this section we examine the effectiveness of our FPD method in the task of isolated Russian vowels recognition. The model database was filled with $R=10$ Russian vowels pronounced by a female speaker. These models were used to recognize the vowel in isolated syllables produced by other (male) speaker. The testing set contained 100 syllable realizations per each vowel (i.e., 1000 utterances recorded with built-in microphone). The following parameters were chosen: sampling frequency F=*8* kHz, length of each segment M=120 ($\tau=0.015$ s.), LPC-model order p=20. To recognize syllables, we, first, performed phonetic segmentation [6] and, second, the largest regular segment (vowel) was recognized with the described methods, namely, the PD (1), the PD with clustering and the proposed FPD (2)-(4). In PD with clustering the vowels were united into $C=5$ clusters: {а, я}, {у, ю}, {о, ё}, {э, е}, {ы, и} (2 phonemes per each cluster). Next, these ASR methods are compared by the following quality indicators.

1. *The count of false phonemes K (in %) checked prior to the true phoneme* - the count of phonemes which grade of membership exceeds the grade of true phoneme $\mu(\gamma)$. Close phonemes in the PD with clustering method have been grouped in clusters, which should lower the number of confusions. Hence, it is incomparable with other methods as the value of K cannot be estimated for this method. Therefore, for this particular algorithm we evaluate the count K_c of *clusters* which grade of membership exceeds the grade of true phoneme $\mu(\gamma)$ and estimate the distribution of K

with the formula $P(K=k)=P\left(K_c=\left\lfloor\frac{k\cdot C}{100\%}\right\rfloor\cdot\frac{100\%}{C}\right)\cdot\frac{C}{R}$ by assuming that all phonemes are equiprobable. Here $\lfloor\cdot\rfloor$ is the floor round function. The distribution of K is shown in Fig. 1. Here $k\in\{0,10,20...,90\}$ are the possible values of K. The recognition accuracy is equal to $P(K=0)$. Value $k=90\%$ indicates the phonemes count whose $\mu(\gamma)=0$ (i.e., $P(K=90\%)$ is the FRR).

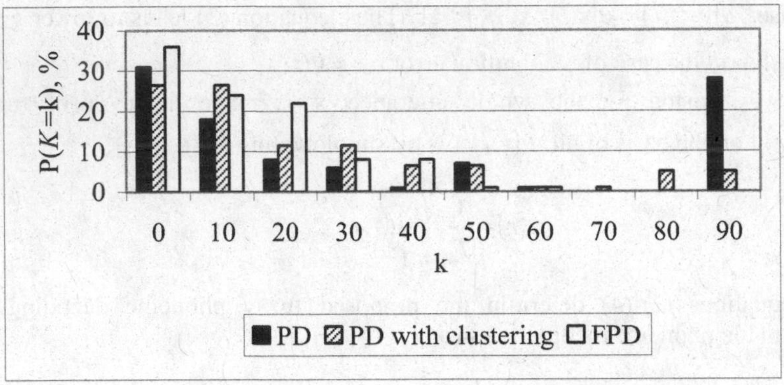

Fig. 1. Distribution of the random variable K

We can see that the probability $p_1=P(K\le 10\%)=P(K=0)+P(K=10\%)$ that no more than one phoneme has grade of memberships more than $\mu(\gamma)$ for the FPD is 60% (36%+24%). In comparison with other methods it is 7%-11% higher than p_1 for other methods (49% and 53% for the PD and the PD with clustering, respectively).

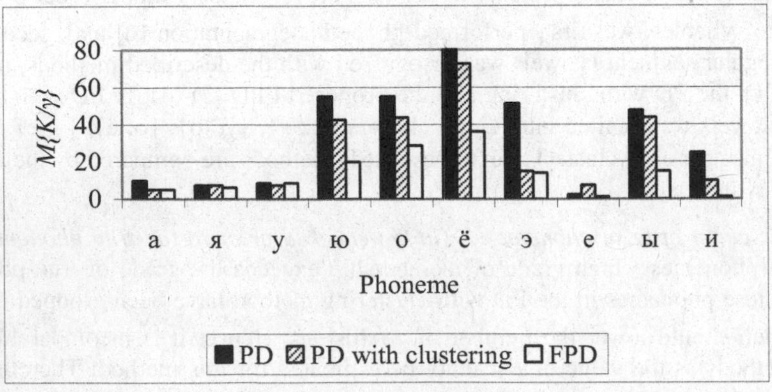

Fig. 2. Dependence of the conditional expectation $M\{K|\gamma\}$ on the true phoneme $\mathbf{x}_\gamma^*$

2. Next, *conditional mean of the count K of false phonemes* $M\{K|\gamma\}$ is examined. This indicator stands for the average count (in %) of incorrectly recognized vowels in test syllables if true phoneme is $\mathbf{x}_\gamma^*$. To estimate this conditional mean for the PD with clustering, at first, $M\{K_c|\gamma\}$ is evaluated. Then, assuming the equal prior probability of each phoneme, it is easy to show that in our case $M\{K|\gamma\}=M\{K_c|\gamma\}+5\%$. The conditional mean $M\{K|\gamma\}$ for each vowel is presented in Fig. 2. As one can see from this figure, $M\{K|\gamma\}$ of the FPD is lower for almost all vowels in comparison with other methods. For instance, for if true phoneme is "ю", $M\{K|\gamma\}=20\%$ for the FPD, while $M\{K|\gamma\}$ is equal to 56% and 42.5% for the PD and the PD with clustering, respectively.

3. *Average count (in %) of incorrectly recognized phonemes*, i.e., $M\{K\}=\frac{1}{R}\sum_{\gamma=1}^{R} M\{K|\gamma\}$, is shown in Table 1. Here $M\{K\}$ of our FPD is 9%-16% lower than the same indicator for other methods.

Table 1. The average count $M\{K\}$ (in %) of incorrectly recognized test phonemes

ASR method	PD	PD with clustering	FPD
$M\{K\}$	33%±12.1%	26%±8.6%	17%±6.3%

In the last experiment we explore the isolated words recognition task for Russian language. To simplify the experiment, we require speaker to pronounce words/phrases in isolated syllable mode. In such case, the vowel in each syllable is stressed so the mapping of the word's textual representation to its phonetic transcription becomes straightforward. Three vocabularies were used: price-list of one fast-food restaurant, consisting of 289 words/phrases (hereinafter "Menu"); list of 1913 drugs sold in one pharmacy of Nizhny Novgorod ("Pharmacy"); list of 1830 Russian cities with the corresponding regions, e.g., "Kstovo (Nizhegorodskaya)" ("Cities"). The phonetic database from the first experiment was used (i.e., it contains only vowels of a female speaker). Male speaker 3 times produced each word from each vocabulary (speaker-independent mode). The borders of syllables were obtained with a simple amplitude detector. The vowel phonemes were recognized in each syllable with the procedure described above (see the first experiment). Finally, each word is associated with the mean of grades of memberships of syllables contained in this word. The word with the highest mean of grades is put into solution. If there are several words which grades of memberships are equal, the decision is made in favor of the first word (in lexicographical order). The words recognition error rate (mean±standard deviation) is presented in Table 2. Here the FPD accuracy is 3%-5% higher than the accuracy of the PD with clustering and 6%-9% higher than the PD accuracy.

Table 2. The word recognition error rate

Vocabulary \ ASR method	PD	PD with clustering	FPD
Menu	13%±7.3%	11%±6.2%	6%±4.0%
Pharmacy	22%±12.8%	19%±9.7%	16%±6.8%
Cities	21%±10.1%	16%±8.6%	12%±5.5%

According to our results in both experiments we could draw the following conclusions. The usage of our method allows to significantly improve the phoneme recognition quality over the conventional implementations of the PD method. For example, the probability p_1 that no more than one phoneme has the grade of membership higher than the that of the true phoneme is equal to 60% for the FPD (Fig. 1), which is 7%-11% higher than p_1 for other methods. The average count of incorrectly recognized test phonemes prior to the true is equal to 17% for the FPD, which is 9%-16% phonemes lower than the same indicator for other methods (Table 1). Finally, we demonstrated that the FPD method can be successfully used in isolated words recognition problem (Table 2). In this case the recognition error rate is 3%-9% lower than error rates of the PD and PD with clustering methods.

5 Conclusion

It is well-known that Russian speech recognition is a challenging problem due to the following reasons [13]. First, one Russian word usually has dozens of word forms as the language is characterized by a combination of several lexical and grammatical morphemes in one word-form. Second, Russian's language model perplexity is 2-3 times higher than the perplexity of English [13]. Finally, the number of distinct vowels in Russian (clusters in the PD with clustering) is much lower (5-6 in comparison with 17 vowel with a lot of diphthongs in English). Thus, the phoneme recognition accuracy is usually [5, 13] low (30%-40%, see Fig. 1).

However, state-of-the-art approach to isolated words recognition [14] is usually applied even in Russian. According to this approach, at first, phonetic segmentation [6] is performed. Next, each regular segment (minimal speech unit, phoneme) extracted by segmentation procedure is recognized (i.e., phonetic transcription is built). Finally, transcription of the query utterance is compared with transcriptions of the words from the vocabulary with the HMM or the dynamic time wrapping (DTW) [1]. Thus, the accuracy of speech recognition may significantly exceed the accuracy of phonemes recognition because semantic, syntactic, lexical and prosodic knowledge sources may be additionally applied [14]. For instance, though the phoneme recognition accuracy in our experiments is quite low (35%, see Fig. 1), we obtained 6%-16% error rate in words recognition task (Table 2).

In this paper we proposed the novel FPD method (2)-(4) of automatic phonemes recognition on the basis of operations with fuzzy sets. Improving the recognition quality is caused by the usage of the model phonemes distance matrix (3). We demonstrated that the fuzzy approach, widely used in various artificial intelligence tasks [15], can be successfully combined with the Kullback-Leibler minimum information discrimination principle [4].

Our further research on proposed FPD will continue in the following directions. First, it is an application to the words recognition task with HMMs or DTW to overcome the drawback of our current solution, namely, the isolated syllable mode. Second, it is necessary to investigate the performance of our method if conventional phoneme features (MFCC, LPC cepstrum) are used. Other possible direction is an enhancement of the FPD (2)-(4) if several model sounds of each phoneme are available.

Acknowledgements. This study was carried out within "The National Research University Higher School of Economics' Academic Fund Program in 2013-2014, research grant No. 12-01-0003" and the Federal Grant-in-Aid Program "Research and development on priority directions of scientific-technological complex of Russia for 2007-2013" (Governmental Contract No. 07.514.11.4137).

References

1. Benesty, J., Sondh, M., Huang, Y. (eds.): Springer Handbook of Speech Recognition. Springer (2008)
2. Ramirez, J., Segura, J.C., Benitez, C., de la Torre, A., Rubio, A.J.: A new Kullback-Leibler VAD for speech recognition in noise. IEEE Signal Processing Letters 11(2), 266–269 (2004)
3. Gruhn, R., Raab, M., Brueckner, R.: US Patent №8301445, Speech Recognition Based on a Multilingual Acoustic Model. Nuance Communications, Inc., Assignee (2012)
4. Kullback, S.: Information Theory and Statistics. Dover Pub. (1997)
5. Savchenko, V.V.: The Method of Words Phonetic Decoding in Automatic Speech Recognition Problem Using the Minimum Information Discrimination Principle, Izvestia vuzov Rossii. Radioelectronika 5, 31–41 (2009) (in Russian)
6. Qiao, Y., Shimomura, N., Minematsu, N.: Unsupervised optimal phoneme segmentation: Objectives, algorithm and comparisons. In: IEEE International Conference on Acoustics, Speech and Signal Processing (ICASSP), pp. 3989–3992 (2008)
7. Rasipuram, R., Magimai-Doss, M.: Improving Articulatory Feature and Phoneme Recognition Using Multitask Learning. In: Honkela, T. (ed.) ICANN 2011, Part I. LNCS, vol. 6791, pp. 299–306. Springer, Heidelberg (2011)
8. Zadeh, L.A.: Fuzzy Sets. Information Control 8, 338–353 (1965)
9. Marple -Jr., S.L.: Digital Spectral Analysis: With Applications. Prentice-Hall Series in Signal Processing (1989)
10. Hill, J.E.: The Minimum of n Independent Normal Distributions, `http://www.untruth.org/~josh/math/normal-min.pdf`
11. Bezdek, J.C.: Pattern Recognition with Fuzzy Objective Function Algorithms. Plenum Press (1981)
12. Koutroumbas, K., Theodoridis, S.: Pattern Recognition, 4th edn. Elsevier Inc. (2008)
13. Ronzhin, A.L., Yusupov, R.M., Li, I.V., Leontieva, A.B.: Survey of Russian Speech Recognition Systems. In: SPECOM 2006, pp. 54–60 (2006)
14. Reddy, D.R.: Speech recognition by Machine: A Review. Proceedings of the IEEE 64(4), 501–531 (1976)
15. Jensen, R., Cornelis, C.: Fuzzy-rough nearest neighbour classification and prediction. Theoretical Computer Science 412(42), 5871–5884 (2011)

Improved EMD Usable Speech Detection for Co-channel Speaker Identification

Wajdi Ghezaiel[1], Amel Ben Slimane[2], and Ezzedine Ben Braiek[1]

[1] CEREP, ESSTT University of Tunis, Tunisia
[2] ENSI University of Mannouba, Tunisia

Abstract. The speech signal is the result of many nonlinearly interacting processes; therefore any linear analysis has the potential risk of missing a great amount of information content. Recently the technique of Empirical Mode Decomposition (EMD) has been proposed as a new tool for analysis of non linear and non stationary data. This paper deals with this new tool, to detect usable speech in co-channel speech. We applied EMD analysis to decompose co-channel speech signal into intrinsic oscillatory modes. Detected usable speech segments are organized into speaker streams, which are applied to speaker identification system (SID). The system is evaluated on co-channel speech across various Targets to Interferer Ratios (TIR). Performance evaluation has shown that EMD performs better than the linear dyadic wavelet decomposition based methods for usable speech detection.

Keywords: co-channel, usable speech, multi-resolution analysis, empirical mode decomposition, speaker identification.

1 Introduction

Speaker identification plays an important role in electronic authentification [1]. In an operational environment, speech is degraded by many kinds of interference. The interference can be classified as stationary or non stationary. Stationary interference is noise which can be dealt with by using denoising and noise reduction techniques; whereas non stationary interference is a noise caused by another speech from a different speaker [2]. Such interference is frequent and the corrupted speech is known as co-channel speech [3]. Usable speech is a new approach to resolve co-channel speech processing problem. The idea of usable speech is to identify and extract portion of degraded speech that are considered therefore useful for a particular speech processing application. Yantormo performed a study on co-channel speech and concluded that the target to interferer ratio TIR was a good measure to quantify the usability for speaker identification [3]. The TIR is a power ratio of the target speech to the interfering speech. This ratio can be expressed for entire utterances or individual frames of speech. For usability, frames above 20 dB TIR are considered usable. However the TIR is not an observable value from the co-channel speech data. Hence, a number of methods for usable speech detection which refer to the TIR have been developed and

T. Drugman and T. Dutoit (Eds.): NOLISP 2013, LNAI 7911, pp. 184–191, 2013.

studied under co-channel condition [4][5][6][7]. In these methods, usable speech frames are composed of voiced speech. In [5], the Spectral Autocorrelation Ratio method was developed to detect usable speech segments. This takes advantage of the structure of voiced speech in the frequency domain. In [7], the Peak difference autocorrelation of wavelet transform (PDAWT) method is applied in order to detect pitch information in usable speech. This method applies autocorrelation on approximation component obtained by filtering co-channel speech at one discrete wavelet transform (DWT) scale. In our previous work [8][9], we have developed a multi-resolution dyadic wavelet (MRDWT) method to detect usable voiced speech frames. MRDWT method applies dyadic wavelet transform (DWT) iteratively to co-channel speech in order to detect usable voiced frames. Pitch periodicity is tracked in all lower frequency sub-bands of co-channel speech until the pitch band. Evaluation of the MRDWT method gives good hits percentage, but false alarms have to be decreased. In fact, DWT is a linear tool well suited for stationary signal analysis. However, co-channel speech signal is considered as non stationary and a multi-resolution approach which incorporates the Empirical Mode Decomposition (EMD) may be effective. In fact, EMD is a signal processing technique particularly suitable for non linear and non stationary signals which has recently been proposed as a new tool for data analysis [10]. The EMD method is able to decompose a complex signal into a series of intrinsic mode functions (IMF) and a residue in accordance with different frequency bands [11]. These are signal components highlighting distinct time-scales (frequencies) of the input time-series. The IMF represents the natural oscillatory mode embedded in the signal. EMD is self-adaptive because the IMF works as the basis functions determined by the signal itself rather than what is predetermined. Therefore, EMD is highly efficient in non stationary data analysis.

In this paper, we propose to improve performance of a speaker identification system under co-channel noise by improving usable speech detection using EMD. Performance of EMD usable speech detection is compared with MRDWT and PDAWT. The extracted usable segments are separated in time and are organized into two speaker streams [12]. The two speakers are identified using the assigned segments with a baseline SID [1]. Evaluation of the SID is performed on TIMIT database referring to the TIR measure. Discussion of the results is provided basing on the SID performance for EMD and MRDWT.

The outline of the present paper is as follows. The first section presents empirical mode decomposition. In section 3, we describe how to extract usable speech using empirical mode decomposition. In section 4, we present the speaker identification system. Evaluation results are given in section 5. Last section concludes the paper.

2 Empirical Mode Decomposition

Empirical Mode Decomposition is a non linear technique for analyzing and representing non stationary signals [10],[11]. The EMD is data-driven and decomposes a signal, in the time domain, into a complete and finite set of adaptive basis

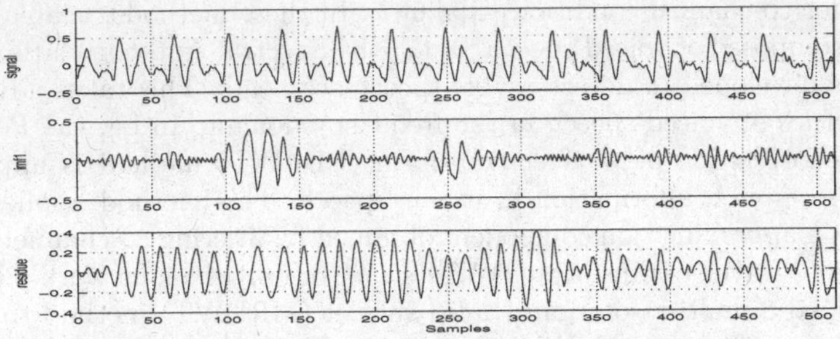

Fig. 1. The IMF components derived from the co-channel speech signal

functions which are defined as Intrinsic Mode Functions (IMFs). The EMD algorithm examines the signal between two consecutive extrema (e.g. minima) and picks out the high frequency component that exists between these two points. The remaining local, low frequency component can then be found. The motivation behind the EMD is to perform this procedure on the entire signal and then to iterate on the residual low frequency parts. This allows identification of the different oscillatory modes that exist in the signal. The IMFs found must be symmetric with respect to local zero means and have the same number of zero crossings and extrema [13]. These criteria led to the development of the EMD in forming IMFs as described by the stages in the following algorithm:

- Determine all extrema of $x(t)$.
- Compute the envelopes of the maxima and minima as $a_{min}(t)$ and $a_{max}(t)$ by interpolation.
- Find the average

$$r_C(t) = \frac{a_{min}(t) + a_{max}(t)}{2} \tag{1}$$

- Extract the detail

$$z(t) = x(t) - r_C(t) \tag{2}$$

- Repeat steps 1-4 for the residue

$$r_C(t) = x(t) - z(t) \tag{3}$$

A sifting process is applied to refine the above procedure corresponding to the steps 1-4 until $z(t)$ can be considered as zero mean according to some stopping criterion [10]. Once this is achieved, $z(t)$ can be considered as an effective IMF. Finally the residue $r_C(t)$ is computed and step 5 is applied. Upon convergence of the algorithm, $x(t)$ is decomposed into a sum of C IMFs and a residue $r_C(t)$,

$$x(t) = \sum_{j=1}^{C} z_j(t) + r_C(t) \tag{4}$$

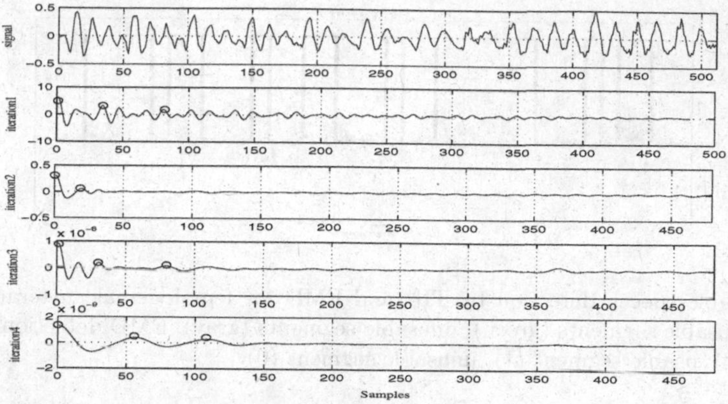

Fig. 2. Analysis of a voiced speech frame for female-female co-channel

where $z_j(t)$ represents the jth IMF component. The EMD can be seen as a type of wavelet decomposition whose sub-bands are built up as needed to separate the different components of $x(t)$. Each IMF replaces the signals detail, at a certain scale or frequency band. The EMD picks out the highest-frequency oscillation that remains in $x(t)$. In our simulation, we decompose co-channel speech signal in one IMF ranging the high-frequency in signal, and residue ranging the low-frequency. Figure 1 gives an example for a voiced speech frame decomposed by EMD into details (IMF1) and approximation (residue).

3 Usable Speech Detection

Usable frames are characterized by periodicity features. These features should be located in low-frequency band that includes the pitch frequency. Multi-resolution analysis based on EMD is applied iteratively in order to determine the suitable band for periodicity detection. In this band, periodicity features are not much disturbed by interferer speech in case of usable frames. In case of unusable frames, it is not possible to detect periodicity in all lower sub-bands. At each iteration, autocorrelation is applied to the approximation coefficients in order to detect periodicity [14]. Three dominated local maxima are determined from the autocorrelation signal with a peak-picking algorithm which uses a threshold calculated from local maxima amplitudes. A difference of autocorrelation lag between the first and second maximum and between the second and third maximum is determined. If this difference is less than the threshold, periodicity is detected and co-channel speech frame is classified as usable. This threshold is empirically fixed according to the best evaluation results. The optimum threshold value of 8 samples is chosen at 16 kHz sampling frequency. If at this iteration, periodicity is not detected, EMD is applied to approximation signal in order to detect hidden periodicity feature in finer band frequency. For unusable frames, it is not possible to detect periodicity in all lower sub-bands. A maximum of 5

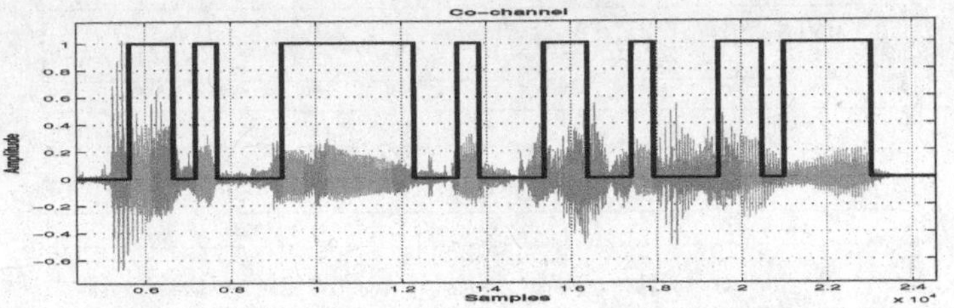

Fig. 3. Usable speech detection by TIR and EMD for female-female utterance. TIR detection: usable segments (green), unusable segments (gray). EMD detection (rectangular curve): usable segment (1), unusable segment (0).

iterations are allowed. This limit is fixed empirically basing on evaluation results, the lowest band should correspond to pitch band. Figure 2 shows that periodicity cant be detected up to the third iteration. In this case, periodicity is detected only at the fourth iteration. Hence this frame is classified as usable. Figure 3 shows usable and unusable speech frames detected by EMD method and TIR reference method, for a female-female co-channel speech utterance. Note that many frames lie in a transition region from voiced to unvoiced silence are detected as usable. Those false alarms could be reduced if such transition frames were identified and eliminated from processing.

4 Speaker Identification System

In order to identify the target and the interferer speakers, the detected usable segments are organized into two speaker streams by a speaker assignment system [12]. The speaker assignment system organizes usable speech segments under co-channel conditions. It has extended probabilistic framework of traditional SID to co-channel speech. It uses exhaustive search algorithm to maximize the posterior probability in grouping usable speech. Then, usable segments are assigned to two speaker groups, corresponding to the two speakers in the mixture. The two speaker streams are used as input for speaker identification system. The SID is performed with a baseline system [1]. Modeling is assured by Gaussian Mixture Model (GMM) and estimated through the Expectation Maximization (EM) algorithm that maximizes the likelihood criterion[1]. A set of 16 mixtures are used for speaker model. In our experiment, we use the classical parameterization based on 16 Mel Frequency Cepstral Coefficients (MFCC). These coefficients are computed from the speech signal every 10 ms using a time window of 25 ms. Each feature vector is presented by the middle windows of every utterance. Speaker model is trained using the EM algorithm with the features calculated from training samples. In testing phase, the organized usable speech, with speaker assignment system, are used as test speech samples for SID system. The same features are derived from the test speech samples and are input to every speakers GMM.

Table 1. Evaluation results for EMD usable speech detection

Co-channel Speech	% hits	% False alarm
Female-Female	98.20	15.34
Male-Male	98.69	18.60
Male-Female	99.03	13.62
Average	98.64	15.85

The speaker with the highest likelihood score represents the identified speaker. Here, speaker identification experiments are close-set and text-independent.

5 Evaluation Results

The TIMIT database is used for all the simulation experiments. The TIMIT database is just used for illustration purposes like in [4]. The speaker set is composed of 38 speakers from the DR1 dialect region, 14 of which are female and the rest are male. Each speaker has 10 utterance files, 5 out of 10 files are used for training and the remaining 5 files are used to create co-channel mixtures for testing. For each speaker deemed as the target speaker, 1 out of 5 test files is randomly selected and mixed with randomly selected files of every other speaker, which are regarded as interfering utterances. For each pair, the TIR is calculated as the energy ratio of the target speech over the interference speech. Three different sets of co-channel speech are considered: male-male, female-female, and male-female. Thus, for each TIR, a total of 1406 co-channel mixture files are created for the testing purpose.

5.1 EMD Evaluation and Comparison to Related Method

The Target to Interferer Ratio TIR measure is used to label voiced frames as usable or unusable. For usability decision, frames that have above 20 dB TIR are considered as usable. Evaluation is based on hits and false alarms percentages. Decision provided by the EMD method is said to have a hit if as well as TIR a frame is labeled as usable. This decision is said to have a false alarm if a frame is classified as usable by the EMD method, but labeled as unusable referring to TIR. The performance of the proposed method is given in Table.1 the EMD gives good results of usable speech detection. On an average the proposed method for usable speech detection system detects around 98.64% of usable speech with false alarms around 15.85%. In this section, we compare the proposed method with two related approaches in [7] and [9]. Peak difference autocorrelation of wavelet transform (PDAWT) method [7] is based on pitch information detection. This method applies DWT once only to co-channel speech to detect pitch information. On average the PDAWT method detects at least 80%of the usable speech with a false alarm rate of 30%. In multi resolution dyadic wavelet (MRDWT) method [9] DWT is applied iteratively to detect pitch periodicity in lower band

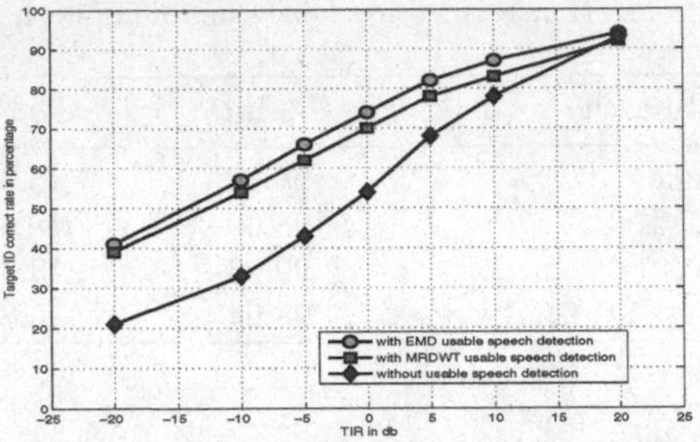

Fig. 4. Performance of the proposed speaker identification under co-channel conditions compared with related methods

frequency. On average the MRDWT method detects at least 95.76% of the usable speech with a false alarm rate of 29.65%. EMD achieve a minimum of false alarm compared to MRDWT and PDWAT methods. We consider the effectiveness of EMD usable speech detection, to reduce the percent of false alarm.

5.2 Speaker Identification Evaluation

The SID identifies the target and the interferer speaker. The evaluation system aims to evaluate the identification of the speaker referred as target. Its clear from figure 4 that the EMD performs significantly better than the MRDWT usable speech method. This effectiveness is due to reduction of false alarm by our proposed method. The target SID correct rate with usable speech detection is better than the target SID correct rate without usable speech detection. The proposed usable speech detection improves speaker identification performance. The average improvement is about 16% in terms of SID correct rate. Also the improvements are consistent across all TIR levels. Performance improvement increases at higher TIRs because the target speaker dominates the mixture. However, target speaker is dominated by interference at negative TIRs, resulting in better performance after usable speech extraction. The accuracy degrades sharply when TIR decreases because the target speech becomes increasingly corrupted.

6 Conclusion

In this paper, we have proposed a new usable speech extraction method based on multi-resolution analysis by empirical mode decomposition EMD. Usable speech is extracted by tracking the pitch information at sub-band residues obtained non linearly using empirical mode decomposition. Our usable speech extraction method produces segments that are useful for co-channel SID across various TIR conditions. EMD achieves a good percent of usable speech detection.

In comparison with wavelet linear filtering based methods, our proposed method achieves a minimum of false alarms. We note the effectiveness of EMD to reduce the percentage of false alarms. We have shown that the proposed usable speech detection achieves good SID performance and it performs significantly better than alternative methods for usable speech detection. Some extracted usable frames still contain sound energy from both speakers. The speaker information can be distorted. How much does usable speech impact the performance of co-channel speaker identification? This will be investigated in a future work.

References

1. Reynolds, D.A.: Speaker identification and verification using Gaussian mixture speaker models. Speech Commun. 17, 91–108 (1995)
2. Khanwalkar, S., Smolenski, Y.: Robert E. Yantorno and S. J. Wenndt, Enhancement of speaker identification using SID usable speech. EUSIPCO (2005)
3. Yantorno, R.E.: Method for improving speaker identification by determining usable speech. Journal of the Acoustical Society of America 124 (2008)
4. Lovekin, J., Yantorno, R.E., Benincasa, S., Wenndt, S., Huggins, M.: Developing usable speech criteria for speaker identification. In: Proc. ICASSP, pp. 421–424 (2001)
5. Krishnamachari, K.R., Yantorno, R.E., Benincasa, D.S., Wenndt, S.J.: Spectral autocorrelation ratio as a usability measure of speech segments under cochannel conditions. In: IEEE International Symposium Intelligent Sig. Process. and Comm. Sys. (2000)
6. Smolenski, B.Y., Ramachandran, R.P.: Usable Speech processing: a filterless approach in the presence of interference. IEEE Circuits and Systems Magazine (2011)
7. Kizhanatham, A., Yantorno, R.E.: Peak Difference Autocorrelation of Wavelet Trans-form Algorithm Based Usable Speech Measure. In: 7th World Multi-Conference on Systemic, Cybernetics, and Informatics (2003)
8. Ghezaiel, W., Ben Slimane, A., Ben Braiek, E.: Usable speech detection for speaker identification system under co-channel conditions. In: International Conference on Electrical System and Automatic Control JTEA, Tunisia (2010)
9. Ghezaiel, W., Ben Slimane, A., Ben Braiek, E.: Evaluation of a multi-resolution dyadic wavelet transform method for usable speech detection. World Academy of Science, Engineering and Technology Journal WASET, 829–833 (2011) pISSN 2010-376X, eISSN 2010-3778
10. Huang, N.E., Shen, Z., Long, S.R., et al.: The empirical mode decomposition and Hilbert spectrum for nonlinear and non-stationary time series analysis. Proc. R. Soc. Lond. A 454, 903–995 (1998)
11. Flandrin, P., Rilling, G., Goncalves, P.: Empirical mode decomposition as a filter bank. IEEE Signal Process. Letters 11(2), 112–114 (2004)
12. Ghezaiel, W., Ben Slimane, A., Ben Braiek, E.: Usable Speech Assignment for Speaker Identification under Co-Channel Situation. International Journal of Computer Applications 59(18), 7–11 (2012)
13. Jan, T., Wang, W.: Empirical Mode Decomposition for joint denoising and dereverberation. In: Proc. 19th European Signal Processing Conference (EUSIPCO 2011), Barcelona, Spain, August 29-September 2 (2011)
14. Hess, W.H.: Pitch determination of speech signal: Algorithms and devices, Springer-Verlag. Springer, Heidelberg (1983)

Speech Enhancement: A Multivariate Empirical Mode Decomposition Approach

Jordi Solé-Casals[1], Esteve Gallego-Jutglà[1], Pere Martí-Puig[1], Carlos M. Travieso[2], and Jesús B. Alonso[2]

[1] Digital Technologies Group, University of Vic, Sagrada Família 7, 08500 Vic, Spain
{jordi.sole,esteve.gallego,pere.marti}@uvic.cat
[2] Signals and Communications Department, Institute for Technology Development and Innovation in Communications (IDeTIC), LPGA University, Gran Canaria, Spain
{ctravieso,jalonso}@dsc.ulpgc.es

Abstract. Speech signals in real scenario ambient are usually mixed with some other signals, such as noise. This may interfere with posterior signal processing applied to the signals. In this work, a new technique of data denoising is presented using multivariate Empirical Mode Decomposition. Different SNR ratios are tested in order to study the evolution of the improvement of the recovered data. An improvement of the analyzed data is obtained with all the SNR levels tested.

Keywords: Speech enhancement, multivariate EMD, Speech processing.

1 Introduction

When speech signals are recorded there is often other noise signals added to the desired signal. This problem arises especially when we do not have laboratory conditions, i.e., when we are working in real applications. In this case, most of the systems for speech recognition, speaker recognition or speaker verification, for example, can fail due to the presence of noise. Nature of this noise can be variable. In some cases, we can assume additive white Gaussian noise. In other cases, it can be a pure tone due to the supply network or due to some vibrations (produced by machines or other systems near the microphone). Also non-white (colored) noise or others can be present depending on the scenario. In this work we present a new strategy to deal with white Gaussian noise in speech signals (as a first exploratory case), based on multivariate Empirical Mode Decomposition (mEMD). mEMD is an extension of EMD, which at this turn is a data-driven decomposition which can analyze nonlinear and non-stationary data [1]. Some work has been done these last recent years in order to use EMD for speech enhancement. For example, Kais Khaldi et al [2] present two approaches. The first one combines EMD and the minimum mean-squared error (MMSE) filter while the second one associates the EMD with hard shrinkage. In [3] an empirical mode decomposition-based filtering (EMDF) approach is presented as a post-processing stage for speech enhancement in order to suppress low-frequency

T. Drugman and T. Dutoit (Eds.): NOLISP 2013, LNAI 7911, pp. 192–199, 2013.

residual noise from speech signals that were previously enhanced by other system. More complex systems are for example proposed in [4], where a combination of Hilbert-Huang transformation of the empirical mode decomposition (EMD) and wavelet analysis is proposed. In some cases, EMD is used in VAD detectors [5-6], as presented in [7], where the use of EMD allows enhancing the speech signal into the noisy environment. Our proposed method uses mEMD in order to simultaneously decompose several channels (recordings) of the same scenario, in a similar way done in blind source separation (BSS) algorithms [8] or blind (linear or non-linear) deconvolution algorithms [9]. The analysis of the obtained modes will allow us to eliminate (as a first initial approach) the modes related to noise and thus recover an enhanced version of the speech signals. To the best of our knowledge, this is the first proposed method using mEMD.

This paper is organised as follows: First, methods used, including speech data, synthetic noisy data generation, EMD and mEMD description are presented in Section 2. Section 3 describes the cleaning proposed method. Experimental results obtained with this method are presented in Section 4. Finally, discussion and conclusions are presented in Section 5.

2 Material and Methods

2.1 Speech Signals and Noise

For our experiments, we have used subcorpora of the Gaudi database that follows the design of [10]. The database consists of 49 speakers. Signals were acquired with a simultaneous stereo recording with two different microphones (AKG C-420 and SONY ECM66B). The speech is in wave format at fs = 16 kHz, 16 bit/sample and the bandwidth is 8 kHz. We have applied the potsband routine, public available, in order to obtain narrow-band signals. This function meets the specifications of G.151 for any sampling frequency. The speech signals are preemphasized by a first-order filter whose transfer function is $H(z) = 1 - 0.95z^{-1}$. Two speakers of the database are selected, one male and one female, and only one sentence from one of each is used. The sentence lasts about 3 seconds.

In order to generate noisy signals we will use Gaussian white noise, generated with *randn*(·) Matlab function. This noise is added to the (clean) speech signals, the same noise in both channels, controlling the SNR of each observation. Different SNR values will be analyzed.

2.2 Empirical Mode Decomposition

EMD algorithm is a method designed for multiscale decomposition and time–frequency analysis, which can analyze nonlinear and non-stationary data [1].

The key part of the method is the decomposition part in which any time-series data set can be decomposed into a finite and often small number of Intrinsic Mode Functions (IMFs). These IMFs are defined so as to exhibit locality in time and to represent a single oscillatory mode. Each IMF satisfies two basic conditions: (i) the number of zero-crossings and the number of extrema must be the same or differ at most by one in the whole dataset, and (ii) at any point, the mean value of the envelope defined by the local maxima and the envelope defined by the local minima is zero [1].

The EMD algorithm [1] for the signal $x(t)$can be summarized as follows.

(i) Determine the local maxima and minima of $x(t)$;

(ii) Generate the upper and lower signal envelope by connecting those local maxima and minima respectively by an interpolation method;

(iii) Determine the local mean $m_1(t)$, by averaging the upper and lower signal envelope;

(iv) Subtract the local mean from the data: $h_1(t) = x(t) - m_1(t)$.

(v) If $h_1(t)$ obeys the stopping criteria, then we define $d(t) = h_1(t)$ as an IMF, otherwise set $x(t) = h_1(t)$ and repeat the process from step (i).

Then, the empirical mode decomposition of a signal $x(t)$ can be written as:

$$x(t) = \sum_{k=1}^{n} IMF_k(t) + \epsilon_n(t) \tag{1}$$

Where n is the number of extracted IMFs, and the final residue $\varepsilon_n(t)$ is the mean trend or a constant.

2.3 Multivariate Empirical Mode Decomposition (mEMD)

EMD has achieved optimal results in data processing [11 - 12]. However, this method presents several shortcomings in multichannel datasets. The IMFs from different time series do not necessarily correspond to the same frequency, and different time series may end up having a different number of IMFs. For computational purpose, it is difficult to match the different obtained IMFs from different channels [13]. To solve these shortcomings, an extension of EMD to mEMD is required. In this approach the local mean is computed by taking an average of upper and lower envelopes, which in turn are obtained by interpolating between the local maxima and minima. However, in general, for multivariate signals, the local maxima and minima may not be defined directly. To deal with these problems multiple n-dimensional envelopes are generated by taking signal projections along different direction in n-dimensional spaces [14]. mEMD is the technique used in this paper to compute all the decompositions.

The algorithm [14] can be summarized as follows:

(i) Choose a suitable pointset for sampling on an $(n-1)$ sphere (this $(n-1)$ sphere resides in an n-dimensional Euclidean coordinate system).

(ii) Calculate the projection, $p^{\theta_k}(t)\}_{t=1}^{T}$, of the input signal $v(t)_{t=1}^{T}$ along the direction vector, x^{θ_k} for all k giving $p^{\theta_k}(t)\}_{t=1}^{K}$.

(iii) Find the time instants $t_i^{\theta_k}$ corresponding to the maxima of the set of projected signals $p^{\theta_k}(t)\}_{t=1}^{T}$.

(iv) Interpolate $\left[t_i^{\theta_k}, v\left(t_i^{\theta_k}\right)\right]$ to obtain multivariate envelope curves $e^{\theta_k}(t)\}_{t=1}^{K}$.

(v) For a set of K direction vectors, the mean of the envelope curves is calculated as $m(t) = (1/K)\sum_{k=1}^{K} e^{\theta_k}(t)$.

(vi) Extract the detail $d(t)$ using $d(t) = x(t) - m(t)$. If the detail $d(t)$ fulfills the stopping criteria for a multivariate IMF, apply the above procedure to $x(t) - m(t)$, otherwise apply it to $d(t)$.

Then, the mEMD of a signal $x(t)$ can be written as detailed in equation 1.

2.4 Study Data Generation

Real speech signals are used in our experiments, but as they were recorded in optimal conditions, different kind of noise/interferences are artificially generated and added to the speech signals. The scenario we consider contains two speech sources $s_1(t)$ and $s_2(t)$, plus a noise source $n(t)$ that will interfere with the speech signals. We use two microphones in order to get two different observation signals, $e_1(t)$ and $e_2(t)$, as a mixture of speech signals and noise.

Two (clean) speech signals $s_1(t)$ and $s_2(t)$ (one male, one female) are used from the Gaudi database. White Gaussian noise is added to the speech signals in order to obtain the observation signals as follows:

$$\begin{aligned} e_1(t) &= s_1(t) + \alpha s_2(t) + \beta_1 n_1(t) \\ e_2(t) &= s_2(t) + \alpha s_1(t) + \beta_2 n_2(t) \end{aligned} \tag{2}$$

Where α=0.1 is a fixed parameter that models the interference of one speech signal to the secondary microphone, and β_1 and β_2 are tuned in order to test different SNR values in the observation signals. The considered SNR values for the observation signals are: -20 dB, -10 dB, -5 dB, -3 dB, 0 dB, +3 dB, +5 dB, +10dB.

3 Cleaning Method

Our hypothesis is that having strong noise interfering to our recordings, the noise will be present in both mixtures but (almost) only one of the speech signals will appear in each one, i.e., one microphone will record (almost) one speech signal with noise, and the second one will record the other speech signal with the same previous noise. In this study different levels of noise are tested. This will allow us to compare the signal-to-noise ratio (SNR), and the results of the cleaning method with the observed (noisy) speech signals and the clean ones.

The key idea of the proposed method is to consider that, after applying mEMD, if a mode appears in all the channels, this mode cannot be from speech activity and therefore it's considered as interfering noise. Note that now the only data we use are the observed signals (mixed), and common modes are sought in the mEMD decomposition of these data.

mEMD cleaning method can be summarized as it follows:

(i) Apply mEMD to raw observed data (channels of speech signals with noise, i.e. $e_1(t)$ and $e_2(t)$), in order to obtain oscillatory modes of the multivariate data.

(ii) Construct a matrix containing the same mode of the channels. Therefore the total number of matrices will be equal to the number of modes we obtained.

(iii) Calculate the correlation matrix of each one of these previous matrices.

(iv) Calculate the mean correlation of each channel for each mode, obtaining a vector that contains the degree of communality of each mode (i.e. a measure of how this mode is present in all the channels). Normalize this vector in order to have values between 0 and 1.

(v) Threshold the previous vector in order to find which of these modes is common within all the channels. Modes with high correlation (|r|>T) are eliminated.

(vi) Reconstruct clean signals without taking into account the eliminated modes.

4 Experimental Results

After the observation signals $e_1(t)$ and $e_2(t)$ were cleaned, we calculate the performance by simply correlating the recovered speech signals $\widehat{s_1}$ and $\widehat{s_2}$ with the original ones. Comparing these correlations between the correlations of the observation signals and original speech signals will allow us to quantify the amount of improvement introduced by our system as:

$$E_i = \frac{R_{\widehat{s_i} s_i}}{R_{e_i s_i}} \tag{3}$$

In all the experiments we explored different values for the threshold T used for deciding if two modes are common or not (see step (V) of the cleaning method described in Section 3). Values of threshold considered are: {0.80, 0.85, 0.90, 0.91, 0.92, 0.93, 0.94, 0.95, 0.96, 0.97 and 0.98}. Figure 1 shows the evolution of $R_{\widehat{s_i} s_i}$ (black triangles) and $R_{e_i s_i}$ (gray squares) for both two speakers (y-axis), depending on the value of the threshold T (x-axis), and for the different SNR. In all the cases we can obtain better results with the cleaning method. The worst case of -20 dB shows that the threshold must be high (over 0.95) in order to clean some noise, but in all the other cases this improvement is (almost) constant for all the values of T, which can facilitate very much the automatisation of the cleaning method. The effect of the threshold can be observed in figure 2, where all the correlations between modes of the mEMD decompositions, for different SNR values, are plotted (*x*-axis corresponding to number of the mode and *y*-axis corresponding to correlation $|r|$). Adjusting the threshold will result in a different selection of modes to be discarded. In all the cases, central modes are kept as they contain the important part of the speech signal, while firsts and lasts modes are eliminated as they are related to noise frequencies. We can also observe that the improvement is important when dealing with noisy observations and decrease when SNR increases. This evolution is shown in figure 3, where E is plotted against SNR value for both channels (excluding the case of $SNR = -20\ dB$ for the sake of clarity). At $SNR = -10\ dB$ there is a maximum in E for all the values of threshold T in both channels, where the correlation of recovered speech signals are more than 2 times the correlation of the observation signals.

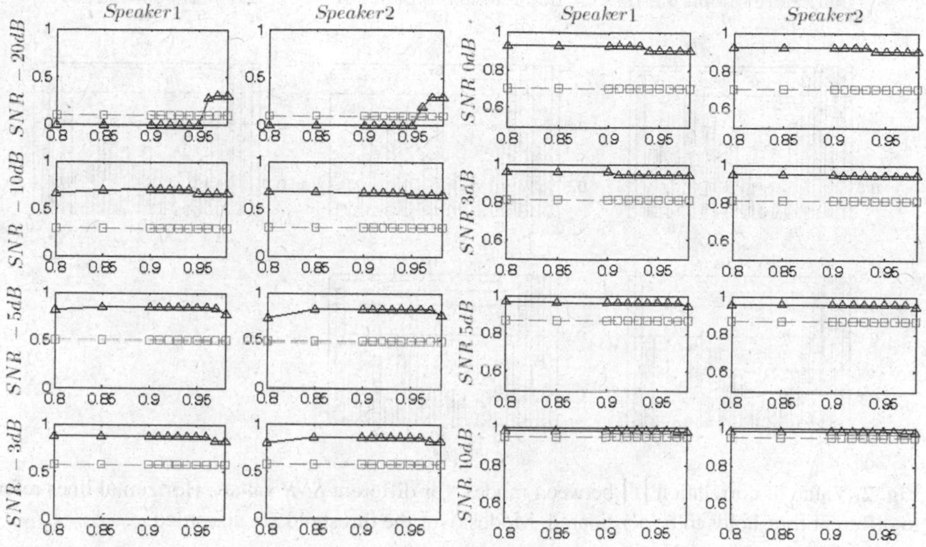

Fig. 1. $R_{\hat{s}_i s_i}$ (black triangles) and $R_{e_i s_i}$ (gray squares) for both speakers (y-axis), depending on the value of the threshold T (x-axis) and for the different considered SNR

5 Discussion and Conclusions

In this work we have presented a first approach on mEMD for speech enhancement. The system decomposes at the same time all the observed signals that contain speech signals and noise. Then, some of the IMFs are discarded according to the correlation between them into the observed signals. The rest of the modes are added together in order to reconstruct the original signal (eq. 1).

In the performed experiments we can see how the system is able to enhance the speech signals. If the SNR is low, noise can be well detected and eliminated from the observed signals, as shown in figure 1 (left). If SNR is high, the system tends to maintain all the modes and then the recovered signal is similar to the observed one. This fact is easily explained through figure 3 where the improvement E tends to 1 as SNR increases, indicating that there is a little enhancement in that case. It is interesting to note that the system is fully data-driven; hence no parameterization or tuning is needed, as the only parameter (threshold T) was very stable during all the experiments we performed. Also, even if not shown here for the lack of space, if there are other interferences, like sinusoids, the mEMD decomposition catch them in one or several modes, that can be easily removed from the observation signals in order to recover better speech signals.

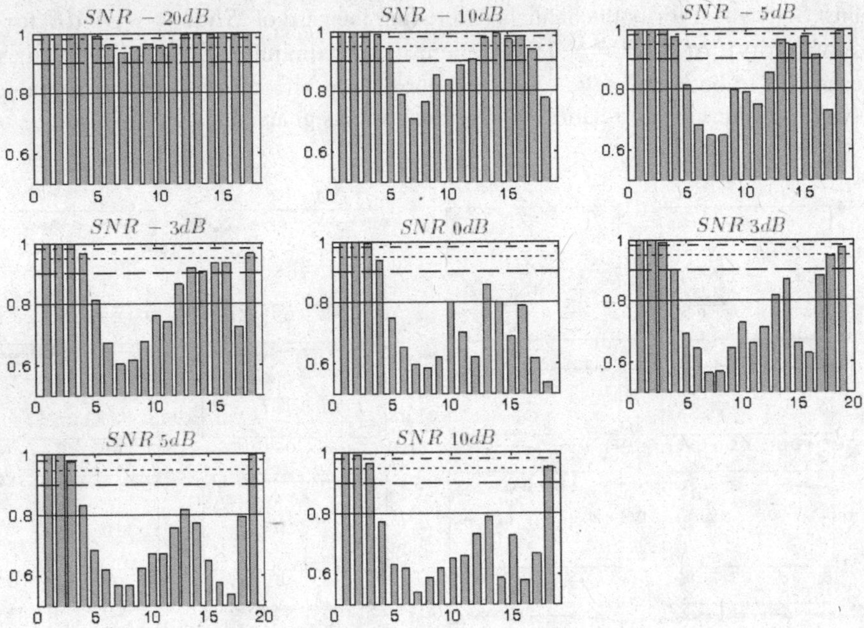

Fig. 2. Value of correlation $|r|$ between modes, for different *SNR* values. Horizontal lines refer to different thresholds to be considered. Modes over the threshold are discarded.

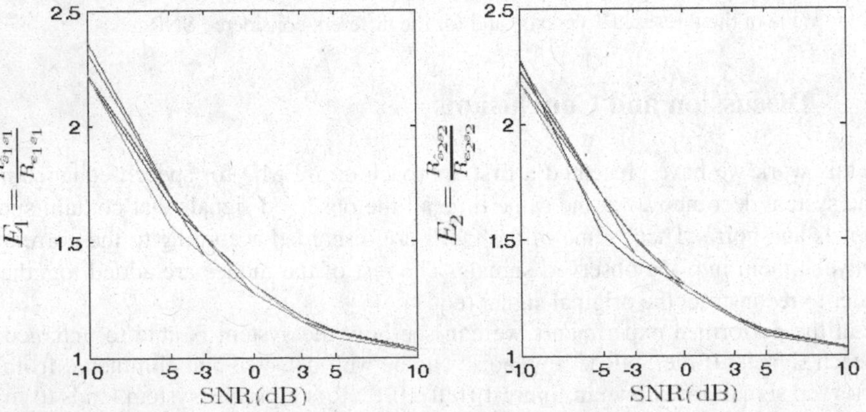

Fig. 3. Evolution of E for all the threshold values and SNR values

This first attempt to use mEMD for speech enhancement was successfully, opening a new way to explore in order to clean speech signals. Future work must include other strategies in order to decide which modes must be eliminated, the study of other kind of noise and the automatisation of the whole procedure in order to develop a real time system for speech enhancement totally data-driven.

Acknowledgments. This work has been partially supported by the University of Vic (grant R904), the funds with reference "e-Voice", from "Cátedra Telefónica" (ULPGC 2012/13), and under a predoctoral grant from the University of Vic to Mr. Esteve Gallego-Jutglà ("Amb el suport de l'ajut predoctoral de la Universitat de Vic").

References

1. Huang, N.E., Shen, Z., Long, S.R., Wu, M.C., Shih, H.H., Zheng, Q., Yen, N., Tung, C.C., Liu, H.H.: The Empirical Mode Decomposition and the Hilbert Spectrum for Nonlinear and Non-Stationary Time Series Analysis. Proceedings of the Royal Society of London. Series A: Mathematical, Physical and Engineering Sciences 454, 903–995 (1998)
2. Khaldi, K., Boudraa, A., Bouchikhi, A., Alouane, M.T.: Speech Enhancement Via EMD. EURASIP Journal on Advances in Signal Processing 2008, 873204 (2008)
3. Chatlani, N., Soraghan, J.J.: EMD-Based Filtering (EMDF) of Low-Frequency Noise for Speech Enhancement. IEEE Transactions on Audio, Speech, and Language Processing 20, 1158–1166 (2012)
4. Li, J., Liu, F., Xu, H., Wang, F.: Speech Enhancement Algorithm Based on Hilbert-Huang and Wavelet. Informatics and Management Science III, 173–178 (2013)
5. Solé-Casals, J., Zaiats, V.: A Non-Linear VAD for Noisy Environments. Cognitive Computation 2, 191–198 (2010)
6. Comas, C., Monte-Moreno, E., Solé-Casals, J.: A Robust Multiple Feature Approach to Endpoint Detection in Car Environment Based on Advanced Classifiers. Computational Intelligence and Bioinspired Systems, 1–10 (2005)
7. Shi, W., Zou, Y.: A Novel Instantaneous Frequency-Based Voice Activity Detection for Strong Noisy Speech, 956–959 (2012)
8. Comon, P., Jutten, C.: Handbook of blind source separation: Independent component analysis and applications. Academic press (2010)
9. Solé-Casals, J., Faundez-Zanuy, M.: Application of the Mutual Information Minimization to Speaker Recognition/Identification Improvement. Neurocomputing 69, 1467–1474 (2006)
10. Ortega-Garcia, J., Gonzalez-Rodriguez, J., Marrero-Aguiar, V.: AHUMADA: A Large Speech Corpus in Spanish for Speaker Characterization and Identification. Speech Commun. 31, 255–264 (2000)
11. Diez, P.F., Mut, V., Laciar, E., Torres, A., Avila, E.: Application of the Empirical Mode Decomposition to the Extraction of Features from EEG Signals for Mental Task Classification, 2579–2582 (2009)
12. Molla, M.K., Tanaka, T., Rutkowski, T., Cichocki, A.: Separation of EOG Artifacts from EEG Signals using Bivariate EMD, 562–565 (2010)
13. Ali Yener, M., Selin, A.: Multivariate Empirical Mode Decomposition for Quantifying Multivariate Phase Synchronization. EURASIP Journal on Advances in Signal Processing 2011 (2011)
14. Rehman, N., Mandic, D.P.: Multivariate Empirical Mode Decomposition. Proceedings of the Royal Society A: Mathematical, Physical and Engineering Science 466, 1291–1302 (2010)

Speech Denoising Based on Empirical Mode Decomposition and Improved Thresholding

Issaoui Hadhami and Aïcha Bouzid

LSTS, National Engineering School of Tunis,
Le Belvédère. B.P. 37, 1002, Tunis, Tunisia
{issaouihadhami,bouzidacha}@yahoo.fr

Abstract. The goal of this paper is to introduce a new speech enhancement algorithm using empirical-mode-decomposition (EMD). A mode selection approach and an improved thresholding technique are proposed. In the first stage, the noisy speech is adaptively decomposed into intrinsic oscillatory components called Intrinsic Mode Functions (IMFs) by means of a sifting process. In the second stage, an energy criterion, based on the minimization of the consecutive mean square error (CMSE), is applied to find the IMF from which the energy distribution of the original signal is greater than the noise. In the third stage, the previously selected IMFs are thresholded through an improved thresholding process by means of a detection function. Finally, the enhanced speech signal is reconstructed from the processed IMFs, the remaining ones and the residue. The proposed approach is evaluated using speech signals taken from the NOISEUS database corrupted with additive white Gaussian noise. Our algorithm is compared to other state of the art speech enhancement algorithms and the results are provided.

1 Introduction

In communications and other speech related systems, the background noise is a classical problem that degrades the quality and the intelligibility of the speech signals. To overcome this problem, it is important to improve the speech signal quality, mainly through noise reduction algorithms. Over the past two decades the developments in digital signal processing have resulted in a wide variety of techniques for the removal of noise in degraded speech depending on the type of the application and the the noise characteristics.

Due to its simplicity, the spectral subtraction is one of the earliest and most popular noise reduction methods. It was first proposed by Weiss et al in 1974 [1]. The additive noise is assumed to be stationary or slightly varying. The principle of this approach is to estimate the noise signal spectrum during the silence periods and to subtract it from that the noisy speech signal to obtain the enhanced speech. Then the spectral subtraction has been improved by many authors such as in Natalie Virag [2], [3] and [4]. Despite these improvements, the spectral subtraction has remained a limited method by the appearance of distortion and musical noise in the enhanced signal. Another denoising technique

T. Drugman and T. Dutoit (Eds.): NOLISP 2013, LNAI 7911, pp. 200–207, 2013.

is to estimate the speech by applying a linear filter, called optimal Wiener filter [5]. This approach uses also the spectrum energy and therefore an estimate of the signal from the noisy speech in the spectral domain is required. Although these traditional denoising techniques are frequently used because of their easy implementation and design, they remain not so effective in the case of speech signals which are nonlinear are non stationary.

In recent years, many authors have proposed various nonlinear methods notably those using the wavelets thresholding [6]-[7]. The main idea of this approach is to threshold the wavelet coefficients by keeping only those which are supposed to correspond to the signal. This method has shown a good agreement. However, the drawback of the wavelet approach is that the analyzed functions are predetermined in advance and it is not often optimal to describe the signal as non stationary. In the last decade, a new technique, termed empirical mode decomposition (EMD) has been introduced by Huang et al. [8] to adaptively analyze the nonstationary and nonlinear data process. The main advantage of the EMD analysis is that the basic functions are derived from the signal itself. Therefore the analysis is adaptive in contrast to traditional methods where the basic functions are fixed. Thus the EMD allows the decomposition of a signal into a finite sum of components, called Intrinsic Mode Functions (IMFs). The EMD has been applied in the speech signal enhancement field.

This work presents a new speech enhancement approach based essentially on the EMD algorithm and an improved thresholding process with a detection function that is applied on selected modes. The main idea is to fully reconstruct the signal with all IMFs by thresholding only the first noisy IMFs (low order components) and keeping unthresholded the last ones.

2 Empirical Mode Decomposition Basics

The principle of the EMD algorithm is to decompose iteratively a given signal $x(t)$ into series of fast oscillating components (high frequency) superimposed on slower oscillating components (low frequency) called empirical modes (or Intrinsic Mode Functions (IMFs)). Each of these oscillations is considered as a distinct time scale. Every IMF satisfies the two basic conditions: (**C1**) in the whole data series, the number of extrema and the number of zero crossings must be the same or differ at most by one, (**C2**) at any point, the mean value between the upper envelope, defined by the local maxima, and the lower envelope, defined by the local minima, is equal to zero.

Therefore, each IMF contains locally lower frequency oscillations than the one just extracted before. The EMD algorithm does not require any predetermined filter or wavelet function and it is fully data driven method [8]. To determine the IMFs, denoted $imf_i(t)$, an algorithm called sifting process is applied. This algorithm can be summarized as follows:

1. Initialize: $r_0(t)$ = x(t), i=1,
2. Extract the ith IMF:
   (a) Initialize: h_0(t) = $r_{i-1}(t)$, j = 1,

(b) Identify the extrema (both maxima and minima) of the signal, $h_{j-1}(t)$,
(c) Interpolate the local maxima and the local minima by a cubic spline to form upper and lower envelopes of $h_{j-1}(t)$,
(d) Compute the local mean, $m_{j-1}(t)$, by averaging the envelopes,
(e) $h_j(t) = h_{j-1}(t)$ - $m_{j-1}(t)$,
If the stopping criterion is satisfied then set $imf_i(t) = h_j(t)$
Else go to (b) with j = j+1

3. $r_i(t) = r_{i-1}(t)$ - $imf_i(t)$,
4. If $r_i(t)$ still has at least two extrema then goes to 2 with i=i+1.
Else the decomposition is finished and $r_i(t)$ is the residue.

This leads to a decomposition of the following form:

$$x(t) = \sum_{i=1}^{n} imf_i(t) + r_n(t) \tag{1}$$

Where n is the mode number and $r_n(t)$ is the residue of the decomposition.

3 Mode Selection Approach

The mode selection approach is based on the assumption that the first IMFs are heavily contaminated by noise and are not representative for information specific to the original speech. Therefore, the enhanced speech signal is reconstructed only by the few IMFs dominated by the pure signal. Thus, there will be a mode, denoted $IMF_{j_s}(t)$, from which the energy distribution of the original signal is greater than the noise. This idea is used in order to separate the signal from the noise. According to [9], the principle of this approach is to set to zero the first $(j_s - 1)$ IMFs and to partially reconstruct the signal from the remaining ones. The mode selection approach aims to find an approximation $\tilde{x}_{j_s}(t)$ of the original signal x(t).

$$\tilde{x}_{j_s}(t) = \sum_{j=j_s}^{n} imf_j(t) + r_n(t), \qquad j_s = 2, ..., n \tag{2}$$

In order to find j_s, a distortion measure, termed consecutive mean square error (CMSE) [9] has been applied. This distortion measure CMSE is defined as:

$$CMSE(\tilde{x}_k, \tilde{x}_{k+1}) \triangleq \frac{1}{N} \sum_{i=1}^{N} [\tilde{x}_k(t_i) - \tilde{x}_{k+1}(t_i)]^2, k = 1, ..., n-1 \tag{3}$$

The CMSE is reduced to the energy corresponding to the k^{th}IMF. It is also the classical empirical variance approximation of the IMF:

$$CMSE(\tilde{x}_k, \tilde{x}_{k+1}) \triangleq \frac{1}{N} \sum_{i=1}^{N} [imf_k(t_i)]^2, k = 1, ..., n-1 \tag{4}$$

Finally j_s is calculated as:

$$j_s = argmin[CMSE(\tilde{x}_k, \tilde{x}_{k+1})], \qquad 1 \leq k \leq n-1 \qquad (5)$$

Where $\tilde{x}_k$ and $\tilde{x}_{k+1}$ are respectively the signals reconstructed starting from the IMFs that are indexed by k and $(k+1)$. By applying the CMSE criterion, the IMF order corresponding to the first significant change in the energy distribution is identified.

4 Thresholding Algorithms

The Hard and the Soft thresholding are the two most widely used thresholding ways [10]. In order to improve these methods, other thresholding variant techniques have been developed.

4.1 Hard Thresholding Algorithm

Concerning the hard thresholding, on a given signal, if its absolute amplitude is less than the predefined threshold τ, it will be considered as the noise and be made equal to zero; if the absolute amplitude is greater than the threshold τ, it will be considered as the real signal information and remain unchanged. The mathematical formulation is as follows:

$$x_{hard} = \begin{cases} x & \text{si } |x| > \tau \\ 0 & \text{si } |x| \leq \tau \end{cases} \qquad (6)$$

The error of the hard thresholding is relatively small, but it is easy to produce a discontinuity and parasitic oscillation at the threshold critical point.

4.2 Soft Thresholding Algorithm

Concerning the soft thresholding, if the absolute amplitude of the signal is less than the threshold τ, it will be also considered as the noise and be made equal to zero; if the absolute amplitude is greater than the threshold τ, it will be considered as the real signal information too. The mathematical formulation is as follows:

$$x_{soft} = \begin{cases} sgn(x)(|x| - \tau) & \text{si } |x| > \tau \\ 0 & \text{si } |x| \leq \tau \end{cases} \qquad (7)$$

In contrast of the hard thresholding, the soft thresholding has good continuity at the threshold critical point. However, there are τ difference between the enhanced signal and the original one. So if applied on a set of IMFs, it will cause a larger error after reconstruction. In order to overcome these drawbacks, various improvements have been proposed in the literature. In our work, we retain essentially what is proposed by L. She et al. in [11] for the ECG signal denoising.

4.3 Improved Thresholding Algorithm

In our proposed approach, we use a new technique called improved thresholding which combines the advantages of both the soft thresholding and the hard thresholding. As proposed in [11], the mathematical formulation of the improved thresholding is given by the following equation:

$$x_{imp} = \begin{cases} 0 & \text{if } |x| < \frac{\tau}{2} \\ sgn(x)(\frac{\tau}{2} - \sqrt{(\frac{\tau}{2})^2 - (x - sgn(x)\frac{\tau}{2})^2}) & \text{if } \frac{\tau}{2} \leq |x| \leq \tau \\ sgn(x)(\frac{\tau}{2} + \sqrt{(\frac{\sqrt{2}+1}{2}\tau)^2 - (x - sng(x)\frac{\sqrt{2}+3}{2}\tau)^2}) & \text{if } \tau \leq |x| \leq \frac{4+\sqrt{2}}{4}\tau \\ x & \text{if } \frac{4+\sqrt{2}}{4}\tau \leq x \end{cases} \tag{8}$$

As it has been shown by [11] the improved thresholding not only minimizes the parasitic oscillation to some extent, but also it doesn't have the τ difference. It improves the signal to noise ratio of the enhanced signal.

4.4 Threshold Value Selection

To denoise speech signal by thresholding, the threshold value choice is an important task. In the literature, the most used threshold value is the universal threshold proposed by Donoho and Johnstone [6] for removing added Gaussian noise and given by:

$$\tau = \tilde{\sigma}\sqrt{2logN} \tag{9}$$

Where N is the signal length and $\tilde{\sigma}$ represents the noise level estimation of the signal. The expression of $\tilde{\sigma}$ is:

$$\tilde{\sigma} = \frac{MAD}{0.6745} \tag{10}$$

MAD represents the absolute median deviation of x.

In our work, we use a new threshold [12], proposed by Atto to a better estimation of a corrupted signal. This threshold is the result of a nonparametric statistical approach dedicated to the detection of a signal with unknown probability distribution and in the presence of additive white Gaussian noise. This threshold is called the detection threshold.

In the case of denoising the IMFs issued from the EMD speech analysis, we calculate the threshold for each considered IMF, as follows:

$$\tau_j = \tilde{\sigma}_j(\sqrt{log\frac{N}{2}} + \frac{log(1 + \sqrt{1 - \frac{1}{N^2}})}{\sqrt{2logN}}) \tag{11}$$

Where $\tilde{\sigma}_j$ is given in equation 10 and MAD_j defined by:

$$MAD_j = Median\{|IMF_j(t) - Median\{IMF_j(t')\}|\} \tag{12}$$

5 Proposed Denoising Approach

As the Mode Selection proposal implies secluding the first (j_s-1) IMFs and considering the other ones, this can deteriorate the signal quality. The new approach consists on maintaining and thresholding the first (j_s-1) IMFs [13] through an improved thresholding process. The enhanced signal is constituted by the thresholded IMFs, the remaining ones and the residue.

The proposed denoising approach is summarized as follows:

- Decomposition of the noisy speech $x_n(t)$ into a series of IMFs via the EMD algorithm (equation 1),
- Applying the Mode Selection criteria to find the index j_s minimizing the CMSE (equations 4 and 5),
- Denoising the first (j_s-1)IMFs by the improved thresholding algorithm and the detection threshold function to obtain the enhanced $imf_i(t)$ versions $\tilde{f}_i(t)$, i=1,...,j_s-1,
- Reconstructing the enhanced following signal as follows

$$\tilde{x}(t) = \sum_{i=1}^{j_s-1} \tilde{f}_i(t) + \sum_{i=j_s}^{n} imf_i(t) + r_n(t) \tag{13}$$

6 Results

To illustrate the effectiveness of our proposed denoising algorithm, deep computer simulations were carried out with 10 sentences, which were selected from the NOISEUS database and degraded by additive white Gaussian noise. The simulations were performed with various SNR levels -5, 0 and +5. Here, the use of white Gaussian noise is justified by the fact that it has been reported that this type of noise is more difficult to detect and remove than any other type [14].

To evaluate our method, we calculate the SNR level and the weighted spectral slope measure (wss). Besides, the proposed approach is compared to other techniques using the EMD process.

About the output SNR the used mathematical expression is:

$$SNR = 10log_{10} \frac{\sum_{i=1}^{N}(x(t_i))^2}{\sum_{i=1}^{N}(x(t_i) - \tilde{x}(t_i))^2} \tag{14}$$

About the Weighted Spectral Slope the used mathematical expression is:

$$d_{wss} = K_{SPL}(K - \hat{K}) + \sum_{k=1}^{36} w_a(k)[x(k) - \tilde{x}(k))]^2 \tag{15}$$

Where $(K - \hat{K})$ is the difference between overall sound pressure level of the original and processed utterances. K_{SPL} is a parameter which can be varied to increase the overall performances.

The obtained results of our method are illustrated in tables 1 and 2 for the output SNR and the Weighted Spectral Slope respectively.

Table 1. Comparison of the output SNR for various denoising method

	Output SNR			
Input SNR	First IMFs elimination	EMD Soft Thresholding	Mode Selection Approach Soft	Proposed Method
-5	0.30	0.90	0.35	0.45
0	1.26	1.35	1.64	1.82
5	3.56	4.06	6.02	11.16

Table 2. Comparison of *wss* measure for various denoising method

	wss			
Input SNR	First IMFs elimination	EMD Soft Thresholding	Mode Selection Approach Soft	Proposed Method
-5	82.84	118.93	82.74	80.74
0	64.90	107.13	66.28	64.71
5	59.90	86.19	56.35	51.81

Referring to tables 1 and 2, one can clearly notice the following interpretations:

- Table 1 shows the effectiveness of the proposed algorithm compared to the other speech denoising methods for a wide range of SNRs. It can be observed that our method gives better results for all SNR levels (except for SNR=-5dB). The effectiveness of the method can be better observed for high SNR values.
- Table 2 shows the wss evaluation criteria for our approach and the three others. It can be clearly noticed that our approach gives the least wss measure for almost all the SNR levels showing its convenience for speech enhancement.

7 Conclusion

In this present work, a new speech enhancement method based on the empirical mode decomposition and improved thresholding has been proposed. This method follows four stages. In the first stage, the noisy speech signal is decomposed via the EMD algorithm into series of IMFs. In the second stage, the mode selection approach is applied to find the IMF_{j_s} by using an energy criterion. In the next stage, the first (j_s -1) IMFs are thresholded by an improved thresholding technique. In the last stage, the enhanced speech is reconstructed by adding the thresholded IMFs, the remaining IMFs and the residue. Referring to the SNR and the WSS parameters, our approach shows its efficiency when compared to other approaches using also the EMD technique. Owing to their promising features in speech signal enhancement, the EMD will be applied with a noise power estimation technique in future works.

References

1. Weiss, M.R., Aschkenasy, E., Parsons, T.W.: Processing speech signal to attenuate interference. In: Proc. IEEE Symp. Speech Recognition, pp. 292–293 (1974)
2. Virag, N.: Single channel speech enhancement based on masking properties of the human auditory system. IEEE Trans. Speech Audio Process 7, 126–137 (1999)
3. Paliwal, K., Jcicki, K.W., Schwerin, B.: Single-channel speech enhancement using spectral subtraction in the short-time modulation domain. Speech Communication 52, 450–475 (2010)
4. Lu, Y., Loizou, P.C.: A geometric approach to spectral subtraction. Speech Communication 50, 453–466 (2008)
5. Proakis, J.G., Radar, C., Ling, F.: Advanced digital signal processing. Macmillan, New York (1992)
6. Donoho, D.L., Johnstone, I.M.: Ideal spatial adaption via wavelet shrinkage. Biometrika 81, 425–455 (1994)
7. Donoho, D.L.: De-noising by soft-thresholding. IEEE Trans. Inform. Theory 41(3), 613–627 (1995)
8. Huang, N.E., Shen, Z., Long, S.R., Wu, M.C., Shin, H.H., Zheng, Q., Yen, N.C., Tung, C.C., Liu, H.H.: The empirical mode decomposition and the Hilbert spectrum for nonlinear and non-stationary time series analysis. Proc. R. Soc. Lond. A, Math. Phys. Sci. 454(1971), 903–995 (1998)
9. Boudraa, A.O., Cexus, J.C.: EMD-Based Signal Filtering. IEEE Trans. on Inst. and Meas. 56(6), 2196–2202 (2007)
10. Ghanbari, Y., Karami, M.R.: A new approach for speech enhancement based on the adaptive thresholding of the wavelet packets. Speech Comm. 48, 927–940 (2006)
11. She, L., Xu, Z., ZhangS., S.Y.: Denoising Of ECG Based On EMD Improved-thresholding And Mathematical Morphology Operation. In: Proc. IEEE BMEIN, pp. 838–842 (2010)
12. Atto, A.M., Pastor, D., Mercier, G.: Detection threshold for non-parametric estimation. SIViP 2, 207–223 (2008)
13. Issaoui, H., Bouzid, A., Ellouze, N.: Noisy Speech Enhancement Using Soft Thresholding on Selected Intrinsic Mode Functions. S.P.J.I. 5(3), 93–100 (2011)
14. Soon, I.Y., Koh, S.N., Yeo, C.K.: Noisy speech enhancement using discrete cosine transform. Speech Communication 24, 249–257 (1998)

A Fast Semi-blind Reverberation Time Estimation Using Non-linear Least Squares Method

Neda Faraji, Seyed Mohammad Ahadi, and Hamid Sheikhzadeh

Speech Processing Research Lab., Amirkabir University of Technology, Tehran, Iran

Abstract. Reverberation Time (RT) estimation is of great importance in de-reverberation techniques and characterizing room acoustics. Estimating and updating the RT parameter of an enclosed environment could be carried out either continuously or discretely in the free-decaying regions of recorded reverberant signal. In this paper, we present a novel continuous sub-band-based RT estimation method which employs the general model for the Power Spectral Density (PSD) of the reverberant signal. The temporal envelope of the observed reverberant PSD in each sub-band is fitted to the temporal envelope of the proposed theoretical PSD of the reverberant signal to estimate the RT value. In Comparison to a well-known method for RT estimation, the proposed approach performs both more accurately and faster, so that it can be used in real-time applications for fast tracking of the RT value with high accuracy.

1 Introduction

Consider an enclosed environment, such as a classroom or corridor, in which a sound from a source is radiated. The receiving object, for example microphone or human being, in addition to the original radiated sound receives reverberated sounds from the surfaces in the room. In fact, the receiving microphone records the convolution of the original radiated signal with a decaying function called Room Impulse Response (RIR). Reverberation Time (RT) is an important parameter to quantify the total reverberation effect of the enclosed environment. It is defined as the time interval during which the energy of the reverberant signal decreases 60dB after playing off the radiated signal.

Identifying the RT parameter of an RIR is a challenging subject in signal processing. Some dereverberation techniques use an estimate of RT value [1][2][3]. RT estimation is also of interest for acousticians in architectural design of auditoriums and large chambers. There are some approaches for off-line measurement of the RT by radiating either a burst of noise [4] or brief pulse [5] into the test enclosure to determine the RIR. The RT can be inferred from the slope of the measured RIR. These methods require careful experiments and sufficient excitation signals. Therefore, RT estimation from a recorded reverberant signal with speech as the excitation signal is more preferable. In completely blind approaches of this category, no prior information of the room and the radiated speech is

T. Drugman and T. Dutoit (Eds.): NOLISP 2013, LNAI 7911, pp. 208–215, 2013.

available. Hence these methods can be incorporated in hearing-aids or hands-free telephony devices [6]. Generally, blind methods for RT estimation from the recorded reverberant speech can be categorized in two classes. The first class consists of locating free-decay regions in the reverberated signal, which carry more information of the RIR [1] [7] [8]. However, these methods are more vulnerable in noisy conditions as the free-decay regions have the lowest SNRs. Moreover, a large number of these free-decay parts are required for reliable estimation of RT. To overcome the need for long data recording, so that fast tracking of RT would be possible, the approach proposed in [9] utilized a sub-band decomposition to estimate RT in each sub-band of the free decay parts. In the second class, RT is estimated continuously for each arbitrary frame of the reverberant signal [6] [10]. The final RT estimate is obtained using an order-statistics filter on a number of accumulated RT estimates.

In this paper, we propose a continuous RT estimation method where the excitation signal is an available speech signal. Therefore our approach is semi-blind. We derive a theoretical model for the Power Spectral Density (PSD) of the reverberated speech [11]. The PSD of the reverberant speech depends on the RT parameter which is the desired parameter to be estimated. Through fitting the theoretical PSD to the observed reverberant PSD, RT estimation algorithm can be run segment-by-segment in each sub-band without need to seek for free-decay parts. As the theoretical PSD non-linearly depends on RT, a Non-linear Least Squares (NLS) method is employed in the estimation algorithm. Finally, statistics can be inferred from the histogram constructed based on a number of estimated RTs. Comparing different statistics, we show that the most frequently occurring estimated RT during a time interval (mode of histogram) is an accurate approximation to the real RT. We compare our continuous algorithm with a rather newly developed method [7] which estimates RT only during free-decay regions of the reverberant speech. Assuming that the offsets of speech signal occur sharply, [7] uses an approximate model which stands for free-decay parts of the reverberant speech and utilizes a Maximum Likelihood (ML) approach for RT estimation. On the other hand, our approach utilizes an exact model which stands for any arbitrary segment of the reverberant speech and therefore will be shown that outperforms [7] in accuracy. Moreover, compared to [7], our continuous approach speeds up tracking of RT.

Our proposed method can be incorporated in Public Address Systems (PAS) in which the original signal is assumed to be available. For example, [11] proposed a noise PSD estimator employed in the intelligibility improvement algorithm of a PAS, assuming reverberant enclosure. In [11], it was assumed that reverberation time of the enclosure is available. Using the RT estimation method we present in this paper, the noise PSD estimator [11] would be applicable for the environments with time-varying RT.

This paper is organized as follows. In Sec. 2, we derive a closed-form equation for the PSD of reverberated signal. Then, the proposed RT estimation algorithm and experimental results are presented in Sec. 3. Finally, we draw our conclusions in Sec. 4.

2 PSD of the Reverberated Speech

2.1 Time-Domain Model of Reverberant Speech

Assume a clean speech signal, s, is radiated through a loudspeaker in an enclosure. A microphone at a specified distance from the loudspeaker records the direct-path signal along with the reflections from the surfaces in the enclosure. We can define the observed signal at the receiver side by the following equation

$$x(l) = g(l) * s(l), \tag{1}$$

in which l is the sample index, $*$ stands for convolution operator and $g(l)$ models both the late reverberation and the direct-path as below

$$g(l) = \begin{cases} \alpha & l = 0 \\ h(l-1) & l \geq 1, \end{cases} \tag{2}$$

where h is the RIR excluding the direct path. In Polack's statistical model [12] of the RIR, a specific RIR is an ensemble of the following stochastic process

$$h(l) = b(l)e^{-\eta l} \text{ for } l \geq 0, \tag{3}$$

in which $b(l)$ is a zero-mean Normal stochastic process with variance ν^2 modulated with an exponential function with the decay rate η. The decay rate is defined as $\eta = \frac{3ln(10)}{RT f_s}$ in which RT and f_s are reverberation time and sampling frequency, respectively. Assuming that the attenuation factor α and clean speech signal s are available, we can rewrite (1) as

$$z(l) = g(l) * s(l) - \alpha s(l) = z(l) = \sum_{p=0}^{\infty} h_l(p)s(l-p-1), \tag{4}$$

in which $z(l)$ is the reverberated speech signal excluding the direct path.

2.2 Derivation of the Reverberated PSD

It has been shown [13] that

$$Z(i,k) \approx \sum_{p=0}^{\infty} h_{i+\frac{L}{2}}(p)S(i-p-1,k), \tag{5}$$

where $S(i-p-1,k)$ is the kth Short Time Discrete Fourier Transform (STDFT) coefficient of a frame of clean speech starting at sample point $i-p-1$. $Z(i,k)$ is the kth STDFT coefficient of the reverberated speech frame with sample index i and L shows the frame length. We derive a new equation for the PSD of reverberated speech based on (5). By definition of PSD as $\sigma_Z^2(i,k) = Var\{Z\} = E\{Z^2(i,k)\} - E^2\{Z(i,k)\}$, the first two moments of Z have to be derived.

We assume the clean signal, and therefore its spectrum, to be available. The first moment of Z is determined as follows:

$$m_Z(i,k) = E\{Z(i,k)|\mathbf{S}\} = \sum_{p=0}^{\infty} E\left\{h_{i+\frac{L}{2}}(p)S(i-p-1,k)|\mathbf{S}\right\}$$
$$= \sum_{p=0}^{\infty} E\left\{h_{i+\frac{L}{2}}(p)\right\} S(i-p-1,k) = 0, \qquad (6)$$

in which $\mathbf{S} = \{S(i-1,k), S(i-2,k), ..., S(1,k)\}$. For the second moment we have:

$$\sigma_Z^2(i,k) = E\left\{Z^2(i,k)|\mathbf{S}\right\} = E\left\{\sum_{p=0}^{\infty}\sum_{q=0}^{\infty} h_{i+\frac{L}{2}}(p)h_{i+\frac{L}{2}}(q)S(i-p-1,k)S(i-q-1,k)|\mathbf{S}\right\}$$
$$= \sum_{p=0}^{\infty}\sum_{q=0}^{\infty} E\left\{h_{i+\frac{L}{2}}(p)h_{i+\frac{L}{2}}(q)\right\} S(i-p-1,k)S(i-q-1,k). \qquad (7)$$

Refering to Polack's model (3), the expectation $E\left\{h_{i+\frac{L}{2}}(p)h_{i+\frac{L}{2}}(q)\right\} = \nu^2_{i+\frac{L}{2}} e^{-2\eta_{i+\frac{L}{2}} p}, q = p$ and $E\left\{h_{i+\frac{L}{2}}(p)h_{i+\frac{L}{2}}(q)\right\} = 0, q \neq p$. Finally, we obtain

$$\sigma_Z^2(i,k) = \sum_{p=0}^{\infty} \nu^2_{i+\frac{L}{2}} e^{-2\eta_{i+\frac{L}{2}} p} S^2(i-p-1,k). \qquad (8)$$

3 Experiments on the RT Estimation Algorithm

We tested our algorithm on six speech files of TIMIT database which were selected from 6 different speakers, 3 males and 3 females and were concatenated to construct the final test file. We generated 6 synthetic RIRs using Polack's model (3) with $RT = [0.1, 0.2, 0.4, 0.6, 0.8, 1]$ sec and $\nu^2 = 0.25$. We made six synthetically reverberated speech signals by convolving the test signal with the RIRs. In all experiments, we set the upper limit of the summation in (8) to 4000. Moreover, the clean and reverberated speech signals are segmented into 16msec frames with the frameshift of one sample at the sampling frequency of 8000 Hz. The hamming-windowed frames of both clean and reverberated speech signals are transformed into Fourier domain with 128 DFT points.

3.1 Verification of the Theoretical Model

Here, we carry out an experiment to verify the theoretically-derived reverberant PSD (8). First, for a synthetic RIR with $RT = 0.3$ sec ($\eta = 0.0028$) and $\nu^2 = 0.25$, we compute the theoretical PSD of the reverberated test speech (σ_Z^2) based

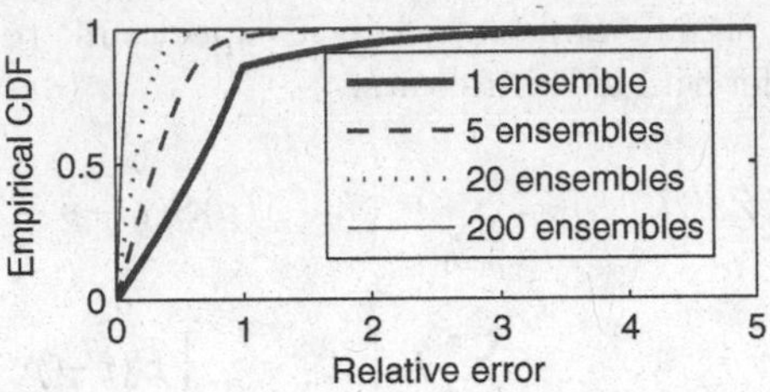

Fig. 1. Emperical CDF of the relative errors

on (8). Then, this theoretical PSD is compared with the observed PSD of the reverberant speech. We can generate an ensemble of the reverberated test speech by making a realization of the RIR with the above parameters. In application, the PSD of the observed reverberant speech is estimated by Periodogram method ($\hat{\sigma}_Z^2$), which is an approximate to the true PSD. A better approximation to the true PSD can be made by ensemble averaging of the Periodogram-based PSDs. In order to generate different ensembles of the reverberated speech, different ensembles of the RIR are realized and convolved with the test signal. Comparing the theoretical PSD with the observed PSD of the reverberated speech, the relative error is defined as follows

$$\text{Relative Error} = \left|\sigma_Z^2(i,k) - \hat{E}\left\{\hat{\sigma}_Z^2(i,k)\right\}\right| / \sigma_Z^2(i,k), \tag{9}$$

in which $\hat{E}\left\{\hat{\sigma}_Z^2(i,k)\right\}$ is the sample mean of the Periodogram-estimated PSDs of reverberant speech. The Cumulative Distribution Function (CDF) of the relative error values of all frames and frequency bins are shown in Fig. 1 with different number of ensembles to obtain the sample mean $\hat{E}\left\{\hat{\sigma}_Z^2(i,k)\right\}$. As the number of ensembles increases, better fitting between the theoretical and the ensemble-averaged PSDs is observed.

3.2 Proposed Method for RT Estimation

As shown in (8), the reverberated PSD non-linearly depends on the decay rate η. The parameter η, and therefore RT, could be simply determined through minimizing the squared error between the observed PSD and the theoretical PSD of (8). In fact, for the observed PSD of reverberant speech estimated in k^{th} frequency bin of the ith frame, $\hat{\sigma}_Z^2(i,k)$, the parameter η is obtained as:

$$\hat{\eta}(i,k) = \underset{\eta}{Min}\left\{\left(\hat{\sigma}_Z^2(i,k) - \sum_{p=0}^{\infty} \nu_{i+\frac{L}{2}}^2 e^{-2\eta_{i+\frac{L}{2}} p} S^2(i-p-1,k)\right)^2\right\}. \tag{10}$$

3.3 Experimental Results of the Proposed RT Estimation Method

For each of 6 synthetically reverberated speech signals, the same experiment is carried out as follows. First, the reverberated speech is segmented into 64 ms

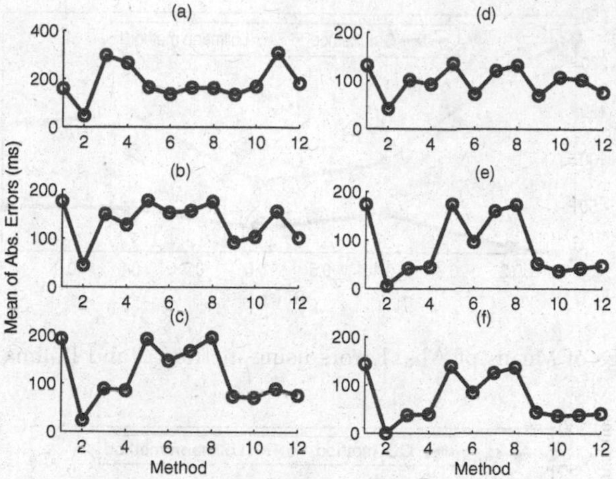

Fig. 2. Mean of Absolute Errors using different statistics (a) RT=1 s; (b) RT=800 ms, (c) RT=600 ms, (d) RT=400 ms, (e) RT=200 ms, (f) RT=100 ms

blocks with a block shift of 3ms. Then each block is divided into frames with the setup mentioned before. As mentioned, in frame scale, η can be estimated using (10). For block scale estimation, the objective function to be minimized is

$$\hat{\eta}(j,k) = \underset{\eta}{Min}\left\{\sum_{i=1}^{M}\left(\hat{\sigma}_Z^2(i,k) - \sum_{p=0}^{4000}\nu_{i+\frac{L}{2}}^2 e^{-2\eta_{i+\frac{L}{2}}p} S^2(i-p-1,k)\right)^2\right\}, \quad (11)$$

where j is the block index and i represents the frame number in the block. For our setup, M is set to 384. To infer the fullband η from the subband block-based estimated η parameters, different statistics could be employed. For example, similar to the method proposed in [9], we employ the Median of Medians method. First, the fullband RT of the j^{th}block is set to the median of the RTs derived in all subbands of the block. Then, the fullband RT of the total reverberant speech is estimated through computing median of all J fullband block-derived RTs

$$\hat{RT} = \underset{j=1,2,\ldots,J}{Median}\,\hat{RT}(j) = \underset{j=1,2,\ldots,J}{Median}\left\{\underset{k=1,2,\ldots,NFFT/2+1}{Median}\quad \hat{RT}(j,k)\right\}. \quad (12)$$

In another approach [7][1] the mode of the histogram of the block-estimated RTs was considered as the final RT estimate. Hence, in our proposed approach we compare different statistics together. First, we create the histogram of all ηs derived from all frequency bands of the N consecutive blocks. We measure four statistics from this histogram that are Median, Mode, Mean and Mean after removing 30 percent of outliers (Trimmed Mean). The inferred statistics constitute

[1] Implemented code is available at `http://www.mathworks.com/matlabcentral/fileexchange/35740-blind-reverberation-time-estimation`

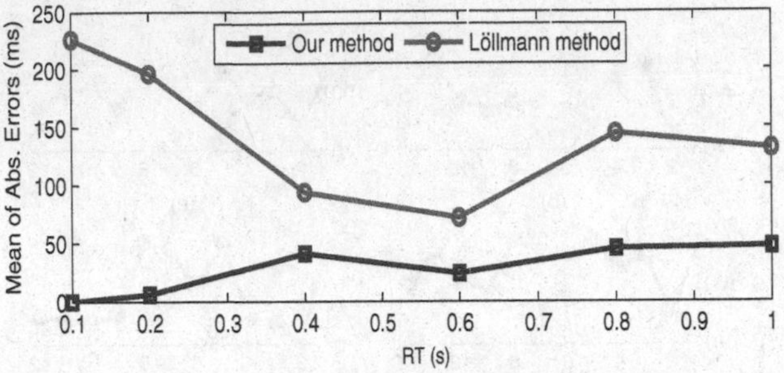

Fig. 3. Average of Means of Abs. Errors using method 2 and Löllmann method [7].

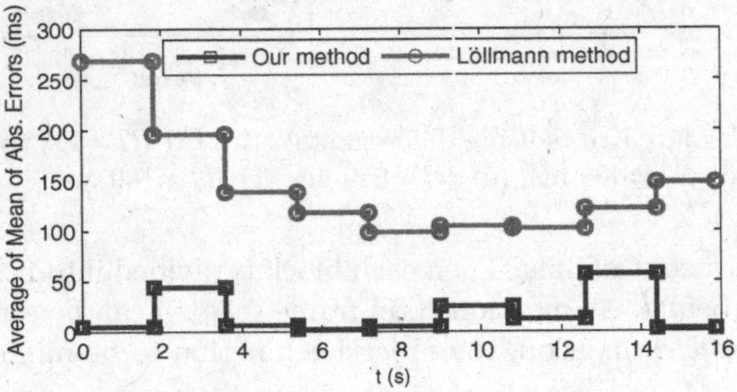

Fig. 4. Trend of the Average of Means of Absolute Errors in the intervals of 1.8 sec

Methods 1 to 4 in the depicted results in Fig. 2. Also, we can extract the Median value of $NFFT/2+1$ estimated ηs in each block and then make the histogram for the N Median values. Hence, the other four statistics 5 to 8 are Median of Medians, Mode of Medians, Mean of Medians and Trimmed Mean of Medians. The same idea can be used for the Mean value of the ηs extracted in each block. Therefore, methods 9 to 12 involve Median of Means, Mode of Means, Mean of Means and Trimmed Mean of Means. In our setup, we used 300 blocks to make the histogram, which for the block shift of 3msec corresponds to the time interval of 900 msec. Then, similar to [7], we smooth η using a recursive averaging filter with the time-constant of 0.996. Finally, we obtain the estimated RT as $\hat{RT} = \frac{3 \times ln(10)}{\hat{\eta} f_s}$. The performance can be quantified by averaging the Absolute Errors between the target RT and the estimated RTs as below

$$\text{Mean of Absolute Errors} = \frac{1}{J} \sum_{j=1}^{J} \left| \hat{RT}(j) - RT \right|. \tag{13}$$

In Fig. 2, Means of Absolute Errors for six reverberated speech signals are demonstrated. The horizontal axis represents different statistics. As shown, method 2 has the minimum Mean of Absolute Errors compared to the other methods. Using method 2, Means of Absolute Errors for 6 reverberated signals are plotted in Fig. 3, in which the performance of the method of Löllmann et al. [7] is depicted too. Besides, in real situations, the reverberation time varies with time, so that it is of advantage to have a fast RT estimation algorithm. As our procedure is able to extract the RT for any arbitrary segment of the reverberated speech, it is considerably faster compared to [7] that estimates the RT in the free decay parts of the reverberated speech. In order to illustrate the high speed of our algorithm, for each of 6 reverberant speech signals, we compute the Mean of Absolute Errors in the interval of 1.8 sec rather than the total reverberated speech. The average of the short-time Means of Absolute Errors over the 6 reverberant signals is computed. Fig. 4 demonstrates the trend of this average over time. Compared to [7], our algorithm is able to detect the RT even in short segments of the reverberated speech.

4 Conclusion

In this paper we have proposed a continuous RT estimation algorithm based on a general model we derived for PSD of reverberant speech. The presented algorithm works on subband domain to extract the RT of any arbitrary segment of the reverberant speech. Compared with a new method of Löllmann et al., our approach achieves superior performance with fast adaptation speed.

References

1. Lebart, K., Boucher, J.M.: A new method based on spectral subtraction for speech dereverberation. Acta Acoustica-ACOUSTICA 87, 359–366 (2001)
2. Habets, E.A.P.: Single-channel speech dereverberation based on spectral subtraction. In: Proc. of Ann. Workshop on Circuits, Systems and Signal Processing (2004)
3. Jan, T., Wang, W.: Joint blind dereverberation and separation of speech mixtures. In: Proc. of EUSIPCO, pp. 2343–2347 (2012)
4. ISO-3382, Acoustics measurement of the reverberation time of rooms with reference to other acoustical parameters, Int. Org. for Standardization, Geneva (1997)
5. Schroeder, M.R.: New method for measuring reverberation time. Journal of the Acoustical Society of America 37, 409–412 (1965)
6. Ratnam, R., Jones, D.L., Wheeler, B.C., O'Brien, W.D., Lansing, C.R., Feng, A.S.: Blind estimation of reverberation time. Journal of the Acoustical Society of America 114, 2877–2892 (2003)
7. Löllmann, H.W., Yilmaz, E., Jeub, M., Vary, P.: An improved algorithm for blind reverberation time estimation. In: Proc. of IWAENC (2010)
8. Vesa, S., Harma, A.: Automatic estimation of reverberation time from binaural signals. In: Proc. of ICASSP, pp. 281–284 (2005)
9. de, T., Prego, M., de Lima, A.A., Netto, S.L., Lee, B., Said, A., Schafer, R.W., Kalker, T.: A blind algorithm for reverberation-time estimation using subband decomposition of speech signals. Journal of the Acoustical Society of America (2012)
10. Wen, J.Y.C., Habets, E.A.P., Naylor, P.A.: Blind estimation of reverberation time based on the distribution of signal decay rates. In: Proc. of ICASSP (2008)
11. Faraji, N., Hendriks, R.C.: Noise Power Spectral Density estimation for public address systems in noisy reverberant environments. In: Proc. of IWAENC (2012)
12. Polack, J.D.: La transmission de l' energie sonore dans les salles (1988)
13. Erkelens, J.S., Heusdens, R.: Correlation-based and model-based blind single channel late-reverberation suppression in noisy time-varying acoustical environments. IEEE Trans. Audio, Speech and Language Processing 18, 1746–1765 (2010)

Author Index